THE OAKWOOD PRESS

MAUNSELL'S SR STEAM CARRIAGE STOCK

by
David Gould

THE OAKWOOD PRESS

ISBN 0 85361 401 6

First published October 1978
Reprinted January 1981
Enlarged revised edition 1990

Typeset by Gem Publishing Company, Brightwell, Wallingford, Oxfordshire.

Printed by Alpha Print, Witney, Oxfordshire.

Title page: 1935-built Corridor Third Brake No. 2838, Diagram 2113. *British Rail*

4-coach set of 8 ft 6 in. stock, No. 220, near Shoreham (Kent) on 21st May, 1938. The rear coach is a replacement of the original Third Brake. *H.C. Casserley*

Published by
The OAKWOOD PRESS
P.O.Box 122, Headington, Oxford.

Contents

7-coach set No. 461 ('Thanet' stock) plus Pullman on a Ramsgate to Victoria service near Bromley South, 31st October, 1931. *H.C. Casserley*

References and Acknowledgements

Most of the information herein has been gathered from official sources and scattered references in books and magazines, too many to list in detail. Carriage Working Notices and their Appendices have been studied, without which it would hardly have been possible to find out where the carriages worked. That they actually did work where they were supposed to has been confirmed by study of many photographs; set numbers can often be seen peeping behind locomotive tenders.

The former British Transport Historical Records now at Kew have been consulted:

SOU 1/28 Locomotive, Carriage and Electrical Committee Minutes
SOU 1/29 Locomotive, Carriage and Electrical Committee Minutes
SOU 1/85 Rolling Stock Committee Minutes
SOU 4/90 Carriages damaged in Wartime
SOU 4/146 Carriage Working Notices, Western Section
SOU 5/27 Coaching stock renumbering book
SOU 5/41 Uncompleted orders of coaching stock
SOU 5/51 Diagram book of carriage stock.

I am greatly indebted to Richard Casserley, who supplied almost all the withdrawal dates; Ray Chorley, for his kind permission to reprint his scale drawings of Maunsell coaches; R.W. Kidner, who having lived through the Southern era was able to furnish notes based on his observations; Mike King, who through his contacts – particularly Denis Cullum and Tony Sedgwick – has made available details of set formations at various periods and clarified many points; and Lawrence Mack (Southern Carriage & Wagon Society), who spotted many errors in the original script – now, I hope, corrected – and freely gave information gathered over the years from many sources.

September, 1990

D. Gould
East Grinstead

Maunsell stock on a 'no-passport' Boulogne excursion, Oxted to Folkestone Harbour. Schoolchildren entrain at Oxted on 25th May, 1960. *Oakwood Collection*

Introduction

This book describes in some detail all steam-hauled carriages built new by the Southern Railway between 1923 and 1936, and it attempts to trace their history right through to their withdrawal or, in a few cases, preservation; special attention being given to the formation of set trains and their workings.

When a renumbering scheme for London & South Western, South Eastern & Chatham, and London Brighton & South Coast Railways' carriages was worked out in about June, 1923, it was decided to arrange everything by class, starting with the Thirds of the LSW followed by blank numbers, the Thirds of the SEC then blank numbers, and the Thirds of the LBSC and blank numbers. This pattern was maintained consistently throughout; next came Third Brakes, followed by Seconds and Second Brakes, Composites, Composite Brakes, Firsts, First Brakes and finally Saloons.

The batches of vacant numbers in the list available for new vehicles were as follows: Thirds – 744–844, 975–1775, 2339–2420; Third Brakes – 3203–33, 3548–3663, 4043–97; Seconds and Second Brakes – 4168–4486; Composites – 5133–77, 5505–5794, 6287–6328; Composite Brakes – 6560–6604, 6643–6922, 6939–86; Firsts – 7192–7232, 7376–7485, 7652–7700; First Brakes – 7715–34, 7748–65, 7776–7800; Saloons, including Kitchen and Dining Cars – 7852–71, 7932–51, 7974–8000. Sometimes it turned out that there were too many blanks, which were never filled; often, however, particularly with Third Brakes, there were not nearly enough and new vehicles had to take the numbers of withdrawn stock.

All new and rebuilt rolling stock to be dealt with in the Southern's own workshops was given a Head Office order number. Sometimes each type of coach ordered would have an individual order number within the batch, just as British Rail coaches do with their lot numbers, but more often the order numbers were given to complete batches of sets. Coaches ordered from contractors did not generally have order numbers. After a few years it became standard practice to build coach bodies at Eastleigh Works of the former LSW and carriage underframes at Lancing Works of the former LBSC. The old SEC's works at Ashford, after doing electric stock conversions, concentrated on building wagons.

Eastleigh always built brake vehicles the same way round; consequently, when the bodies were placed on the underframes that had come from Lancing, half those intended for inclusion in sets required turning. This was done usually by one of the carriage works 'O2' tank locomotives on the triangle behind the shed and locomotive works. It is recorded that Composite Brakes Nos. 6695–9 for Sets 168, 172, 196–8 were turned on 2nd October, 1935; and Third Brakes Nos. 2781/3/5 for Sets 248–50 were turned on 14th October, 1935.

Most stock had a trial run from Eastleigh to Hamworthy Junction and back before being released to traffic. Motive power was usually a 'T9' 4–4–0, with a brake van for the guard if no such accommodation was included in the new or ex-works stock.

The Southern was a firm believer in the principle of set trains, by which groups of carriages not only stayed coupled together for long periods but actually had set numbers prominently painted on the outer ends of the rake.

Short sets of two, three or four coaches would be used for almost any sort of train service and so hardly ever changed their formation, but long sets tended to be used for specific regular services and when those ceased the sets were usually subject to alteration because they were unsuitable for any other service. Pullman and dining cars were never regarded as part of a set but would be added as required. The set number appeared at the brake-end of each set, once on each side of the gangway at about cantrail level; a few set numbers were painted lower down on the ends, examples being Nos. 218 and 461 in the early 1930s.

If a carriage had to be 'stopped' for any purpose the normal practice was to remove it from the set and substitute one of corresponding description temporarily. Occasionally a complete set might be 'stopped'. Substitute vehicles would in any case have to be found when a set booked for a regular daily working had to go in for overhaul.

On every coach-end three metal plates were to be found (low down, on left-hand side of gangway). A large square plate gave details of overall length and width of the coach; above this a small circular plate gave the tare weight; and, from 1934, a further small circular plate under the dimensions plate gave the 'route restriction' number. SR corridor coaches were built in three widths of body. Those 8 ft wide were Restriction '0', which meant they could pass over all routes; those 8 ft 6 in. in width were Restriction '1' stock, which could not pass between Grove Junction (south of Tunbridge Wells Central) and Battle; and those 9 ft over body were Restriction '4', prohibited between Tonbridge and Battle, Hastings and Winchelsea, Gipsy Hill and Crystal Palace Low Level, Charlton and Plumstead, Dartford and Strood. Later, all restrictions except the first were eased for 9 ft stock. No coaching stock of any description was allowed on the Canterbury and Whitstable line.

Tare weights of coaches as shown on the ends were only approximate and did not always agree with the weights shown in the carriage register. A few examples are given here: Corridor Thirds to Diagram 24, 33 tons; Open Thirds to Diagram 2005, 33 tons; Corridor Brake Thirds to Diagram 2101, 32 tons; Corridor Composites to Diagram 317, 34 tons, Diagram 2302, 33 tons and Diagram 2304, 32 tons; Brake Composites to Diagrams 2401 and 2403, 32 tons; Corridor Firsts to Diagrams 476 and 496, 34 tons and Diagram 2503, 33 tons; Kitchen Dining Firsts to Diagram 2651, 34 tons; Saloons to Diagram 2653, 32 tons; and Nondescript Brakes to Diagram 2654, 31 tons. The diagrams to which these refer may be found on pages 26–7, 35, 42, 140–3.

Also painted on every coach-end was the Section letter: 'E' for Eastleigh indicating Western Section, and 'A' for Ashford or Eastern Section. Misleadingly, these letters indicated not the Section to which the coach was allocated but the works responsible for maintenance. The 1925 Eastern section stock bore the letter 'A', but all standard Maunsell coaches were 'E'. After 1931 Section letters were discontinued.

Who actually designed 'the Maunsell coach'? Richard Maunsell was the chief mechanical engineer during the period, but it is not thought he had very much to do with design. He did, however, report to the Rolling Stock Committee with regular requests for authorisation to construct numbers of coaches each year. Surrey Warner from the London & South Western was assistant mechanical engineer for carriages, wagons and road motors until his retirement in 1929; he had been responsible for the 'Ironclad' coaches, and the SR standard coaches were only a lengthened and tidied-up version of those. Perhaps the actual designer was Lionel Lynes, who was chief draughtsman from 1923 and, from 1929, as technical assistant (carriages and wagons) to Maunsell, directed carriage design. The chief rolling stock clerk was C.W. Pepper, and presumably his was the responsibility of working out the carriage renumbering scheme and finding suitable numbers for both vehicles and sets and seeing that the carriage registers were accurately maintained.

Destination Boards

During the time of the SR all the 'best' corridor trains carried large destination boards – two each side per coach – which were held in place by brackets fixed to the carriage roofs. The lettering was painted on each green board in yellow, shaded black to right and base. Some boards were blank for paper destination labels to be pasted upon; these boards were kept for use as required at Charing Cross, London Bridge, Victoria and Waterloo.

Examples of some of the wording used on destination boards are shown below; it is interesting that, whereas the Central Section specified Victoria or London Bridge for its services, the Eastern Section contented itself with showing merely 'London' to save having a considerable stock of boards lettered 'Charing Cross', 'Cannon Street' or 'Victoria'.

First Board		*Second Board*	
VICTORIA *or*	LONDON BRIDGE	EASTBOURNE	
"	"	EASTBOURNE	HASTINGS
"	"	BOGNOR REGIS	
"	"	CHICHESTER	PORTSMOUTH
"	"	HOVE	LITTLEHAMPTON
"	"	HOVE	WORTHING
LONDON	FOLKESTONE	CENTRAL	EXPRESS
LONDON	FOLKESTONE	DOVER	DEAL
LONDON	TUNBRIDGE WELLS	ST. LEONARDS	HASTINGS
LONDON	TUNBRIDGE WELLS	SIDLEY	BEXHILL
LONDON	MARGATE	BROADSTAIRS	RAMSGATE
CONTINENTAL	EXPRESS	GRAVESEND	ROTTERDAM
CONTINENTAL	EXPRESS	NEWHAVEN	DIEPPE
WATERLOO	SALISBURY	EXETER	CENTRAL
WATERLOO	SALISBURY	EXETER	ILFRACOMBE
WATERLOO	SALISBURY	EXETER	TORRINGTON
ATLANTIC COAST EXPRESS		WATERLOO	BUDE*
WATERLOO	PORTSMOUTH	ISLE OF WIGHT	
WATERLOO	SOUTHAMPTON	BOURNEMOUTH	SWANAGE
WATERLOO	SOUTHAMPTON	BOURNEMOUTH	WEYMOUTH
BOURNEMOUTH	LIMITED	DORCHESTER	WEYMOUTH

*Or EXETER CENTRAL *or* ILFRACOMBE *or* PADSTOW.

When the Southern Railway became the Southern Region of British Railways in 1948, all coach numbers were given an 'S' prefix; some set numbers were as well. From 1951, when the first of the BR standard coaches were constructed, the numbers of Southern coaches received in addition an 'S' suffix to avoid confusion. The first 'S' indicated a coach operated by the Southern Region and the second 'S', one formerly owned by the Southern Railway. Should a coach be transferred to another Region, such as the Western, the number would be altered from S 1234 S to W 1234 S.

On 3rd June, 1956, third class was abolished and the former third class accommodation was re-designated second class. All coaches referred to in this book as Seconds after that date are actually the former Thirds.

It was in 1961 that I became interested in Southern coaching stock and began to distinguish the many different types. To me, the fact that the trains ran in sets, with the numbers painted in enormous figures each side of the gangway, made them so much more fascinating than the coaches of any other railway. Not for me locomotive numbers; instead, I *had* to obtain a record of carriage sets and their formations because I imagined that no one else would bother to record the coach numbers. Hours were spent at Oxted, East Croydon, Redhill and Tonbridge observing sets. So I was well acquainted with the later Maunsell Restriction '4' stock, as well as nearly all those bearing Restriction '1'; but the Restriction '0' and the very early Maunsell stock I knew not. A great find at Oxted station was a thrown-out Appendix to Carriage Working Notice for 1958, which showed the official formation and allocation of sets and forced me to realise that 'sets' were not permanent but suffered alteration from time to time. Nevertheless, it was clear that many of the three- and four-coach sets I was seeing were still in their original, as-built, formations.

In September, 1961, the sidings at Gatwick Airport were found quite by chance, stuffed full of coaches from withdrawn sets, most of which I had never seen before. There were some gems there and, having no camera at the age of fifteen, I made valiant attempts to sketch some of these vehicles, being well aware of the significance of the cross-within-circle with which all were branded: the mark of condemnation. There were 'Ironclads', completely new to me: No. 754 from Set 433 and No. 3205 from Set 442. There was a 'Thanet' coach, easily seen to be non-standard because it had a different type of gangway from the Pullman one I was accustomed to: No. 3566 from Set 465. Above all there was a 'Continental' coach, the strangest vehicle I had ever seen, with its large door windows and small corridor windows and gangway at one end only: No. 3550. All were sketched on visits up to April, 1962; most of them were still there then. There were several Maunsell vehicles of differing widths, some with high corridor windows and some with low windows. Buffet car No. 7944 was there; Set 397 complete; four coaches from Set 271 (Nos. 844, 5650, 5649 and 6568); and six of the 8 ft Maunsell coaches (Nos. 1023, 3676, 5579, 5578, 1019 and 3677).

Actual journeys in Maunsell coaches were made in 1961/2 between Oxted and East Croydon, Redhill and Tonbridge. I usually stood in the corridor, leaning on one of the droplights safe in the knowledge that the 'door' could not possibly fly open! The cream panels contrasting with the varnished woodwork in these corridors are well remembered. Traces of cream paint could often be seen on the droplights where the green had not quite covered. By 1961 the only remaining sets still in crimson and cream were a couple of BR standard 3-sets.

After June, 1962, when the Oxted line was turned over to diesel operation, I did not take so close an interest; there were few steam-hauled sets left and those that remained were altered in formation. It did not seem worth attempting to keep up with the changes. Fortunately others were still taking careful note of the Southern coaching stock scene and so the account that follows can be reasonably complete.

Maunsell Carriages and the Holidaymaker

by R.W. Kidner

Maunsell's coaches were the last to be designed for the Southern with the absolute right of passenger preference in mind. Thereafter, other considerations gradually supervened. This meant that his coaches were kept clean, inside and out. The seat numbering system was not allowed to go wrong. If a family with children and nursemaid booked a compartment when going on holiday, the guard would have readily thrown out anyone who attempted to enter, however full the train. Destination boards were turned without fail, defective light bulbs quickly replaced. Sufficient luggage space was provided on trains such as the 'Atlantic Coast Express' to allow for at least three trunks per family, and it was rare for them to get into the wrong portion of the train. In other words, the carriages themselves were part of a 'package' designed to appeal to the person who had not yet got a motor-car, or, if he had one, did not care to do long journeys in it. The summer holidaymaker, for all that he appeared for only ten weeks in the year, received every consideration (more so than the regular traveller) on the Southern, which considered its role as the gateway to the Sunny South as paramount.

Some three years after the new stock first appeared, things began to change. When paid holidays became general there were far more holidaymakers, and with many middle-class parents now buying motor-cars the passengers tended to become less worthy of obsequious attention. Numbers became the name of the game, with the railway and the resorts notching up records all the time.

By the mid-thirties this vast increase in summer holiday traffic was placing a strain on carriage capacity. The six-wheeled excursion stock was gone, and much of the pre-grouping bogie stock had a low passenger/coach ratio. How important Maunsell's policy of building a good number of straightforward Thirds was can be judged from the stock observed on various relief trains of the period; for example, a Bognor train on 28th March, 1937 (Easter), comprised one of his SE&CR 100-seaters, two of his re-framed LSW coaches, just one of his new Thirds, and seven assorted SE&CR short bogie coaches. One can imagine that the high-capacity stock was carefully apportioned, a coach here and a coach there, to reduce the very obvious gap between the regular train, probably all-Maunsell, and the trains which the unfortunate overspill passengers found waiting for them.

The 1938 summer season, the last full peacetime one, saw perhaps the biggest call on Maunsell's new stock. The most elastic services from the point of view of loadings were the three morning 'groups' from Waterloo. The 9.30 am 'Bournemouth Group' was increased to five trains by an additional one to Swanage; the 11.00 am 'West of England Group' now comprised six trains leaving between 10.24 and 11.06; and the 12.00 noon 'West of England Group' was also strengthened. Enough Maunsell stock could not always be found, especially on Saturdays, and there was also a 'knock-on' effect on race specials and the increasing number of Territorial camp specials, for which trains were formed from early short ex-LSW corridor stock and ex-SEC non-corridor stock. Nevertheless, stock was still well-cleaned, and when the new livery for the Bournemouth trains was introduced it was still possible to present it as some contribution to gracious living, which was certainly still going on in Bournemouth. That particular resort, with its large population of visitors too old to drive cars, was rightly the apple of the railway management's eye.

After World War II, much of the Maunsell stock on the Eastern Section was in use on the British Army of the Rhine (BAOR) leave trains, mixed in with 'Continental' stock; and again, as in the 1930s, the occasional Maunsell loose coach or rebuild helped to eke out the wasteful ex-SE&CR excursion sets. A typical example was a relief Margate train in July, 1946, with one Maunsell Third and two re-framed LSW coaches cut in with five SE&CR bogies which included two long luggage compartments. Things had changed in many ways, but the problem of matching carriage availability to demand had not gone away.

'Ironclad' Corridor Composite (built Lancing 1925) No. 6287, Diagram 284; seen in crimson and cream livery at Maze Hill, 19th September, 1956. *H.C. Casserley*

Chapter One

LSW and SR 'Ironclad' Corridor Stock

Only a small quantity of modern carriage stock was inherited from the constituent companies that made up the Southern Railway on 1st January, 1923. The South Eastern & Chatham had turned out an eight-coach corridor boat train in 1921; the London, Brighton & South Coast had nothing that could be described as modern (which here implies flush-sided corridor stock); and the London & South Western had built four 5-coach pantry sets for the Bournemouth line in 1921, followed in 1922 by two boat trains. Coaches for six more 5-coach sets were under construction at Eastleigh Carriage Works and were completed in 1923.

The so-called 'Ironclad' coaches were in fact steel-clad, with a body length of 57 ft, body width of 9 ft and a height from rail to rooftop of 12 ft 5 in. Screw couplings and British Standard gangways were fitted at each end of the vehicles. Bogies, of 9 ft wheelbase, had outside frames and double bolster, the whole giving an air of solid construction. Indeed, the coaches themselves had a heavy look about them and were wider and higher, although not longer, than any previous LSW stock.

Each Third Brake had four compartments with a large area for luggage. The guard's duckets, and the way the bodysides of the luggage compartment were swept in, were notable features. Each set was made up with a Third Brake at one end having a right-hand corridor and one at the other end with a left-hand corridor. There was an eight-compartment Third, plus a seven-compartment Third that incorporated a small pantry compartment that occupied the space that would otherwise have been taken up by one compartment and lavatory. A seven-compartment First completed the formation. Sets were numbered 1C to 4C ('C' standing for 'corridor'); the Southern renumbered them 431 to 434.

Sets 1C and 2C were dated July, 1921; Set 3C September; and Set 4C November, 1921. In the lists below the original LSW numbers, the later SR numbers and dates of renumbering are shown.

	Set 1C	**Set 431**	
	LSW	*SR*	
Third Bke	1277	3182	2.24
Ptry Third	930	713	2.24
First	3867	7170	2.24
Third	773	717	2.24
Third Bke	1276	3181	2.24

	Set 3C	**Set 433**	
	LSW	*SR*	
Third Bke	1279	3184	4.27
Ptry Third	932	715	4.27
First	3922	7171	4.27
Third	778	719	4.27
Third Bke	1280	3185	4.27

	Set 2C	**Set 432**	
	LSW	*SR*	
Third Bke	1275	3180	12.24
Ptry Third	931	714	12.24
First	3864	7168	12.24
Third	774	718	12.24
Third Bke	1278	3183	12.24

	Set 4C	**Set 434**	
	LSW	*SR*	
Third Bke	1282	3187	2.25
Ptry Third	933	716	2.25
First	3923	7172	2.25
Third	929	720	2.25
Third Bke	1281	3186	2.25

Regarding the Third Brakes, viewed from the guard's compartment the corridor was on the right-hand side of Nos. 3180/2/4/7 and on the left-hand side of Nos. 3181/3/5/6. This makes sense only when it is realised that the

South Western liked to marshal its coaches so that the corridors alternated from one side to the other down the train; if the set had an odd number of vehicles, as these did, then inevitably brake coaches had to be in left-hand and right-hand versions.

A new type of coach was introduced in 1922: the Pantry Brake First, which was designed for Southampton boat trains and had three first class compartments, a lavatory, and a kitchen/pantry between the compartments and the brake-end. To go with them were 16 Firsts: sufficient stock to run two 10-coach trains, although not in permanent sets, some of the coaches standing spare at slack times. Original LSW numbers, building dates, SR numbers and dates of renumbering are shown below.

FIRSTS

LSW	*Built*	*SR*		*LSW*	*Built*	*SR*	
3854	5.22	7166	5.28	3929	6.22	7178	9.27
3858	"	7167	1.28	3930	"	7179	3.28
3866	"	7169	3.28	3931	8.22	7180	7.28
3924	"	7173	5.28	3932	"	7181	1.28
3925	"	7174	6.28	3933	"	7182	7.28
3926	6.22	7175	2.28	3934	"	7183	6.28
3927	"	7176	7.28	3935	"	7184	7.28
3928	"	7177	7.28	3936	"	7185	3.28

PANTRY FIRST BRAKES

LSW	*Built*	*SR*		*LSW*	*Built*	*SR*	
4061	6.22	7711	11.27	4063	8.22	7713	2.28
4062	5.22	7712	11.27	4064	8.22	7714	2.28

A further six 5-coach sets were completed in 1923; these did not have a Pantry Third, its place being taken by an additional eight-compartment Third. The intention was to run the trains as 6-coach dining sets, using either wooden-bodied dining cars or two new steel-clad dining cars. The first four sets were turned out in LSW livery (sage green) with LSW numbers, but the last two had Southern lettering and numbers (the green was the same), the numbering system having been worked out by September 1923. Sets 5C and 6C were dated March, 1923; Sets 7C and 8C June; and the final two were October, 1923. Below are given formations, LSW and SR numbers and dates of renumbering.

	Set 5C	**Set 435**			**Set 7C**	**Set 437**	
	LSW	*SR*			*LSW*	*SR*	
Third Bke	1353	3190	5.28	Third Bke	1356	3192	11.28
Third	67	724	5.28	Third	69	725	11.28
First	3938	7187	5.28	First	3939	7188	11.28
Third	66	723	5.28	Third	70	726	11.28
Third Bke	1354	3191	5.28	Third Bke	1357	3193	11.28

	Set 6C	**Set 436**			**Set 8C**	**Set 438**	
	LSW	*SR*			*LSW*	*SR*	
Third Bke	1310	3188	12.27	Third Bke	1365	3195	2.28
Third	64	722	12.27	Third	73	727	2.28
First	3937	7186	12.27	First	3940	7189	2.28
Third	62	721	12.27	Third	74	728	2.28
Third Bke	1325	3189	12.27	Third Bke	1366	3196	2.28

		Set 439 SR
Third Bke	—	3194
Third	—	729
First	—	7190
Third	—	730
Third Bke	—	3197

		Set 440 SR
Third Bke	—	3198
Third	—	731
First	—	7191
Third	—	732
Third Bke	—	3199

In all cases seating was four-a-side in the third class compartments and three-a-side in the firsts. Third Brakes Nos. 3188/90/2/4/5/8 had right-hand corridors (viewed from the brake-end) and Nos. 3189/91/3/6/7/9 had left-hand corridors. Bogies were as before, but from Set 437 on the coaches had 9 ft wheelbase inside-frame, double bolster bogies with laminated side bearing springs and large helical bolster springs.

The two dining cars, numbered 7850 and 7851, were completed towards the end of 1923. They had 57 ft bodies. Each had two dining saloons for a total of 29 third-class diners, and there was a kitchen and pantry.

Some more loose 'Ironclads' were built in 1924. They ran on the 9 ft inside-frame bogies described above. Thirds Nos. 745–750 were completed in April and 751–754 in May, 1924; Firsts Nos. 7192–7199 in March and 7200 and 7201 in April, 1924. Another new type was the Composite, of which there were four built in May, 1924, and numbered 5133–5136; each had three first and four third class compartments.

At a meeting of the Southern's Locomotive, Carriage and Electrical Committee on 30th April, 1924, more coaches to the South Western design were authorised: six dining cars, eleven Corridor Firsts, one Corridor Composite, five Corridor Brake Composites, nine Corridor Thirds, eight Third Brakes with four compartments and seven Third Brakes with six compartments. These were to be turned out as four 5-coach sets for Waterloo–Bournemouth services, five 2-coach sets for Waterloo–Lymington and Swanage through portions, and one 11-coach train for London–Brighton services. The dining cars would run in the 5-coach sets, although not permanently formed in them.

The Bournemouth sets, Nos. 441 to 444, were built in 1925: No. 441 in July, 442 in August, and 443/4 in September. Original formations were:

	Set 441	Set 442	Set 443	Set 444			
Third Bke	3203	3205	3207	3209	Order	No	E23
Third	755	757	760	762	"	"	E21
First	7202	7203	7204	7205	"	"	E17
Third	756	758	759	761	"	"	E21
Third Bke	3204	3206	3208	3210	"	"	E23

In this batch, Third Brakes 3203/6/7/9 had right-hand corridors and Nos. 3204/5/8/10 left-hand corridors. Bogies of the Firsts only were the SEC single-bolster type, 8 ft wheelbase. Body width was 9 ft 1 in. over duckets.

The dining cars, Nos. 7852 to 7857, were to the same design as the earlier two, with 9 ft inside-frame double bolster bogies, and were built in 1925: 7852–4 in July and 7855–7 in August (Order No E16).

Each of the 2-coach sets, Nos. 381 to 385, was made up of a six-compartment Third Brake and a Composite Brake with two first class and four third class compartments; both vehicles had left-hand corridors. The Composite Brake continued LSW practice of placing the two first class compartments in the centre of the coach rather than at one end as in later practice. Why the Third Brakes of Sets 381 and 382 were numbered in the 'Central Section' series is unknown. All were completed in October, 1925, although Set 382 did not enter traffic until the following April.

	Set 381	**Set 382**	**Set 383**	**Set 384**	**Set 385**	
Third Bke	4052	4053	3211	3212	3213	Order No E24
Compo Bke	6560	6561	6562	6563	6564	" " E20

Lancing Carriage Works had the task of building the coaches for the Central Section, and they were the last to be built there; in future only carriage underframes would be built and carriage repairs and repaints carried out. The 11-coach train, intended for the 'City Limited' Brighton–London Bridge fast, was completed in December, 1925. Little third class accommodation was provided because the patronage of the 'City Limited' was largely by wealthy businessmen and stockbrokers. The vehicles built, and Order Nos, were:

> Third (eight compartments) 2341 (L22); Third Brakes (six compartments) 4043, 4044 (L24); Composite (three first and four third class compartments) 6287 (E19); Firsts (seven compartments) 7652–7658 (E18).

All the coach numbers were in the 'Central Section' series. Bogies were the 9 ft wheelbase inside-frame type.

The last 'Ironclad' train was authorised at the Rolling Stock Committee meeting of 6th April, 1925: it was to be an 11-coach train for the Bognor, Worthing and London service and was built at Eastleigh Carriage Works. It

'Ironclad' 5-coach set on up West of England service in the 1920s. The second coach is a Pantry Third. *Locomotive Publishing Co.*

was ready for traffic in January, 1926. Coaches ran on 8 ft wheelbase single bolster bogies. The vehicles were:

Thirds 2346 to 2348; Third Brakes 4046, 4047; Firsts 7659 to 7664. All to Order No. E85.

They were to the same design as the Lancing-built train. It is perhaps surprising that an 'Ironclad' train should have been built as late as 1925 as the Southern had already decided (in January, 1924) to adopt Pullman gangways, and the 'Ironclads' all had British Standard gangways, many of which had subsequently to be fitted with adaptors to allow them to work with Pullman-gangwayed stock. However, as a 'stop-gap' while the standard Southern coaches were being designed, the South Western's 'Ironclad' stock was excellent.

The two Central Section trains were numbered 471 and 472, and ran slightly reduced in formation with Pullman cars added. Formation and working as from 24th September, 1928, were:

	Set 471		Set 472
Third Bke	4043	Third Bke	4046
Composite	6287	Third	2346
First	7652	First	7661
First	7653	First	7662
First	7654	3rd Pullman	—
1st Pullman	—	First	7663
First	7656	First	7664
First	7657	Third	2348
First	7658	Third Bke	4047
Third	2341		
Third Bke	4044		

Set 471: 8.45 am Brighton–London Bridge, 5.00 pm return.
Set 472: 9.20 am Brighton–London Bridge, 6.00 pm return.

Three of the spare 'Ironclads', along with three ex-LSW wooden-bodied corridor coaches, were included in Set 455, which was made up for Brighton line services. This set ran in service formed Third Brake 3162, Third 2347, First 7659, First Pullman, Third Pullman, First 7660, Third 690 and Third Brake 3174. It was scheduled to work: 8.55 am Brighton–Victoria, 2.05 pm Victoria–Brighton; 5.05 pm Brighton–Victoria, 7.05 pm Victoria–Brighton; 10.05 pm Brighton–Victoria, 12.05 mdt Victoria–Brighton.

On the Western Section by 1929 Pullman adaptors had been fitted to the gangways of all the Third Brakes of sets 431–444 and to the Firsts in sets 431–5 and 444 only. In these sets one Third or Pantry Third had been replaced by a 1927-built Open Third with Pullman gangways coupled to a Kitchen/Dining First of 1927, also with Pullman gangways. One of the sets was running in 1929 as three coaches only (Third Brake, First, Third Brake) as the Bournemouth portion of the 'Bournemouth Limited' and shown in the Waterloo Carriage Workings as 'Part 4 cor. set (431 class)'. Nos. 431 and 432 were both noted in this form by R.W. Kidner in 1929.

The altered sets were referred to as 6-dining sets 'A' type. Those with their original formation, Nos. 436–43, ran with either LSW or 'Ironclad' dining cars and were designated 6-dining sets 'B' type. They were similarly altered in 1931, losing one of the Thirds and running either as 4-sets or 6-dining sets as required by traffic.

Workings of 6-dining sets Nos. 431 to 444 as from 21st September, 1931, were:

Working No.

1. 8.30 am W'loo–Bournemouth West and 2.25 pm return.
3. 11.30 am W'loo–Bournemouth West and 5.08 pm return.
4. 12.30 pm W'loo–Bournemouth West and 6.26 pm return.
5. 7.24 am Bournemouth West–W'loo and 1.30 pm return.
6. 12.21 pm (FSO)* Bournemouth West–W'loo. On Sundays worked 6.40 pm W'loo–Salisbury.
7. 8.10 am (MO) Salisbury–W'loo. 2.30 pm (FSO) W'loo–Bournemouth.
9. 8.35 am Bournemouth West–W'loo and 4.45 pm return.
10. 10.17 am Bournemouth West–W'loo and 5.30 pm return.
11. 10.55 am Bournemouth West–W'loo and 6.30 pm return.
12. 1.15 pm Bournemouth West–W'loo and 7.30 pm return.

Four spare sets.

Workings of these sets as from 1st May to 4th June, 1936, were little changed:

9. 8.30 am W'loo–Bournemouth West and 2.20 pm return.
10. 9.30 am W'loo–Bournemouth West and 3.25 pm return.
11. 11.30 am W'loo–Bournemouth West and 5.10 pm return.
13. 7.25 am Bournemouth West–W'loo and 1.30 pm return.
14. 12.17 pm (FO) Bournemouth W–W'loo and 2.30 pm (SO) return.
15. 10.42 am (WO) (Excursion) W'loo–Weymouth and 7.32 pm (WO) return.
    11.08 am (ThO) (Excursion) W'loo–Weymouth and 6.23 pm (ThO) return.
    2.30 pm (FO) W'loo–Bournemouth West and 12.17 pm (SO) return.
16. 7.33 am Bournemouth West–W'loo and 3.30 pm return.
18. 10.18 am Bournemouth West–W'loo and 5.30 pm return.
20. 1.20 pm Bournemouth West–W'loo and 7.30 pm return.
25. (7-dining set 443) 8.00 am Portsmouth Harbour–W'loo, 12.50 pm W'loo–Portsmouth Hbr, 3.48 pm Portsmouth Hbr–W'loo and 6.50 pm return.

Two 5-sets were on the Brighton–Cardiff service and two 4-sets stood spare at Clapham Yard.

The Pantry Thirds, on being removed from 'Ironclad' sets 431–4, were assembled into un-numbered 5-pantry sets Type 'D', used only during the summer season. Workings from 7th July to 20th September, 1930, included the 10.30 am (SX), 10.35 am (SO) Waterloo to Bournemouth and 3.30 pm (SX), 3.07 pm (SO) return; and the 8.36 am Bournemouth to Waterloo and 3.30 pm return. In later years use of the Pantry Thirds declined and in 1936 they were withdrawn for conversion into ordinary eight-compartment Thirds: this work was completed in July 1936.

On 15th August, 1936, fire broke out on the Jersey special boat train when near Micheldever and the bodies of Firsts 7169 and 7180 were completely destroyed. The underframes were stated by the chief mechanical engineer to be 're-useable' and, sure enough, they turned up a couple of years later in 'new' push and pull sets 657 and 656.

*FSO–Fridays & Saturdays Only; MO–Mondays Only; WO–Wednesdays Only (etc).

After the electrification of the Portsmouth line it was found possible to work all Bournemouth dining car train services with Maunsell stock, except during the summer season, and the 'Ironclad' sets were all re-formed and transferred to secondary services. All were reduced to 4-coach sets; the Third in each one was replaced by a Pullman-gangwayed vehicle of more recent construction. Sets 431 to 444 now had, in set number order, Thirds Nos. 1194, 1185, 1854, 1843, 1184, 1204, 1902, 1903, 842, 1831, 1826, 1814, 1230 and 1901. Those with flush windows and quantities of screw-heads visible on the bodysides did not go very well with the 'Ironclad' body style. The sets still could be, and were, made up to 6-dining sets by the addition of a Maunsell kitchen car and Open Third; and to seven-, eight-, or ten-dining sets by adding Corridor Thirds as required.

Some examples of 'Ironclad' Saturday workings in the summer of 1938 were:

Working No.

74. (6-dining set). 7.22 am Basingstoke–W'loo, 9.17 am W'loo–Wareham, 2.25 pm Bournemouth Central–W'loo.
75. (6-dining set). 7.10 am Southampton Docks–W'loo, 9.40 am W'loo–Lymington Pier, 1.35 pm return.
76. (6-dining set). 11.47 am W'loo–Exmouth.
77. (6-dining set). 1.48 pm Exmouth–Waterloo.
80. (7-dining set). 12.22 pm W'loo–Swanage, 6.40 pm return.
81. (8-dining set). 9.22 am W'loo–Bournemouth West, 2.33 pm Bournemouth Central–W'loo.
82. (10-dining set). 6.39 am Basingstoke–W'loo, 8.27 am W'loo–Bournemouth West, 1.11 pm return.

By September, 1938, none of the eight 'Ironclad' restaurant cars had any regular working but were kept in reserve. Three of the 4-coach sets ran on Portsmouth–Salisbury–Bristol services, all others being spare. Pantry Brake Firsts Nos. 7711–4 were used only on Southampton boat trains. Of the five 'Ironclad' 2-sets Nos. 381–5, two were used on the Bournemouth West –Manchester through portions and two on a Bournemouth West–Guildford service (which included a through coach to/from Margate).

Sets 431–44 were kept busy in wartime. Seven ran as 5-dining sets without Open Thirds; six on Waterloo–Plymouth services and one between Exeter and Waterloo, from 1st March, 1941. 'Ironclad' restaurant cars were 'temporarily' withdrawn and Pantry Brake Firsts ran in service unstaffed. Later in the War, *all* restaurant cars were withdrawn, and the workings for 2nd October, 1944, show that 4-sets 431–44 were booked for many Weymouth and West of England services as well as the Brighton–Plymouth services, only one set being spare at Clapham Yard for cleaning. The 'Ironclad' 2-coach sets also appeared on West of England trains as there were no Swanage or Lymington through portions in wartime.

Restaurant cars Nos. 7850/1/2/4 were fitted up, between May and July, 1944, as canteens for the Civil Engineer's Department war damage mobile repair parties, and Nos. 7855/6/7 were similarly converted about October, 1944, being renumbered in the Service Vehicles list as 624S to 630S, in the same order, late in 1947, when they began to be used for various departmental purposes.

In 1946 there was once again a major change in the formation of Sets 431 to 436. The Maunsell Thirds were removed and to replace them were 'Ironclad' Thirds scraped up from the pool of 'loose' coaches. Once again the Third Brakes and First in each set were unchanged. Sets 431–3 ran on Southampton and Exeter services; Nos. 434–6 were special traffic sets.

	Set 431	**Set 432**	**Set 433**
Third Bke	3181	3180	3184
Third	715	747	755
First	7170	7168	7171
Third	720	759	751
Third Bke	3182	3183	3185

	Set 434	**Set 435**	**Set 436**
Third Bke	3186	3190	3188
Third	716	726	713
Third	721	728	748
First	7172	7187	7186
Third	722	752	718
Third	727	760	719
Third	754	761	2346
Third Bke	3187	3191	3189

By 1947 Nos. 431–3/7–9 had also been strengthened to 8-sets in a similar manner to Nos. 434–6 and all were relegated to special traffic working. Sets 440–4, remaining as 4-coach sets, worked on Brighton/Portsmouth–Cardiff services.

On the Central Section, Sets 455, 471 and 472 were reduced to four coaches after the Brighton electrification in 1933 and were transferred to London–Bognor/Portsmouth services until they were in turn electrified in 1938. After that it is believed that the three began working on the Oxted line. The Carriage Working Notice for 5th May, 1941, shows that Set 455 was booked to work the 8.30 am Tunbridge Wells West to London Bridge; except on Saturdays it returned on the 4.40 pm to Uckfield and 6.50 pm thence to Tunbridge Wells. On Saturdays it ran empty from London Bridge via Eardley to Victoria, picking up two extra Thirds on the way, then returned 'home' on the 1.25 pm from Victoria. By June 1947, it was a 7-set berthed at New Cross Gate for special traffic.

Four-sets 471/2 in 1941 had no booked workings and were berthed at New Cross Gate. However, the improved post-War services saw their return into traffic, No. 471 as 6-coach and No. 472 as 5-coach, on Oxted line services. On 29th July, 1947, K. Nunn photographed the 5.20 pm London Bridge –Tunbridge Wells West, formed of a very crowded Set 471 hauled by class 'J2' locomotive No. 2326.

Changes to the set formations are summarised below:

455: Reduced to 4-set; 7659 and 690 to 'Loose', c.1933. Ex-LSW panelled Corridor Third 699 added by 1941; ditto Cor. First 7162 in 1946; ditto Cor. Comp 5077 in 1947.

471: Reduced to 4-set; 7653/4/6/7/8, 6287, to 'Loose', c.1933. 6287 to Set 422, 1945. 757, 5134 ex-'Loose' added c.1942. 4043 to Set 465, replaced by Maunsell Brake Compo 6582 ex-'Loose', c.1946.
472: Reduced to 4-set; 2346, 7661/2/3 to 'Loose', c.1933. 7663 restored c.1944.

Some more of the spare 'Ironclad' coaches were used to replace ex-LSW panelled corridor coaches in Set 457, which had been made up originally in 1931 for Southampton Docks–Waterloo services. Formations varied with traffic requirements and are not known for certain until 1944; Third No. 724 was transferred to the set from loose stock by May 1943, and Composite 5133 by May 1944. Formation from 1944 was:

	Set 457
Third Bke	3101 (CA)
Third	723 (CA)
Third	724 (CA)
First	7173 (CA)
Compo	5133 (CA)
Third	725 (CA1)
Third	758 (C)
Third Bke	3167 (CA1)

C: British Standard gangways.
CA: British Standard gangways, adaptor fitted.
CA1: British Standard gangways, adaptor fitted at one end.

Only the Third Brakes were LSW corridors. After being taken off boat train services in the mid-1930s it became a special traffic set. The Thirds went to Set 438 in 1948, the Composite to Set 442 and the First to loose stock.

Of the 154 'Ironclads' built, including 40 by the LSW, only two had not survived to become part of British Railways stock on 1st January, 1948.

The four Pantry Brake Firsts, Nos. 7711–4, were converted to six-compartment First Brakes in 1949 by stripping the pantry compartment in each and building three first class compartments in the space.

During 1949, 2-sets 381–4 were converted to push-and-pull for use on Western Section branch lines. Each Third Brake was given an extra compartment with consequent reduction in length of the luggage compartment, the lavatory was altered to a coupé with six seats and the corridor connections were removed. A standard driving end with four windows in groups of two was fitted at the brake end of the coach and there was a droplight in each side ducket. Composite Brakes merely had their lavatories altered to coupés seating six and the gangways were removed. Sets 381/3 were in service by May 1949, and 382/4 by September. The 1949 allocations were: 381, Seaton; 382, Gosport; 383, Yeovil Town; 384, Bordon. By 1951 Set 382 was on the Lymington branch. Unconverted Set 385, running with two extra Thirds, worked Bournemouth West–Chester services from 1949 to 1952, when it too was withdrawn for conversion to a push-and-pull set in the same manner as the other four; from June 1952, it was based at Bournemouth West as relief set.

All five sets remained on the Western Section. No. 382 suffered fire damage at Bournemouth West on 20th August, 1959, and was withdrawn; but the others all lasted until 1962.

It will be recalled that all save one of the 'Ironclad' restaurant cars had been altered to service vehicles with the numbers 624 S to 630 S. The fate of these was noted by Mr L.A. Mack, who states that 624 S was last noted about 1948, 625 S became DS 625 in the early 1950s, 626 S may have been withdrawn as early as 1947, 627 S was last noted in mid-1949, 628 S withdrawn probably between 1947 and 1949, 629 S became DS 629 and 630 S was last observed about 1952. 624 S was officially withdrawn about October 1955.

No. 625 S was used at Ilfracombe as a dormitory coach for the 'Devon Belle' Pullman car staff until the demise of that train in September 1954. It was painted green for the Operating Department in 1956 and again in 1960, when it was noted at Grove Park. It was used for parcels traffic in December 1961, and was moved to Woking in 1963. Overhauled at Selhurst in 1972 it was sent to Fratton; then from 1975 to 1979 it stood at Guildford. On being withdrawn and offered for sale it was purchased by the Mid Hants Railway, arriving there in December 1980.

No. 629 S was also a dormitory coach (at Padstow c.1948 and for the 'Devon Belle' c.1952). It was painted red in 1955 and used for the Chief Civil Engineer's department at Orpington, Woking, Faversham in 1959, Hythe (Hants) in 1960, Basingstoke and Ascot in 1963. In that year it appeared in 'gulf red'; when seen at Micheldever in July 1970, it was blue on one side only. It was sold for scrap to Cohen of Morriston in October 1970.

No. 7853 was repainted in 1949 in the new British Railways standard livery of crimson and cream. It was rebuilt into a Cafeteria Car in 1950 and from September 1952 was allocated to the Western Region, presumably numbered in the style W 7853 S. There it remained until its withdrawal in January 1963.

Four-coach sets 442/3 were used on Brighton/Portsmouth & Southsea –Cardiff services during 1948 and 1949, the two sets being joined or divided at Fareham and making the single journey outwards on Monday, Wednesday and Friday and returning on Tuesday, Thursday and Saturday. In 1950 and 1951 4-sets 442/4 were used.

In 1948 and 1949 6-set 444 worked the 7.25 am Salisbury–Bristol, 10.27 am Bristol–Portsmouth & Southsea, and 7.17 pm Portsmouth–Salisbury. In 1950 it was reduced to four coaches for the Cardiff services, and in 1952 it became an 8-set for special traffic and summer services on the Western Section.

From 1950 Set 443, now five coaches, worked the Bournemouth–Birkenhead service, in 1952 becoming a 7-dining set. By 1954 it was a special traffic set of eight coaches. In 1952 Set 442 took over the Portsmouth –Salisbury–Bristol service as a 6-set, becoming an 8-coach special traffic set a year later.

Sets 431–41 had been eight-coach for special traffic and summer services from 1948, still mostly made up of 'Ironclad' stock. Gradually they, and Nos. 442–4, metamorphosed into Maunsell sets as coaches were replaced. Most of the sets lasted until 1959, still working on the Bournemouth line on summer Saturdays. Certain vehicles were repainted crimson and cream, others remained green (often examples of both were in the same set).

In 1954 several 'Ironclad' Firsts were downgraded to Thirds and marshalled into three 'new' special traffic sets for the Western Section, Nos. 274 –276. Below is a list showing old and new numbers.

Old No.	*New No.*	*Old No.*	*New No.*	*Old No.*	*New No.*	*Old No.*	*New No.*
7166	2320	7176	2326	7195	2331	7656	2336
7167	2321	7177	2327	7198	2332	7659	2337
7189	2322	7178	2328	7202	2333	7661	2338
7173	2323	7183	2329	7203	2334	7662	2339
7174	2324	7187	2330	7654	2335	7663	2340
7175	2325						

The 10-coach sets were formed with Maunsell Composite Brakes and Composites, one of the latter type being an 'Ironclad'.

	Set 274	**Set 275**	**Set 276**
Compo Bke	6596	6597	6591
Third	2325	2321	2320
Third	2326	2323	2322
Third	2327	2324	2329
Third	2328	2337	2331
Compo	5133	5585	5588
Third	2332	2338	2335
Third	2334	2330	2336
Third	2340	2333	2339
Compo Bke	6598	6600	6593

Nos. 2320/2/9 were withdrawn in March 1958, and replaced by Maunsell Seconds Nos. 1202/15/26. There were no other changes, and all three sets were withdrawn in the summer of 1959.

The 7-set 455 in 1948 comprised mainly ex-LSW panelled coaches, but still included 'Ironclads' Nos. 2347 and 7660. It was berthed at New Cross Gate for special traffic, mainly on the Eastern Section. In 1950 it was strengthened to nine vehicles and comprised Third Brake 3162, Thirds 699 and 2347, Firsts 7660 and 7162, 'Thanet' Composite 5527, Maunsell Third 1906, Third 762 and Third Brake 3174. During summer Saturdays and Sundays it worked Charing Cross–Dover–Ramsgate services. Three vehicles were replaced in 1955, and the set was withdrawn in September 1956.

Until June 1953, 6-set 471 was based at Brighton for regular Oxted line services, Mondays to Fridays only. These were: 6.58 am Brighton–London Bridge via Ashurst; 4.40 pm London Bridge–Uckfield; 6.40 pm Uckfield –Tunbridge Wells West and thence 7.37 pm to Brighton. From June 1953, it was strengthened to eight coaches with Maunsell Open Thirds 1305 and 1345 and berthed at Bellingham, working the following summer-only services: 8.58 am Bromley South–Ramsgate and 7.44 pm Broadstairs–Victoria (SX); 9.45 am Bromley South–Ramsgate and 1.42 pm Dumpton Park–Victoria (SO). Summer services on the Kent Coast line in the 1950s were intensive, and much empty working was necessary. After some re-formations – a crimson and cream liveried coach was in the otherwise all-green set in June 1957 – Set 471 was withdrawn in June 1959.

Set 472 was five coaches in 1948/9, four coaches plus a loose Third from September 1949 to June 1953, and again five coaches until June 1955. During this time it was based at Tunbridge Wells West for the following regular workings, Mondays to Fridays: 8.30 am to London Bridge and 10.45 am return; 1.08 pm to London Bridge and 6.30 pm return. On Saturdays it worked the 10.06 am to Victoria and 1.25 pm return. From June 1955, it too was strengthened to eight coaches and transferred to Blackheath for special traffic, working on summer Saturdays the 10.06 am Victoria–Margate and 4.52 pm return. Now including various Maunsell coaches, it was withdrawn in June 1959, rendered surplus to requirements by electrification.

'Ironclad' Corridor Third No. 721, Diagram 24, built 1923, here formed in Set 434; seen here at Brockenhurst, 20th May, 1957. *H.C. Casserley*

'Ironclad' Corridor Brake Third No. 3180, Diagram 135, built 1921 and withdrawn in October 1957; LSW 9 ft-wheelbase bogies. *Lens of Sutton*

Joining a section from Swanage (which includes an 'Ironclad' 2-set) on to a special train from Weymouth at Wareham. Close view of brake-end of Maunsell Diagram 2101 Third Brake; 13th August, 1932. *R.W. Kidner*

'Ironclad' Corridor First of 1925, No. 7657 (Diagram 476). The vehicle was withdrawn in August 1959. *Lens of Sutton*

Disposition and withdrawal dates of 'Ironclad' corridor coaches

The following list shows coach numbers and the sets in which each vehicle was placed from inception until final withdrawal. The date following each set number is that of the coach's first appearance in the set concerned, according to the Carriage Working Notices or their appendices, but in some cases the actual date of transfer from one set to another may have been some months earlier. 'L' indicates a loose coach.

THIRDS

Coach	Sets	Withdrawn
713	431, L, 437 1948	4.57
4	432, L, 441 1948	6.57
5	433, L, 431 1946	10.57
6	434, L, 434 1946	11.57
7	431, L, 349 1945, 438 1948, 433 6.56	10.57
8	432, L, 436 1947	4.57
9	433, L, 436 1947	6.57
720	434, L, 431 1946	10.57
1	436, L, 434 1946	10.59
2	436, L, 434 1946	10.59
3	435, L, 457, 438 1948	1.59
4	435, L, 457 5.43, 438 1948	10.57
5	437, L, 457, 438 1948, L 1957	12.60
	Re-instated 3.61	2.62
6	437, L, 435 1946	8.59
7	438, L, 434 1946	4.58
8	438, L, 435 1946	8.59
9	439, L, 437 1948, 432 6.56	10.57
	Re-instated 11.58	12.60
	Re-instated 3.61	2.62
730	439, L, 436 1947, 432 6.56	10.57
1	440, L, 422 1945, 411 1946, 441 1948	11.58
732	440, L, 436 1947	10.58
745	L, 343 1945, 437 1948	7.59
6	L, 441 1948	59
7	L, 432 1946, 438 6.57, 426 6.59	10.61
8	L, 437 1948	8.59
9	L, 431 1948	10.59
750	L, 441 1948, 440 6.56	7.59
1	L, 433 1946	12.57
2	L, 435 1946	59
3	L, 349 1945, 437 1948	8.59
4	L, 434 1946, 433 6.56	11.61
5	441, L, 433 1946	12.57
6	441, L, 422 1945, 411 1946, 441 1948	8.59
7	442, L, 471 c.42	7.59
8	442, L, 457 c.42, 438 1948, L 1958	2.62
9	443, L, 432 1946	6.61
760	443, L, 435 1946, 440 6.56	11.59
1	444, L, 435 1946	8.59
762	444, L, 455 1950, 472 6.55	7.59
2341	471	7.59
2346	472, L c.33, 436 1947	12.61
7	455, 436 6.57	9.58
2348	472	7.59

THIRD BRAKES

Coach	Sets	Withdrawn
3180	432, L 6.57	10.57
1	431, L 6.57	10.57
2	431, L 6.57	10.57
3	432	12.58
4	433, L 6.57	12.57
5	433, 434 6.57	1.58
6	434	1.58
7	434, L 6.57	12.57
8	436	9.58
9	436	10.57
3190	435	8.59
1	435	8.59
2	437	8.59
3	437	8.59
4	439	10.59
5	438	1.59
6	438	1.59
7	439	10.59
8	440	10.57
3199	440	10.57
3203	441	8.59
4	441	8.59
5	442	9.61
6	442	6.61
7	443	11.59
8	443	11.59
9	444	11.59
3210	444	11.59
1	383	12.62
2	384	12.62
3213	385	8.62
4043	471, 465 c.46	8.59
4044	471	7.59
4046	472	7.59
4047	472	7.59
4052	381	12.62
4053	382 Damaged 8.59	11.59

COMPOSITES

Coach	Sets	Withdrawn
5133	L, 457 5.44, 442 1949, 274 6.54	7.59

COMPOSITES - Continued

No.	Details		Withdrawn
5134	L, 471 c.42		7.59
5	L, 443 1949, 99 6.50		12.57
5136	L, 405 1945, 309 1952, L 6.57, 341 6.58		12.59
6287	471, L c.33, 422 1945, 411 1946, 444 1949, L 6.52		6.59

COMPOSITE BRAKES

No.	Details		Withdrawn
6560	381		12.62
1	382 Damaged 8.59		10.59
2	383		12.62
3	384		12.62
6564	385		8.62

FIRSTS

No.	Details		Withdrawn
7166	L, to 3rd 2320 6.54.	276	3.58
7	L, to 3rd 2321 7.54.	275	8.59
8	432, 438 6.54, L 1957		10.57
9	L Fire damage		8.36
7170	431, L 1957		10.57
1	433, L 1957		10.57
2	434, L 1957		10.57
3	L, 457 1942, L 1948. To 3rd 2323 6.54.	275	8.59
4	L, to 3rd 2324 7.54.	275	8.59
5	L, to 3rd 2325 6.54.	274	7.59
6	L, to 3rd 2326 6.54.	274	7.59
7	L, 328 1944, L 1947. To 3rd 2327 1954.	274	7.59
8	L, to 3rd 2328 1954.	274	7.59
9	L, 441 6.57, L 1959		10.59
7180	L Fire damage		8.36
1	L, 438 6.57		1.59
2	L, 441 1954		10.56
3	L, to 3rd 2329 6.54.	276	3.58
4	L, 433 6.57		4.58
5	L, 431 6.57		1.58
6	436		10.58
7	435. To 3rd 2330 7.54.	275	8.59
8	437		8.59
9	438. To 3rd 2322 10.54.	276	3.58
7190	439		2.59
1	440		10.57
2	L, 434 6.57		9.59
3	L,		12.58
4	L, 444 1952		2.59
5	L, to 3rd 2331 6.54.	276	8.59
7196	L, 442 1954		1.59

FIRSTS - continued

No.	Details		Withdrawn
7197	L, 201 6.57		12.59
8	L, to 3rd 2332 6.54.	274	7.59
9	L, 432 6.57		12.58
7200	L, 432 1954, L 1957		11.57
1	L, 443 6.54		12.59
2	441, L 1948, to 3rd 2333 7.54.	275	8.59
3	442, L 1948. To 3rd 2334 6.54.	274	7.59
4	443, L 1948		12.58
7205	444, L 1949 234 6.57		11.59
7652	471, L 6.57		11.58
3	471, L c.33. 440 6.58		7.59
4	471, L c.33. To 3rd 2335 6.54.	276	8.59
5	L, 435 1954		8.59
6	471, L c.33. To 3rd 2336 6.54.	276	8.59
7	471, L c.33		8.59
8	471, L c.33, 441 6.59		8.59
9	455, L c.33. To 3rd 2337 7.54.	275	8.59
7660	455, L 6.57		2.62
1	472, L c.33. To 3rd 2338 7.54.	275	8.59
2	472, L c.33. To 3rd 2339 6.54.	276	8.59
3	472, L c.33, 472 c.44, L 1949. To 3rd 2340 6.54.	274	7.59
7664	472, L 1957		2.62

FIRST BRAKES

No.	Details	Withdrawn
7711	L, 354 6.51, L 6.57	11.58
2	L, 355 1951, L 1952	10.58
3	L, 355 1951, L 1952	5.59
7714	L, 356 1951, L 1952	8.59

RESTAURANT CARS

No.	Details	Withdrawn
7850	L	12.47
1	L	47
2	L	c.47
3	L. Cafeteria, 1950	1.63
4	L	c.47
5	L	c.47
6	L	c.47
7857	L	c.47

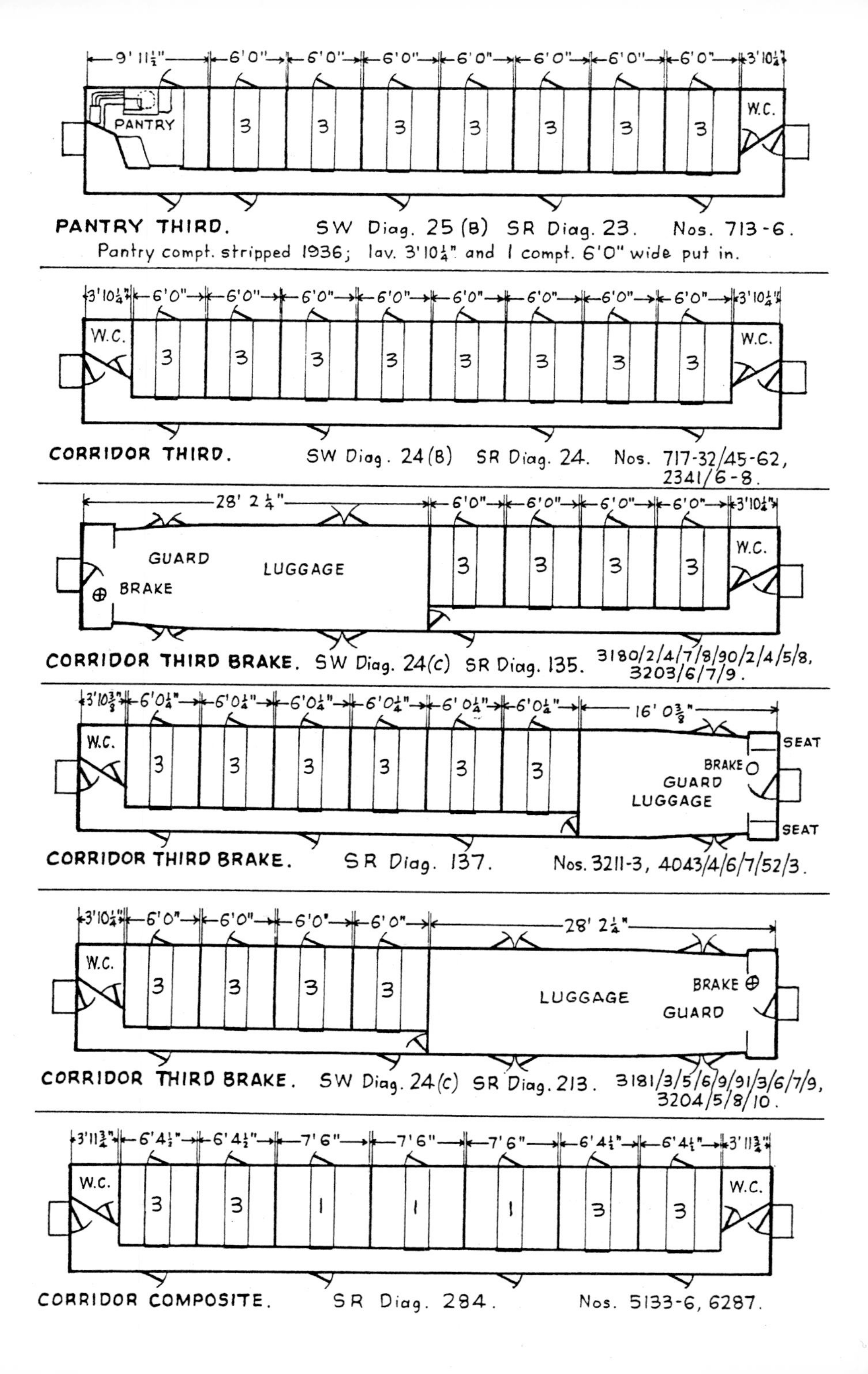

PANTRY THIRD. SW Diag. 25 (B) SR Diag. 23. Nos. 713-6.
Pantry compt. stripped 1936; lav. 3'10¼" and 1 compt. 6'0" wide put in.

CORRIDOR THIRD. SW Diag. 24 (B) SR Diag. 24. Nos. 717-32/45-62, 2341/6-8.

CORRIDOR THIRD BRAKE. SW Diag. 24(C) SR Diag. 135. 3180/2/4/7/8/90/2/4/5/8, 3203/6/7/9.

CORRIDOR THIRD BRAKE. SR Diag. 137. Nos. 3211-3, 4043/4/6/7/52/3.

CORRIDOR THIRD BRAKE. SW Diag. 24(C) SR Diag. 213. 3181/3/5/6/9/91/3/6/7/9, 3204/5/8/10.

CORRIDOR COMPOSITE. SR Diag. 284. Nos. 5133-6, 6287.

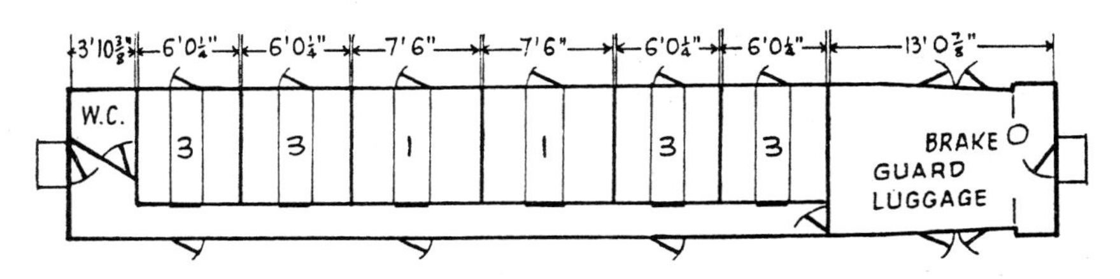

CORRIDOR BRAKE COMPO. SR Diag. 416. Nos. 6560-4.

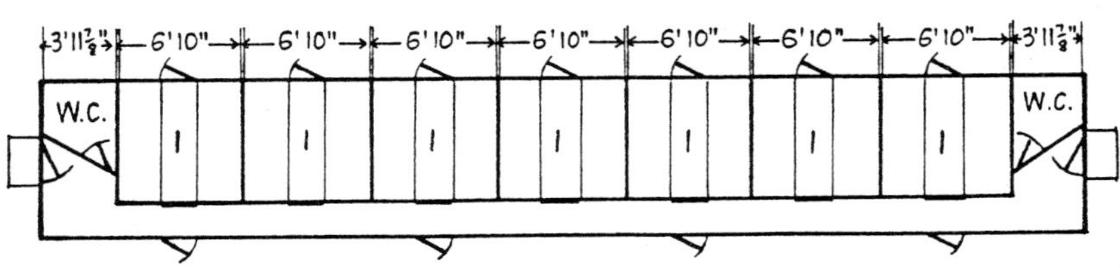

CORRIDOR FIRST. SW Diag. 36(c) SR Diag. 476. Nos. 7166-7205, 7652-64.

CORRIDOR THIRD. Diag. 25 ex 476 (1954). Nos. 2320-40.

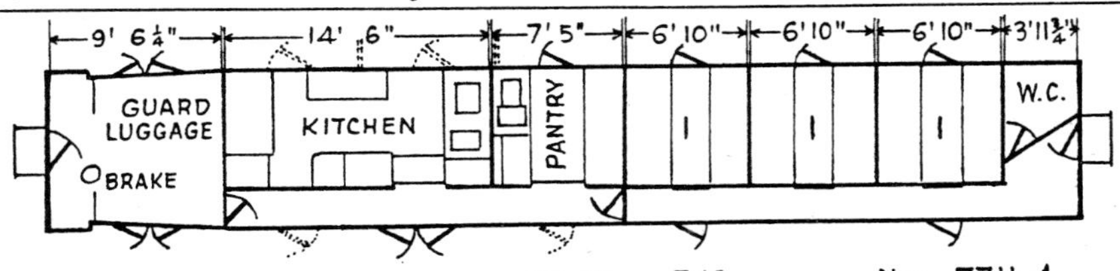

PANTRY BRAKE FIRST. SR Diag. 542. Nos. 7711-4.

Altered 1949 to Cor. Bke First; Kitchen and Pantry stripped and replaced by 3 1st Cl. compts. each 7'3¼" wide. Diag. 542A.

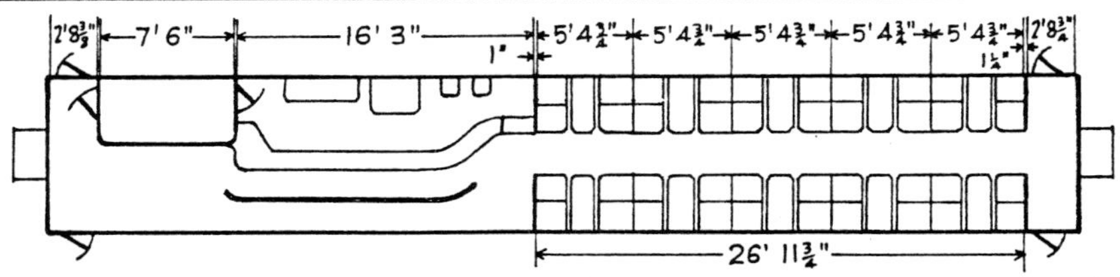

CAFETERIA CAR. Diag. 600. No. 7853.

Rebuilt 1950 from Restaurant Car 7853 (S.R. Diag. 592).
Seats: 40 Third Cl.

STANDARD DIMENSIONS. Body length: 57'0". Length over buffers: 60'7".
Body width: 9'0". Height, rail to roof: 12'5".
Bogie wheelbase: 9'0" (some 8'0"). Bogie centres: 41'0".

'Ironclad' stock converted to service vehicles

A great many 'Ironclads' were converted to service vehicles on being withdrawn from passenger stock, the great majority being used as staff and tool vans for breakdown trains. Here is the list:

SECONDS

713-5 to DS 172-4, c 1958. Breakdown Riding Vans. Condemned pre 82
717 to DS 226, 12.58. Breakdown Staff Van.
718-20 to DS 175-7, c 1958. Breakdown Tool Vans. Condemned pre 82
721 to 081272 Internal Use, 12.60.
722 to 081274 Internal Use, 6.61.
724 to DS 225, 12.58. Breakdown Tool Van.
726 to DS 70127 11.63. Breakdown Van (Tool) Nine Elms ; later Power Supply Section, Horsham.
728 to DS 70011, 9.60. Breakdown Staff Van, Brighton.
730 to DS 228, 11.59. Wimbledon Breakdown Train Unit (Staff)--1976.
745 to DS 70138, 8.61. Dormitory. Condemned 3.81
746 to DS 70012, 10.60. Stewarts Lane Breakdown Train Unit (Staff)--1978
747 to DS 70128, 1961. Eastleigh Breakdown Train Unit (Tool)--1975.
748 to DS 229, c 1959. Breakdown Van Bricklayers Arms 10.60 ; Hither Green 11.68 - 11.75.
749 to DS 70010, 7.60. Breakdown Van. Plymouth WR 6.77. Condemned 4.81
750 to DS 70123, 1962. Breakdown Van (Riding) ; later Power Supply Section, Horsham.
752 to DS 70014, 9.60. Breakdown Van (Tool) Brighton.
753 to DS 230, c 1959. Breakdown Van (Staff) Bricklayers Arms 10.60 ; Hither Green 11.68 - 11.75.
756 to DS 70015, 10.60. Breakdown Van (Tool) Stewarts Lane.
760 to DS 70013, 1959. Breakdown Van (Tool) Exmouth Junct. Cond. 1979
761 to DS 70124, 1962. Eastleigh Breakdown Train Unit (Staff)--1975

SECOND BRAKES

3180 to DS 70024, 6.59. Mess Van, Signals & Telegraphs. Condemned 10.79
3181 to DS 70030, 6.59. Faversham. Condemned 1.69
3182 to DS 231, 1959. Mess & Tool, Wimbledon Breakdown Train.
3183 to DS 70026, 8.59. Condemned in 1960s
3184 to DS 178, 12.57. Staff & Tool. Brighton, 7.78 Condemned c.83
3187 to DS 179, 12.57. Staff & Tool. Breakdown Train Unit. Guildford, Chart Leacon, Stewarts Lane. Sold to Mid-Hants Railway, 1.80.
3188 to 081038 Internal Use (Woking).
3190 to DS 70016, 1959. Breakdown Van, Exmouth Junction. Became DW 70016 after boundary changes. Sold to Mid-Hants Railway 10.78.
3191 to DS 70131, 6.62. Breakdown Van. Condemned 3.73
3193 to DS 70133, 1962. Breakdown Van. At Brighton 1978.
3194 to 081302 Internal Use, c.1961.
3195 to DS 70027, 8.59. Mess Van--Western Division. Condemned 9.72
3196 to DS 70028, 8.59. Condemned 5.69
3197 to 081271 Internal Use, c 1960.
3198 to DS 232, 1959. Brighton Breakdown Train Unit (Staff & Tool)--1978.
3199 to DS 70033, 10.59. Condemned 12.67
3203 to DS 70017, 1959. Breakdown Van. Condemned 2.73
3204 to DS 70085, 8.59. Yeovil Junction. Condemned 6.73 ; sold to Somerset & Dorset Rly Museum Trust.
3207 to DS 70068, 2.60. Lancing Works Train. Condemned 8.64
3208 to DS 70061, 2.60. Lancing Works Train. Re-No DS 70132, 8.62. Power Supply, Horsham--2.81.
4046 to DS 70089, 1960. Mess & Tool Van. Condemned 10.68
4047 to DS 70112, 3.61. Woking, 10.79. Condemned 3.81

FIRSTS

7182 to 080619 Internal Use, c 1957.
7200 to DS 227, 11.59. Wimbledon Breakdown Train Unit (Tool)--1976

Chapter Two

SECR and SR 'Continental' Corridor Stock

In August, 1921, the South Eastern & Chatham Railway had put into service a fine 8-coach corridor train for its Continental boat train services between Victoria and Dover Marine. Body length of each vehicle was 62 ft, width 8 ft 0¾ in. and height from rail to roof 12 ft 2 in. The brake coaches were not gangwayed at the outer ends and ordinary screw couplings and buffers were fitted there; but the rest of the train had Pullman gangways and buckeye automatic couplers. Coaches were 64 ft 8 in. overall, brakes being 65 ft 2¾ in. overall.

There were four types of coach. Seconds, numbered 2501–3, each had seven compartments seating 42 passengers, and two lavatories. The Second Brake, No. 2504, had six compartments for 36 passengers, and one lavatory. Firsts, numbered 2505–7, had six compartments each, seating 24, with two lavatories. Finally came the First Brake No. 2508, with four compartments seating 16, a lavatory, and a small saloon at the brake end with four armchairs.

Entry doors opened inwards, and the lower panels of each vehicle were most beautifully matchboarded. The whole train was renumbered at Ashford in November 1923:

Old No.	*New No.*	*Old No.*	*New No.*	*Old No.*	*New No.*	*Old No.*	*New No.*
2504	4156	2502	4160	2505	7367	2507	7369
2501	4159	2503	4161	2506	7368	2508	7745

The First Brake became a Composite Brake, renumbered 6642 in March 1925; surprisingly the saloon compartment became part of the second class accommodation with eight seats in addition to four in an ordinary compartment, and the remaining three first class compartments seated twelve.

Another two 8-coach boat trains were on order at the time of the Grouping; SEC numbers were allocated but not carried, since by the time the vehicles were completed towards the end of 1923 the Southern carriage renumbering scheme had been worked out. Dimensions were as before, but the Firsts and Seconds were each given an extra coupé compartment in place of one of the lavatories, giving two extra first class seats and three extra second class. The saloon in the First Brake contained six armchairs.

Type	*No.*	*Built*	*Type*	*No.*	*Built*
Second Bke	4157	10.23	First	7370–2	10.23
"	4158	2.24	"	7373–5	2.24
Second	4162–4	10.23	First Bke	7746	10.23
"	4165–7	2.24	"	7747	2.24

The need for more corridor stock on the boat trains being urgent, the next lot were ordered in October 1923 from contractors, who could supply the goods quicker than the Southern's own workshops were able to. Contracts were placed with the Birmingham Railway Carriage & Wagon Co. for eight Firsts at £2,995 each and twelve Seconds at £2,900 each, and with the Metropolitan Carriage, Wagon & Finance Co., Saltley, for nine First Brakes at £2,790 each and twelve Third Brakes at £2,750 each.

By March 1924, six Seconds had been delivered at Ashford, three more in April and the final three in May. The Firsts were delivered in June 1924, by which time MCW&F had delivered only five Third Brakes. Four more came in July and the last three in August. Finally came the First Brakes, of which three had been received in July and the remaining six in August 1924. By October all were in traffic.

Third Brakes were numbered 3548 to 3557, Seconds 4168 to 4179, Firsts 7376 to 7383 and First Brakes 7748 to 7756.

They differed from the earlier stock in having bodies 8 ft 6½ in. wide, and the height from rail to roof was increased to 12 ft 3 in. Each Third Brake had seven compartments seating 45 passengers, three-a-side, being very luxurious for third class. Compartments and seating for the other three types were as for the 1923 stock. Like them, coaches were equipped with Pullman gangways and auto-couplers except at the brake-ends; the bodies were matchboarded; and entry doors opened inwards. On each side of every door was a distinctive long grab-rail.

That took care of the Continental traffic for the moment; however, a surprising feature of the programme of new rolling stock ordered in April 1926 was an order for more 'Continental' vehicles. There were to be six Firsts and four Thirds for the Victoria–Folkestone and Dover boat services (Order No. E162).

By 1927 the bodies were under construction at Eastleigh Carriage Works, and it had been arranged that their underframes should be built by outside contractors. In March 1927, the tender of the Metropolitan Carriage, Wagon & Finance Co. at £766 a frame was accepted.

The Thirds, numbered 779 to 782, were similar to the 1924 series of Seconds, seating 45 passengers in 7½ compartments (three-a-side) and the coach bodies were 62 ft by 8 ft 6½ in. The Firsts, numbered 7384 to 7389 and completed in October 1927, had the same dimensions and accommodation was 26 passengers in 6½ compartments. One source states that the Thirds were built by Birmingham RC&W Co.

These ten vehicles were the last to be built. During the lifetime of the Southern the stock remained exclusively on Folkestone, Dover and Gravesend boat trains, but not in numbered sets (although between 1923 and 1928 Sets Nos. 510–2 were used for 'Continental' stock). Later, formations were made up as required for the particular service and often standard Maunsell stock was mixed in. The Gravesend boat train (for the Rotterdam service) was a real curiosity; often the formation was just one 'Continental' First, a Maunsell 'Nondescript' boarded as Second, and a 'Continental' Third Brake.

Use of second class for through travel to the Continent seemed to be on the decline in the 1930s and so in 1934 all the 'Continental' Seconds and Second Brakes were downrated, being renumbered into the Third Class series. Nos. 4168–79 became Nos. 996 to 1007 in the same order and Nos. 4159–67 became Nos. 1010 to 1018 in the same order. Second Brakes 4156–8 were renumbered 3587 to 3589. Maunsell 'Nondescripts' thereafter provided second class accommodation on boat trains.

Coaches 779 and 7372 were burnt out at Dover Marine in July 1935; and during the War Nos. 1014, 7369 and 7382 were destroyed by enemy action. First Brakes 7750/56 had been given new interiors in about 1939 as part of the 'Improved Boat Stock' scheme.

Of the 75 'Continental' coaches built, eight by the SECR and the rest under Southern auspices, 70 remained to become the property of British Railways in 1948.

A scheme begun during the last years of the Southern was continued by BR: the re-hanging of the entry doors so that they opened outwards instead of inwards. Apparently with the original arrangement it was too easy for a passenger to fall out of the carriage. Many of the doors had their domestic-style panelling covered with steel sheet, and the long, straight, exterior grab-rails beside the doors were removed; the right-hand one was replaced by a kinked hand-rail, presumably so designed to be well clear of a passenger's knuckles as he pulled open the door.

'Continental' stock continued to be seen on boat trains, including by now some of those on the Newhaven services, and in deference to their main-line status several vehicles were repainted in BR's crimson and cream livery, some with the vehicle number at the left-hand end of the body, others with it displayed at the right-hand end. Examples were 3552 (LH), 3554 (RH), 7750 (LH) and 7751 (RH). Boat trains were formed with the Third Brake normally at the country end and the First Brake at the London end.

Composite Brake No. 6642 in 1949 was regularly booked to form the 4.40 am Faversham to Sheerness service, returning attached to other stock at 8.00 am. In 1951 it was still scheduled for the 4.40 am, but returned at 7.55 am (SX), 10.11 pm (SO) to Faversham.

Decline began in 1953, when two 'Continental' Third Brakes were formed in an otherwise non-corridor special traffic set, No. 897. A year later, 13 Firsts were downrated to Thirds, the centre armrests being removed to increase the seating capacity to 39. These were Nos. 7376–81/3–9, which became Nos. 643–655 in the same order. They were formed, with Maunsell Brake Composites and a former First, into two special traffic sets for the Eastern Section, Nos. 261 and 262. At the same time five of the 8 ft Thirds were formed into a 10-coach set, No. 938, for the Hastings line, these being Nos. 1012/3/6/7/8. Formations were:

	Set 261	**Set 262**
Bke Compo	6580	6592
Third	649	644
Third	647	645
Third	648	646
Third	643	650
Third	651	653
Third	652	655
Third	654	656
Bke Compo	6579	6581

	Set 938
Third Bke	3677
Third	1012
Third	1013
Compo	5592
Compo	5593
Compo	5594
Third	1016
Third	1017
Third	1018
Third Bke	3676

Set 261 was berthed at Bellingham from June 1954, and at Blackheath in 1955–7. It worked the 8.06 am Victoria to Margate and 3.34 pm return, summer Saturdays only. In 1956 it was booked for the 9.32 am Gravesend

Central to Ramsgate and 1.46 or 3.40 pm Margate to Victoria, empty to Blackheath, summer Saturdays only. Set 262 was berthed at Folkestone Junction and its only booked services were the 8.45 am to Charing Cross and 10.44 am return on Saturdays during the summer. Set 261 was withdrawn in September 1958, after accident damage at Maze Hill on 4th July, 1958, and Set 262 in May 1959.

Most of the 'Continentals' were withdrawn in 1959, there being no requirement for special traffic sets once the Ramsgate electric services began. Three Second Brakes lasted into 1961; of these No. 3557 became a departmental vehicle, DS 70120, normally kept at Woking; No. 3550 stood in sidings near Gatwick Airport during September 1961, after its withdrawal; and No. 3554 was purchased by Mr Roy Edwards for £250 with the intention of re-selling it to the Westerham Valley Railway Society, of which he was a committee member. It was kept at Hassocks from 20th August, 1962, but when it became clear that the Westerham scheme was going to fail the vehicle was offered for sale to another railway preservation society in the south of England. This body showed no interest, so the coach was purchased by the Keighley & Worth Valley Railway for £237 10s. It left Hassocks for Keighley on 24th February, 1965.

The 'Continental' was as non-standard a coach as it was possible to be. Not only did the doors open inwards but instead of being equipped with droplights as one would expect they had fixed windows. All other Pullman-gangwayed stock was bow-ended but the 'Continentals' had flat ends; this brought the corner pillars of adjoining coaches much closer together than normal. Each compartment had a droplight but no external door. Corridor-side fixed windows and droplights were arranged in a hit-and-miss fashion and it was impossible to judge from the window layout this side how many compartments the coach might have had. In the pre-War period not only was the class written on the doors but in figures beside the doors as well. The unusual panelling (like that of one's kitchen door) has already been referred to. They were, indeed, remarkable vehicles.

'Continental' Third Brake No. 3556 on Gravesend–Rotterdam service passing Bromley South, 27th August, 1937. *H.C. Casserley*

The 2.00 pm Folkestone Harbour service near Shortlands; 'Continental' stock and Pullman cars in lake livery. *A.W.V. Mace*

'Continental' Corridor Third Brake No. 3554 of 1924 with altered doors (Diagram 164A) at Eardley Sidings on 14th June, 1957. *H.C. Casserley*

'Continental' Third No. 646 (formerly First No. 7379 of 1924); withdrawn May 1959. *Lens of Sutton*

Disposition and withdrawal dates of 'Continental' coaches

The following list shows coach numbers and the sets in which certain vehicles were placed. The date following each set number is that of the coach's first appearance in the set concerned, according to the *Appendix to Carriage Working Notice*. 'L' indicates a loose coach.

THIRDS

779	L. Fire, Dover Marine	7.35
780	L, 212 6.56	6.61
1	L, 212 6.56	6.61
782	L, 212 6.56	6.61

SECONDS

4159	To 3rd 1010 1934. 389 6.56	2.59
4160	To 3rd 1011 1934. 389 6.56	2.59
1	To 3rd 1012 1934. 938 6.54	7.59
2	To 3rd 1013 1934. 938 6.54	7.59
3	To 3rd 1014 1934.	c.41
4	To 3rd 1015 1934. L	3.58
5	To 3rd 1016 1934. 938 6.54	2.58
6	To 3rd 1017 1934. 938 6.54	7.59
4167	To 3rd 1018 1934. 938 6.54	7.59
4168	To 3rd 996 1934. 463 6.58	7.59
9	To 3rd 997 1934. L	8.57
4170	To 3rd 998 1934. L	10.59
1	To 3rd 999 1934. L	8.59
2	To 3rd 1000 1934. L	12.58
3	To 3rd 1001 1934. L	8.59
4	To 3rd 1002 1934. L	8.59
5	To 3rd 1003 1934. L	10.59
6	To 3rd 1004 1934. L	6.59
7	To 3rd 1005 1934. L	7.59
8	To 3rd 1006 1934. L	9.59
4179	To 3rd 1007 1934. L	11.58

SECOND BRAKES

4156	To 3rd Bke 3587, 1934. L, 211 9.58	7.59
4157	To 3rd Bke 3588 1934. L, 211 9.58	7.59
4158	To 3rd Bke 3589 1934. L, 696 6.57	7.59

THIRD BRAKES

3548	L, 462 6.58	7.59
9	L, 237 6.57	7.59
3550	L, 468 6.60	7.61
1	L, 237 6.57	7.59
2	L, 263 6.50, L 6.53	10.59
3	L, 917 1956	7.59
3554	L, 468 6.60	7.61

THIRD BRAKES - continued

3555	L	9.59
6	L	7.59
7	L	61
8	L, 263 6.50, L 6.53	10.59
3559	L, 211 6.53, L 9.54	10.59

FIRSTS

7367	L, 937 6.58		2.59
8	L		1.58
9	L Enemy action		12.40
7370	L		2.59
1	L		5.58
2	L Fire, Dover Marine		7.35
3	L		10.58
4	L, 389 6.54.		2.59
5	L		4.58
6	To 3rd 643 6.54.	261	9.58
7	To 3rd 644 6.54.	262	5.59
8	To 3rd 645 6.54.	262	5.59
9	To 3rd 646 6.54.	262	5.59
7380	To 3rd 647 6.54.	261	9.58
1	To 3rd 648 6.54.	261	9.58
2	L Enemy action, Clapham Junction		9.40
3	To 3rd 649 6.54.	261	9.58
4	To 3rd 650 6.54.	262	5.59
5	To 3rd 651 6.54.	261	9.58
6	To 3rd 652 6.54.	261	9.58
7	To 3rd 653 6.54.	262	5.59
8	To 3rd 654 6.54.	261	9.58
7389	To 3rd 655 6.54.	262	5.59

FIRST BRAKES

7745	To Compo Bke 6642 3.25. L, 917 1956	7.59
7746	L	3.59
7	L	8.59
8	L	8.59
9	L	7.59
7750	L	7.59
1	L	7.59
2	L	7.59
3	L	11.58
4	L	2.59
5	L	12.58
7756	L	7.59

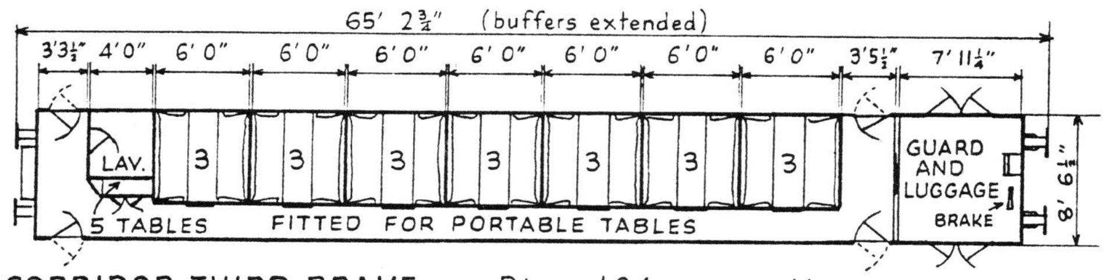

CORRIDOR THIRD BRAKE. Diag. 164. Nos. 3548 - 3559.
Doors altered to open outwards: Diag. 164A.

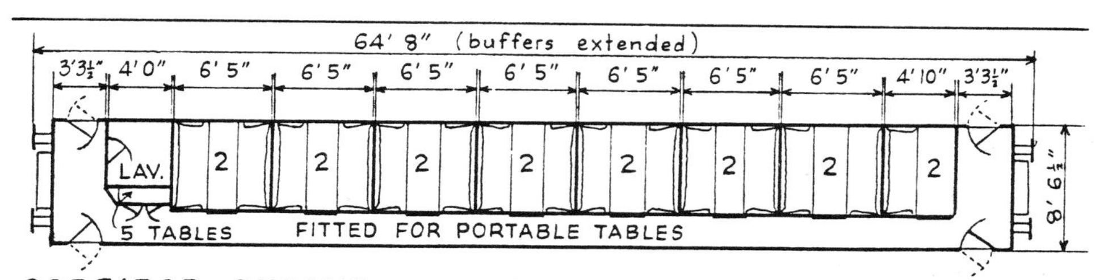

CORRIDOR SECOND. Diag. 235. Nos. 4168 - 4179.
Transferred in 1934 to
CORRIDOR THIRD. Diag. 2002. Nos. 996 - 1007, 779 - 782.
Doors altered to open outwards: Diag. 2002A.

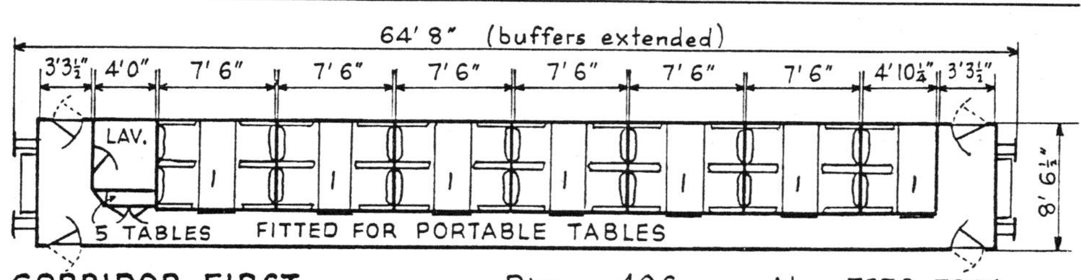

CORRIDOR FIRST. Diag. 496. Nos. 7376 - 7389
Doors altered to open outwards: Diag. 496A. Transferred in 1954 to
CORRIDOR THIRD. Diag. 54A. Nos. 643 - 655.
Centre armrests removed.

CORRIDOR FIRST BRAKE. Diag. 552. Nos. 7748 - 7756.
Doors altered to open outwards: Diag. 552A.

STANDARD DIMENSIONS. Body length: 62' 0". Height, rail to roof: 12' 3". Bogie wheelbase: 8' 0". Bogie centres: 44' 0".

Chapter Three

1924/5 Eastern Section Corridor Stock

The need for corridor stock on the former SE&C main lines to the Kent coast was very great, and so in June 1923, new stock was authorised to be built – the first such authorisation given by the Southern Railway. Although it seems likely that the design, for three types of coach, was worked out at Ashford, work of construction was divided between Eastleigh Works and the former LB&SC carriage works at Lancing: Order Nos. E4 (Composites), E5 (Thirds) and E6 (Third Brakes).

The coaches were peculiarly 'Eastern Section' with many SE&C features in the styling. Commode handles – with their sharp reverse curves – and the door ventilator bonnets were pure SEC style. The roofs had destination board brackets located just below the rainstrip on each side. Coaches were 57 ft over body, 8 ft 6 in. wide and 12 ft 3 in. high from rail to roof. Length over buffers was 60 ft 9½ in. Screw couplings and British Standard gangways were fitted; many of these had subsequently to be fitted with adaptors to allow them to work with Pullman cars and the later Maunsell stock.

Each Third had eight compartments with 64 seats and a lavatory at each end. The Third Brake had five compartments seating 40 also with one lavatory. The Composite had four first and three third class compartments, with 16 and 24 seats respectively, and there were two lavatories. In many ways these 77 coaches were the precursors of the Maunsell/Lynes standard type of carriage, which was to incorporate both LSW and SEC features.

The trains were delivered in 8-coach formations, but it seems certain they were not kept intact for very long. Eastleigh constructed the first five trains and Lancing the final four.

Third Bke	3562	3566	3570	3574	3578
Third	977	981	985	989	993
Compo	5505	5513	5521	5534	5542
Compo	5506	5514	5522	5535	5543
Compo	5507	5515	5523	5536	5544
Compo	5508	5516	5524	5537	5545
Third	978	982	986	990	994
Third Bke	3563	3567	3571	3575	3579

Third Bke	3564	3568	3572	3576
Third	979	983	987	991
Compo	5509	5517	5530	5538
Compo	5510	5518	5531	5539
Compo	5511	5519	5532	5540
Compo	5512	5520	5533	5541
Third	980	984	988	992
Third Bke	3565	3569	3573	3577

The first train was completed in October 1924, the second in November, the third in December, the fourth in January 1925, and the fifth in March. Lancing sent out its first train in March, followed by its second in April and the final two were dated May 1925. Eastleigh also built five spare Composites numbered 5525 to 5529 in May 1925.

The first of the new trains, with a Pullman formed in the centre, entered service on 17th November, 1924, and worked the following services: 8.45 am Ramgate to Victoria, 11.35 am (SO) Victoria to Ramsgate, 3.00 pm (SO) Ramsgate to Victoria, and 7.00 pm Victoria to Ramsgate. The second set was introduced on 20th November, starting with the 3.15 pm Victoria to Ramsgate and returning the next day on the 10.00 am Ramsgate to Victoria.

The introduction of these corridor trains meant that most of the principal Kent Coast services were now supplied with respectable stock. A First Class Pullman car, by 1933 altered to Composite, was usually found in the centre of the set to provide refreshments for those prepared to pay the supplement. The coaches were switched about, the sets were reduced to seven vehicles in most cases (the Pullman making eight in total), and after 1927 one set was deleted altogether.

Disaster overtook three of the 'Thanet' coaches on 24th August, 1927, when the 5.00 pm Cannon Street to Folkestone train became derailed and hit a bridge near Sevenoaks. In the 8-coach train four vehicles were damaged beyond repair, three of these being Third Brake 3564 and Composites 5518 and 5520. Apparently the original formations had been altered as early as 1927, and after that accident they were altered still further. During 1928 Mr R.W. Kidner recorded that each 7-coach train was running as either three or four coaches with the set numbers 386 to 388, 423 to 426 and 460 to 463. Some of these must have been observed at different times as there were not enough Third Brakes to provide for 11 complete sets at any one time. It seems likely that during 1928 there was some renumbering of sets, 11 numbers being used over the whole 1927/8 period although never more than eight at once. By 1929 it was noted that the sets were 'running normally'. Nos. 386, 387 and 426 were deleted and Nos. 388 and 425 remained as 4-sets.

7-coach set No. 460 ('Thanet' stock) plus Pullman on the Sunday 5.10 pm Victoria to Ramsgate service leaving Bromley South on 24th July, 1932. *H.C. Casserley*

These are the formations as shown in the Carriage Working Notice dated 6th January, 1935. 'CA1' indicates 'British Standard Gangways, adaptor fitted at one end of the coach only'.

	Set 388		**Set 425**		**Set 462**
Third Bke (CA1)	3566	Third Bke (CA1)	3565	Third Bke	3576
Compo (CA1)	5513	Compo (CA1)	5535	Compo (CA1)	5534
Compo (CA1)	5514	Compo (CA1)	5539	Pullman Compo	—
Third Bke (CA1)	3573	Third Bke (CA1)	3575	Compo (CA1)	5533
				Third	993
				Compo	5540
				Compo	5523
				Third	987
				Third Bke	3577

	Set 423		**Set 460**
Third Bke	3567	Third Bke (CA1)	3562
Compo	5516	Third	977
Compo	5515	Compo	5507
Compo (CA1)	5543	Third	991
Pullman Compo	—	Compo (CA1)	5506
Third (CA1)	983	Pullman Compo	—
Third Bke	3570	Compo (CA1)	5508
		Third Bke (CA1)	3563

	Set 424		**Set 461**		**Set 463**
Third Bke	3571	Third Bke (CA1)	3568	Third Bke	3572
Compo	5528	Third	980	Third	994
Third	986	Compo	5511	Third	984
Third	982	Compo (CA1)	5510	Compo	5532
Compo (CA1)	5542	Pullman Compo	—	Compo	5526
Pullman Compo	—	Compo (CA1)	5509	Third	990
Compo (CA1)	5536	Compo	5512	Third Bke	3578
Third Bke	3579	Third Bke (CA1)	3569		

Sets 423/4, 460–3 each had a regular 'out-and-home' working on the Kent Coast main line, including the business trains between Ramsgate and Cannon Street via Chatham. Set 460 worked the 5.10 pm (Sundays) from Victoria to Ramsgate during 1932.

The working of Pullman cars in the sets was from 1933 arranged so that Victoria–Ramsgate services normally had a Composite car provided, whilst the Charing Cross–Dover–Ramsgate services still had First Class cars. There was one oddity, however, as the 9.40 am Victoria to Dover via Maidstone East – a working for one of the 4-sets 388 or 425 – included a First Pullman. Third class seating on this train was scarce; probably the train did not load heavily and, typically for the Southern Railway, there was no return trip with Pullman facilities via Maidstone East. At Dover the 4-set with its Pullman (or an identical formation) was attached to the 12.38 pm Margate to Charing Cross, noted in 'Bradshaw' as having a First Pullman between Dover Priory and London. This then formed the 4.15 pm Charing Cross to Ramsgate, which possibly continued as the 7.45 pm Ramsgate to Victoria; this, according to 'Bradshaw', was the only showing of a First Class rather than a Composite Pullman on the Kent Coast.

Composite No. 5537 was burnt out at Swanley early in 1938 and its underframe used for a new Cinema Coach, numbered 1308 S in the service vehicles list. It was completed in November 1939, and made its debut at Bricklayers Arms on 24th July, 1940.

By May 1941, all the Pullmans had been removed from the sets and, with the much-reduced train services then in operation, most of the eight were spare. Nos. 388 and 425 stood at Stewarts Lane or Rotherhithe Road; Nos. 423/4/60/3 were at Eardley; and No. 462 was a standby set at Victoria. Only No. 461, berthed at Rotherhithe Road, had a booked working and then only on Sundays. It formed the 9.15 am Charing Cross to Margate and 6.30 pm Ramsgate to Victoria, returning empty to Rotherhithe Road.

All Third Brakes were now adaptor-fitted at the outer end and all loose coaches were so-fitted at both ends.

After the War the sets were back in traffic. On 20th September, 1946, Set 460 (now 8-coach) was involved in an accident at Catford, with the result that Third Brake 3563 and Thirds 977 and 991 were withdrawn. The war-time and post-War changes to the set formations are set out below.

Set	
388:	5513/4 destroyed by enemy action 1940; replaced by 5523/40 ex-Set 462.
423:	Unaltered.
424:	5528 to 'Loose', c.1941; to Set 463, 1946. Replaced by 5544 ex-'Loose'. 981 ex-'Loose' added, so now 8-set.
425:	Unaltered.
460:	3563 wdn 9/46, replaced by Maunsell 3677 ex-'Loose'. 977/91 wdn 9/46, replaced by 978/9 ex-'Loose'. 5505 added c. 1946.
461:	Unaltered.
462:	5523/40 to Set 388, 1941; 992 ex-'Loose' added, so now 7-set.
463:	5526 to 'Loose', 1941; replaced by 5517 ex-'Loose'. 5528 ex-'Loose' added 1946, so now 8-set.

Of the 77 'Thanet' coaches built no fewer than nine had been lost, leaving 68 to be taken into British Railways ownership on 1st January, 1948.

There were many alterations to the sets from 1948 onwards. Set 423 was reduced from six to four coaches in 1949, increased to eight in 1952 and to nine in 1955. Set 424 was increased from eight to nine coaches from 1949, as was Set 460 – which was further increased to ten from 1957. Set 461 became 8-coach in 1949. 7-set 462 was reduced to four coaches in 1949 and increased to eight in 1952. Finally, 8-set 463 became a 10-set from 1949. The extra coaches were taken from the 'float' of loose stock, and Maunsell standard stock was used too: 9 ft Thirds Nos. 843 and 1153 were in Set 423 from 1952; Nos. 784, 797 and 1833 were in Set 462 from 1952; and 8 ft 6 in. Saloons Nos. 7910 and 7960 were in Set 460 from 1957. Conversely, some of the 'Thanet' stock found its way to other odd sets such as Nos. 211 and 309. Third Brake No. 3677, the Maunsell 8 ft vehicle which had been a replacement due to accident damage, was itself replaced in Set 460 in 1951 by Maunsell 8 ft 6 in. four-compartment Third Brake No. 4066, transferred from Set 468.

Sets 388 and 425, which remained a 4-coach, worked ordinary services in Kent and the Oxted lines from 1948 to 1959; during each summer season from 1950 to 1958, however, they were allocated to Hastings–Western Region through services.

Set 423 also worked through services when four coaches, but from 1952 it was stabled at Stewarts Lane for special traffic and summer Saturday Victoria–Ramsgate services, and at Eardley in winter.

Set 424 was also at Eardley (Grove Park in summer from 1952) for working on summer Saturdays the 8.30 am Victoria to Margate and 3.40 pm return.

Set 460's homes from 1950 to 1959 were Herne Hill Sorting Sidings in summer, and Margate or Westgate-on-Sea in winter. Its regular summer Saturday trains were the 10.10 am Victoria to Ramsgate and 5.26 pm return.

Set 461 was berthed at St Leonards during the summer seasons from 1949 to 1958, and was booked for the Hastings to Walsall service each alternate Saturday, returning seven days later. In winter it was stored at Grove Park for special traffic.

Set 462 when four coaches worked services from Hastings to the Western Region, but from 1952 was stabled at Blackheath, where as a special traffic set it had very little work to do. In summer 1956 it was placed on a Saturday 'rounder' service: 11.26 am Victoria to Ramsgate, empty to Deal, and 3.48 pm Deal to Charing Cross.

Set 463 was stabled at Stewarts Lane in summer and Eardley during the winter in the 1950s, working Saturday Victoria–Ramsgate services at peak times. In the 1954 season it was on the 11.06 am Victoria to Ramsgate and the 5.58 pm Herne Bay to Victoria.

The first withdrawals apart from accident damage were of Nos. 3576 and 5519 from Set 462 early in 1958; they were replaced by 'Continental' Second Brake 3548 and Composite 5538. 'Continental' Second No. 996 replaced in its turn Composite 5538 in Set 463.

All eight sets were 'surplus to requirements' when the Kent Coast line electrified services began on 15th June, 1959, and so, with two exceptions, the 'Thanet' stock was withdrawn during that summer. Two Second Brakes were retained for a couple more years: No. 3566 was placed in Set 465 (then the Margate–Canterbury miners' train) and No. 3573 went to Set 156 (Clapham Junction–Kensington Olympia). After withdrawal No. 3566 was stored at Gatwick Airport sidings from late 1961 until at least April 1962.

'Thanet' Corridor Composite No. 5542, built 1925 (Diagram 317). Withdrawn in May 1959, it bears the mark of condemnation. *Lens of Sutton*

Disposition and withdrawal dates of 'Thanet' Corridor Coaches

The following list shows coach numbers and the sets in which each vehicle was placed. The date following the set number is that of the coach's appearance in the set concerned, according to the *Appendix to Carriage Working Notice*. 'L' indicates a loose coach.

THIRDS

Coach	Sets	Withdrawn
977	460	9.46
8	L, 460 1946, 696 6.57	7.59
9	L, 460 1946	7.59
980	461	7.59
1	L, 424 1941	5.59
2	424	5.59
3	423, 461 5.49	7.59
4	463	7.59
5	L, 333 1946, L 6.51, 423 6.52	7.59
6	424	5.59
7	462, 461 5.48	7.59
8	L, 332 1946, 437 9.58	8.59
9	L, 331 1946, 211 6.54	7.59
990	463	8.59
1	460	9.46
2	L, 462 1941, 460 5.49	7.59
3	462, 463 5.49	7.59
994	463	7.59

THIRD BRAKES

Coach	Sets	Withdrawn
3562	460	7.59
3	460	9.46
4	—	8.27
5	425	5.59
6	388, 465 10.59	11.61
7	423	7.59
8	461	7.59
9	461	7.59
3570	423	7.59
1	424	5.59
2	463	7.59
3	388, 156 11.59	10.61
4	L, 220 1938, 466 1959	11.59
5	425	5.59
6	462	2.58
7	462	8.59
8	463	7.59
3579	424	5.59

COMPOSITES

Coach	Sets	Withdrawn
5505	L, 460 1946	7.59
6	460	7.59
7	460	7.59
8	460	7.59
9	461	7.59
5510	461	7.59
1	461	7.59
2	461, 462 5.48, 463 5.49	7.59
3	388. Enemy action	11.40
4	388. Enemy action	12.40
5	423	7.59
6	423	7.59
7	L, 463 1941	7.59
8	—	8.27
9	L, 462 1952	2.58
5520	—	8.27
1	L, 463 9.53	7.59
2	L, 309 6.50, L 6.57, 341 6.58	5.59
3	462, 388 1941	8.59
4	L, 211 6.55	7.59
5	L, 472 6.53	7.59
6	463, L 1941, 211 6.53	7.59
7	L, 455 6.50, 211 6.55	7.59
8	424, L 1941, 463 1946, 423 9.53	7.59
9	L, 423 6.52	7.59
5530	L, 472 6.57	7.59
1	L, 263 6.55	7.59
2	463, L 9.53, 263 6.55	7.59
3	462	7.59
4	462	7.59
5	425	5.59
6	424	5.59
7	L. Fire, Swanley Jn.	3.38
8	L, 463 9.53, 462 6.58	7.59
9	425	5.59
5540	462, 388 1941	7.59
1	L, 309 6.50, L 6.57, 340 6.58	1.59
2	424	5.59
3	423, 424 5.49	5.59
4	L, 424 1941	5.59
5545	L, 917 6.57	7.59

'Thanet' stock converted to service vehicles

The following coaches were not broken up on withdrawal but instead were converted to departmental service vehicles.

SECOND BRAKES

3568 to DS 70079, 1960. Mobile Office. "Productivity Section" 1975-8.
3569 to DS 70078, 1960. Mobile Office. Condemned at New Cross Gate 1984
3571 to DS 70039, 10.59. Condemned 8.72. Morriston for scrap, 5.73
3572 to DS 70111, 1.61. Mess Van, Herne Hill. Condemned 4.66
3575 to 081133, Internal Use.
3577 to DS 70077, 6.60. Mobile Office. Condemned 7.66
3579 to DS 70040, 1960. Mobile Office. "Work Study Vehicle", 1975.

COMPOSITES

5523 to DS 70117, 3.61. Staff & Tool, New Cross Gate. At Norwood Junction 1971-6. Condemned 7.77
5525 to DS 70113, 5.61. Condemned 4.69
5530 to DS 70116, 1961. Staff & Tool. Woking.
5531 to DS 70115, c 1961. Staff. Basingstoke 1975, Guildford 1979
5532 to DS 70114, 6.61. Three Bridges. Condemned 10.71

In addition, Second No. 981 became a grounded body at Horsham in May, 1959, and Composite No. 5542 was used as a store and staffroom at Newhaven Harbour for some time after its withdrawal.

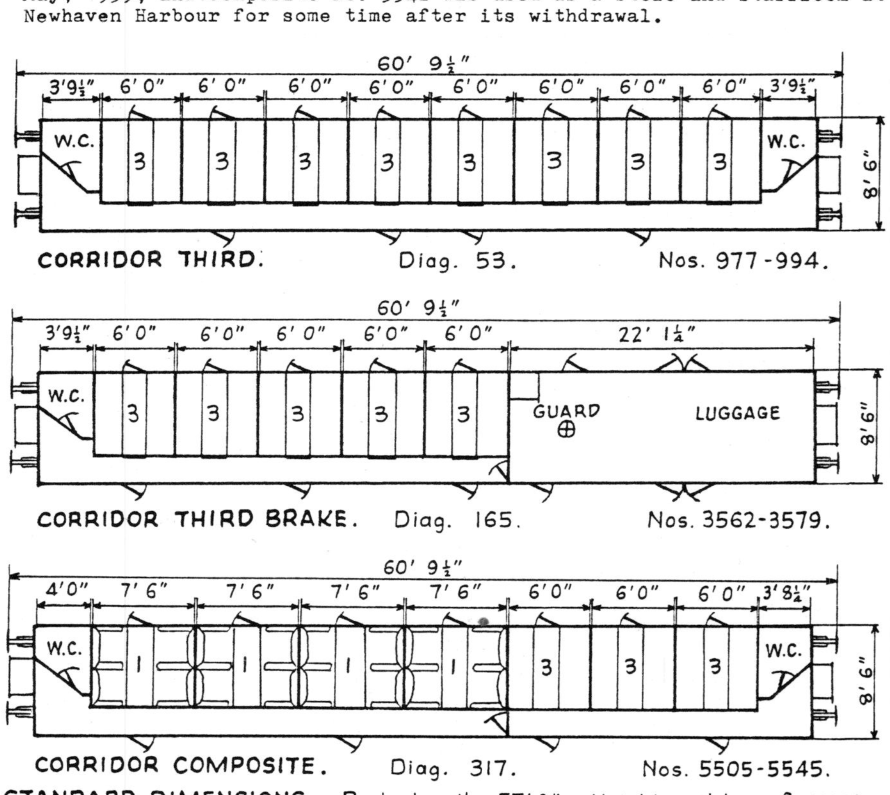

STANDARD DIMENSIONS: Body length: 57'0". Height, rail to roof: 12'3". Bogie wheelbase: 8'0". Bogie centres: 41'0".

Chapter Four

Early 59 ft Corridor Stock

By 1925, designs for a range of standard corridor coaches had been worked out; so, at the Rolling Stock Committee meeting in April, 1925, Mr Maunsell requested authority to go ahead with the construction of the following:

Ten 3-coach trains, for London, Plymouth, Torrington and Ilfracombe services.
One 8-coach train, for the Eastbourne and London service.
One 8-coach train, for the Worthing and London service.
One 11-coach train, for London and Newhaven boat services.
Six First Class Kitchen/Dining cars and six Third Class Dining cars, for the Western Section.
One 10-coach train, for Waterloo–Southampton boat services.
Ten Corridor Brake Composites, for West of England traffic.
Ten General Saloons.

Each coach had a body length of 59 ft (61 ft 7 in. overall), was 9 ft wide over body (9 ft 3 in. overall) and 12 ft 4 in. high. Standard SR bogies of 8 ft wheelbase were fitted. First class compartments were 7 ft 1¾ in. wide, seating three-a-side, and third class ones were 6 ft 3 in. wide, seating four-a-side. The body had rounded sides and bow ends, where Pullman gangways and buckeye automatic couplers were fitted. Body frame was largely of wood covered with steel sheeting; roofs were wood, canvas-covered. Window and droplight frames were stained wood, giving a very pleasing effect. Body profile and the shape of the commode handles continued Eastleigh practice, but the door and lavatory ventilator bonnets, the underframes and bogies showed the influence of Ashford. New features were the window framing, which was neater in appearance than either the LSW or the SEC version; and the guard and luggage compartment, which had straight sides, the body width at this point being only 8 ft 7 in., being finished off with a pressed steel ducket – the shape of which was completely original – on each side.

The compartment side of the coach had a door leading into every compartment, but on the corridor side there was generally a door opposite each alternate compartment. The spaces where the other doors ought to have been were occupied by 'dummy doors' – droplights just like those found on the real doors. The impression of a door was somewhat reduced by the way the lining-out, made to look like imitation panelling, was carried right across, instead of being broken to represent an imitation door panel on the imitation door! Despite the 'No Exit' notices inside, many passengers fumbled for a non-existent door handle.

The decision to adopt Pullman gangways had been made in January 1924; both the Great Western and London & North Eastern Railways had announced that they were doing so and the Southern wanted to conform. Unfortunately the GW changed its mind, with the result that during the whole 'Grouping' period two railways were using the Pullman gangway and the other two the so-called 'Standard' gangway.

The West of England three-coach sets were the first to be built. Each Third Brake, of which there were two per set, had only four compartments, with half the coach given over to a guard and luggage compartment; the half-rounded, half-flat bodysides gave the coach a rather odd appearance. The centre coach was a Composite with four first class and three third class compartments. As with all these early types corridor windows, although wide, were no higher than the door windows. Roof destination board brackets were originally located immediately above the cantrail; some years later they were moved higher up the roof to match later designs. Roofs had a single rainstrip on each side.

Formations of the 3-coach sets, which were built at Eastleigh to Order No. E94, were:

	Set 390	**Set 392**	**Set 394**	**Set 396**	**Set 398**
Third Bke	3214	3218	3222	3228	3230
Compo	5138	5141	5143	5140	5144
Third Bke	3215	3219	3223	3229	3227
	Set 391	**Set 393**	**Set 395**	**Set 397**	**Set 399**
Third Bke	3216	3220	3224	3226	3232
Compo	5139	5137	5146	5142	5145
Third Bke	3217	3221	3225	3231	3233

The Composites were completed first and then stored in sidings; when the Third Brakes were ready the sets were formed without regard to coach numbers, hence the odd order of the Composites. Sets 390–5 were completed in July 1926, and the remainder in October 1926.

Seating capacity was very low for a 3-coach train, being 24 firsts and 88 thirds. It was realised that passengers for the West of England would have mountains of luggage, so plenty of space was provided for it.

Next came the two 8-coach sets for the Central Section; the coaches were numbered in the Central Section series. Third Brakes each had six compartments and a smaller luggage compartment than the Western Section vehicles; these trains were intended for businessmen, who would not have been expected to carry much luggage with them on their daily journeys. As with the earlier 'Ironclad' sets, there was a high proportion of first class, and Pullman cars were marshalled in the middle of the sets.

	Set 469		**Set 470**
Third Bke	4048	Third Bke	4050
Third	2351	Third	2355
Third	2350	First	7674
First	7667	First	7673
First	7665	First	7672
First	7666	First	7671
Third	2349	Third	2354
Third Bke	4049	Third Bke	4051

Set 470, to Order No. E95, was completed in December 1926, and Set 469, Order No. E96, in February 1927. Each First had seven compartments and each Third eight, the layout being similar to that of the 'Ironclads' but with compartments of slightly more generous dimensions.

The running of 9 ft stock through Lewes Tunnel ceased in March 1927, owing to tight clearances, and Set 470 was transferred to Worthing–London services. The clearances were eased in 1935. An exception was made in the case of the Newhaven boat train, the stock of which was completed at

The first style of Maunsell carriage: Corridor Composite No. 5142 at Eastleigh, 1926. *National Railway Museum, Eastleigh Collection*

Pantry First Brake No. 7715 at Eastleigh in 1928, painted in 'photographic grey'. *National Railway Museum, Eastleigh Collection*

Ashford in June 1927. Authority was given to put this 9 ft stock on the Newhaven services on the understanding that no other train would be allowed to enter the tunnel while the boat train was passing through. This train was not run as a set, but the following coaches were allocated to it for use as required: Thirds 2352/3; Second Brakes 4481/2; Seconds 4483–6; Firsts 7668–70. Order No. A97. Second class compartments were the same size as Thirds, but seated three a side.

The First Class Kitchen/Dining Cars were completed in May 1927, at Eastleigh Works. Each car had a dining saloon with 24 seats arranged in four seating bays. The words DINING SALOON were lettered on the bodyside. The other half of the coach had a side corridor; there was a pantry 8 ft 8¾ in. long, a service vestibule 4 ft 3 in. across, and finally the kitchen, 13 ft 3 in. long. Double doors gave access to the transverse vestibule, but passengers could gain access to the vehicle only by means of the end gangways. Numbers were 7858–7863, to Order No. E98. To go with them were six Third Class Dining Cars, without kitchen, numbered 7864–7869, which were completed at Eastleigh in July 1927. Each was divided into three saloon compartments, and there were 64 seats and one lavatory compartment. Wide windows, with louvre-type glass ventilators over them, gave passengers a better view of the scenery than could be had from compartment stock; entry doors were at each end of the vehicle, where the bodyside was slightly recessed. The Order No. was E99.

The cars were stated to be for London–Bournemouth and London–Portsmouth services, but it seems likely that they were also put on Waterloo–Exeter workings.

Order No. E100 was the Southampton boat train, which did not run as a set, coaches being used as required. It included eight Firsts, 7208–7215, and two Pantry Brake Firsts, 7715/6; it was thus an updated version of the two 'Ironclad' 10-coach boat trains of 1922. The Firsts, of which Nos. 7209–14 were built in June and Nos. 7208/15 in July 1927, were the same as those built for the Central Section. The Pantry Brake Firsts, which were not completed until June 1928, had the same layout as the 'Ironclad' ones, except that they had SR-design duckets.

The 10 Brake Composites, Nos. 6565–6574 (Order No. E101), were intended for the single-coach through portions between Waterloo and the West of England, although with their arrival on the scene only a small proportion of these trains as yet had modern stock; the majority were still formed of ex-LSW panelled corridor sets and Brake Composites. The new Maunsell Brake Composite had four third class and two first class compartments, of which the latter were at the guard/luggage end; at the other end was located a lavatory compartment. Nos. 6565–70 came out in August 1926, and 6571–4 in September 1926.

Finally came the ten General Saloons, otherwise known variously as 'unclassed', 'fluid', or 'nondescript' saloons. By means of boards, any class could be shown, but a general guideline was laid down: First Class for race traffic, Second Class for boat train use, and Third Class for school traffic. Unlike all other coaches so far described these were only 8 ft 6 in. wide, and had straight sides. Each was divided into three saloon compartments, with a total of seven seating bays and 42 seats; a lavatory compartment was at each end. There were three doors each side, opposite three of the seating bays. The other four bays had droplights opposite them: dummy doors, in fact. Coach numbers were 7974–7983 (Order No. 102) and the vehicles were built with underframes by the Midland Railway-Carriage & Wagon Co. and bodies by Eastleigh Works, and were completed in January 1928.

The next batch of new stock was authorised at the Locomotive, Carriage and Electrical Committee meeting on 28th April, 1926. In addition to further supplies of 9 ft stock, there was a new design which had been worked out for the Kent Coast and Eastbourne services. These vehicles had the same compartment and window layout as the wide coaches, but had straight sides with just a hint of a curve below the waist, and the guard's compartments were without duckets. Body width was 8 ft 6 in. Roof destination board brackets were located immediately below the rainstrip instead of just above the cantrail. Other variations were in the door droplights, which were counterbalanced with a small tab and spring loaded closure bar at the base of the window; the 1925-ordered stock had droplights operated by the traditional leather strap. The heavy cornice rail at cantrail level was done away with in the 1926-ordered 9 ft stock. The 1926 order was for:

Four 3-coach trains, for London, Plymouth, Torrington and Ilfracombe services.
Two 8-coach trains, for Kent Coast and Eastbourne services.
Twelve Firsts and ten Thirds, for Waterloo–Southampton boat services.
Ten General Saloons.

The 3-coach sets were similar in formation and capacity to the 10 built in 1926, the first two being completed in August 1928, and the other two in September. They were built by Metropolitan Carriage, Wagon & Finance Co. As to numbering, it was no longer possible to maintain separate 'Western Section' or 'Central Section' series because the spaces in the list had been used up; it was now a matter of using up any spare numbers that were available. There were two rainstrips on each side of the carriage roofs; destination board brackets were located *above* the lower rainstrip.

Formations of the West of England sets were:

	Set 445	**Set 446**	**Set 447**	**Set 448**
Third Bke	4055	4057	4059	4060
Compo	5147	5148	5149	5150
Third Bke	4056	4058	4061	4062

The Kent Coast and Eastbourne sets each had two Third Brakes with only four compartments and large luggage compartment (the only narrow coaches with this feature ever to be built by the SR); four Composites each with four first class compartments seating two-a-side and three third class compartments; and two 8-compartment Thirds. Numbers and formations when new were:

	Set 467	**Set 468**
Third Bke	4063	4065
Third	765	767
Compo	5151	5155
Compo	5152	5156
Compo	5153	5157
Compo	5154	5158
Third	766	768
Third Bke	4064	4066

Set 467 was completed in October 1928, and 468 in November, both to Order No. E160. In normal service they ran with a Pullman car in the centre of each set.

The 9 ft coaches intended for the Southampton boat services were Firsts Nos. 7216–7227, completed in November 1927, by the Midland Railway-Carriage & Wagon Co.; and Thirds Nos. 769–778, built at Eastleigh in July and August 1927. Like all coaches so far constructed, they had low windows in the corridors.

The order was completed by the construction of 10 more General Saloons, to the same design and layout as the original 10 but built by Midland Railway-Carriage & Wagon Co. They were numbered 7984–7993; Nos. 7985–7 were delivered in January and 7984/8–93 in February 1928.

In March 1927, orders were placed for:

Six 4-coach sets, for London, Folkestone, Deal and Ramsgate services.
Two 8-coach sets, for the 8.10 and 8.33 am Eastbourne to London and 4.05 and 5.05 pm London to Eastbourne services.
Fifty Corridor Thirds, for Southampton boat trains, Bournemouth and West of England services.

There was as yet very little corridor stock on the former South Eastern main line, even important trains being worked by ex-SECR 3-coach lavatory sets. The new four-coach sets, which were numbered 449 to 454 and appeared early in 1929, must have effected a vast improvement in passengers' travelling conditions.

The coaches were 8 ft 6 in. wide, had low windows in the corridors and were similar to previous batches in having the roof destination board brackets directly below the rainstrip. Each Third Brake had six compartments and the Composite had four first class and three third class compartments. Sets

The 5.40 pm (Saturdays) Victoria to Angmering enters Haywards Heath on 19th July, 1930. It is formed of 8-set 469 plus 2 Pullmans. *H.C. Casserley*

449 and 450 were turned out in January 1929, 451/2 in February, and 453/4 the following month, to Order No. 288:

	Set 449	Set 450	Set 451	Set 452	Set 453	Set 454
Third Bke	4067	4069	4071	4073	4075	4077
Compo	5159	5161	5163	5165	5168	5169
Compo	5160	5162	5164	5166	5167	5170
Third Bke	4068	4070	4072	4074	4076	4078

Two such sets would make up the formation of trains such as the 4.15 pm Charing Cross to Ramsgate, and a First Class Pullman would be placed between the Composites in one set. Most trains detached a portion at either Folkestone Central or Dover Priory, and it was because of this that the trains were made up of two short sets instead of one long one, as on the Kent Coast services where the whole train ran through to Ramsgate.

The new Eastbourne sets were also 8 ft 6 in. stock with roof board brackets under the rainstrip. Being designed for business services the trains had a high proportion of first class accommodation, although in later years this was somewhat reduced. The set numbers and original formations were:

	Set 465	Set 466
Third Bke	4079	4081
Third	833	835
First	7390	7394
First	7391	7395
First	7392	7396
First	7393	7397
Third	834	836
Third Bke	4080	4082

Set 465 was built in March 1929, and Set 466 followed in April, both to Order No. 286. Both worked on the Eastbourne services as intended, with one or two Pullman cars added. No 466 was the regular set on the 5.05 pm London Bridge to Eastbourne until electrification in 1935; in its reduced formation at that time it included two Pullman cars.

It was originally intended that the 50 Corridor Thirds (9 ft stock) should be built by outside contractors; but the quotation was so high that the horrified Board quickly decided that only the underframes were to be built by the contractor, Metropolitan Carriage, Wagon & Finance Co., at £687 each, and Eastleigh Works would build the bodies itself. This is what the Locomotive, Carriage and Electrical Committee minutes state, but somewhere along the line something must have been changed. Of the 50 (Nos. 783 to 832), 783 to 812 were built by Birmingham Railway Carriage & Wagon Co., 813 to 822 by MCWF Co., and 823 to 832 by Eastleigh. All were completed in 1928. Every one was a loose coach, used for strengthening trains as required, particularly during the summer services. (Nos. 783–96, 804–12 were dated March and Nos. 797–803 dated April 1928.)

The completion of these coaches saw the end of what may be termed the 'early period' of Maunsell carriage design, as the next batches were built with the corridor windows extended up to the cantrail, ushering in the 'middle period'.

WORKING OF EARLY CORRIDOR STOCK ON THE CENTRAL SECTION, 1928

Six years after Grouping the quantity of Maunsell corridor stock on the Central Section was negligible, and what trains there were in most cases did only one return trip per day. Here are the workings as from 24th September, 1928:

8-set 469, plus First Class Pullman, Third Class Pullman: 9.44 am West Worthing –Victoria, 5.40 pm return.

8-set 470, plus First Class Pullman: 8.38 am Worthing–London Bdg, 5.08 pm London Bdg–Angmering.

Loose stock: 4481, First Class Pullman, 7669, 4484, 4482, plus 2353 (night only): Newhaven Harbour–Victoria services.

WORKING OF EARLY CORRIDOR STOCK ON THE WESTERN SECTION, 1929

The fourteen 3-coach sets 390–9 and 445–8 were referred to in carriage working notices as '3 P corridor sets', P standing for Pullman gangwayed. They worked mainly on the Weymouth trains in conjunction with 'Ironclad' dining sets, whose standard gangways had been fitted with adaptors to allow them to be coupled to Pullman gangways. One of the '390' class sets was running as a 5-coach portion of the 'Bournemouth Limited', with an adaptor-fitted dining car and an Open Third of the 7864–9 series marshalled between the Composite and one of the Third Brakes. This 5-coach formation left Weymouth at 7.32 am for Waterloo, returning at 4.30 pm.

All 10 of the loose Corridor Brake Composites were scheduled, five being formed in the Down 'Atlantic Coast Express' and five in the Up train, one each to and from Ilfracombe, Torrington, Plymouth, Padstow and Bude as from 23rd September, 1929. Any coach that had to be 'stopped' would have been replaced by an adaptor-fitted ex-LSW vehicle.

Five dining cars and five Open Thirds were formed into 'Ironclad' sets selected from sets 431–5/44, one of the original Thirds in these having been removed. The Firsts in these sets were adaptor-fitted, as were the Third Brakes. These sets were referred to in notices as 6-dining sets 'A' type, with the formation Third Brake, Third, First, SR dining car, SR Open Third, Third Brake. There were five return workings daily on Waterloo–Bournemouth services. The remaining 'Ironclad' sets, 436–43, retained their original make-up including an ex-LSW restaurant car and were known as 6-dining sets 'B' type.

Remaining Western Section main line services were worked by ex-LSW corridor stock, loose non-corridor vehicles normally being used for strengthening the trains.

Chapter Five

59 ft Corridor Stock, 1929 to 1934

It is not known why the design of Maunsell's coaches was modified to incorporate high windows in the corridors, but perhaps there had been complaints from standing passengers who found it difficult to see out without stooping. The corridor windows at both ends of the coaches remained at the original height to allow the placing of destination board brackets above them. The wording 'Southern Railway' had perforce to be transferred to the waist. Full lining-out of the bodysides was still indulged in.

A large number of coaches to the modified design was authorised in April 1928, and included for the first time some new stock for the ex-South Eastern's Hastings line. It was similar in appearance to the Folkestone line stock, but coaches had a body width of 8 ft 0¾ in. and were 12 ft 3 in. high from rail to roof. The bodyside doors did not extend to the base of the body as they did on both 9 ft and 8 ft 6 in. stock. However, like the 8 ft 6 in. coaches, bodies had almost straight sides and guard's compartments were without side lookouts. First class compartments sat only two-a-side and third class three-a-side. Roof-board brackets were *above* the rainstrip.

Also included in the 1928 order were further 8 ft 6 in. coaches for Folkestone trains; 9 ft stock for the Central Section; and several vehicles intended for use in through services to other railways. All had high corridor windows.

For the London, Bexhill and Hastings services 24 vehicles were constructed. The intended formation was to be:

3-set, First, First, 3-set – two trains. A Pullman to be formed between the two Firsts.

3-set, Third, Third, 3-set – one train. A Pullman to be formed between the two Thirds.

Original formation of the 3-sets:

	Set 475	**Set 477**	**Set 479**
Third Bke	3672	3676	3680
Compo	5592	5594	5596
Third Bke	3673	3677	3681

	Set 476	**Set 478**	**Set 480**
Third Bke	3674	3678	3682
Compo	5593	5595	5597
Third Bke	3675	3679	3683

Sets 475–8, along with loose Firsts Nos. 7400 to 7403, were completed in September 1929, to Order No. 376. The other two sets, plus loose Thirds Nos. 1115 and 1116, were dated October 1929, to Order No. 377. These Thirds, oddly enough, did have low corridor windows, and were the only 8 ft stock with this feature. Sets 478–80 may not have run for long in their intended formations, Firsts 7403, 7402 and 7400 being used instead of the Composites, which then became loose coaches.

The Hastings trains were made up of short sets because at that time most of them had a through portion for Bexhill West, detached at Crowhurst. This would have been the rear 3-set.

Four further 4-coach sets were built for London, Folkestone, Deal and Ramsgate services; these coaches were 8 ft 6 in. wide. The big jump in the numbering of the Composites is due to the fact that the numbers from 5178 to 5581 were already occupied by pre-Grouping carriages.

	Set 181	**Set 182**	**Set 183**	**Set 184**
Third Bke	4087	4089	4091	4093
Compo	5173	5175	5177	5583
Compo	5174	5176	5582	5584
Third Bke	4088	4090	4092	4094

All were completed in November 1929, to Order No. 362.

For the Central Section two 3-sets and two loose Firsts (7398 and 7399) were completed in December 1929, to Order No. 361. They were placed in service on the 7.18 am Bognor to Victoria and 3.20 pm Victoria to Bognor and Chichester. The sets were formed:

	Set 387	**Set 456**
Third Bke	4085	4083
Compo	5171	5172
Third Bke	4086	4084

The 9 ft stock built for through services was unusual in that most of the brake coaches had standard gangways (adaptor-fitted) at the outer ends, although gangways within the sets were the Pullman type. They were so fitted to allow them to run with LMS and GW stock. The intended formations are quoted, but whether all the coaches actually worked in these services is not known. In particular, the SR never supplied coaches for the

4-coach set 181 is at the front of a Victoria to Dover service as it passes Bromley South on Sunday 24th July, 1938. *H.C. Casserley*

'Sunny South Express' as far as is known; it was always LMS stock.

Vehicle	Service
Third Bke	Bournemouth/Newcastle
Compo	
Third	
Dining	
Compo	
Third	
Third Bke	
Bke Compo	Bournemouth/Bradford
Bke Compo	Bournemouth/Leeds

To alternate with LNE stock.

Vehicle	Service
Third Bke	Bournemouth/Birkenhead
Third	
Compo	
Dining	
Compo	
Third	
Third Bke	
Third Bke	Bournemouth/Manchester
Compo	
Third Bke	

To alternate with GW stock.

Vehicle	Service
Bke Compo	Eastbourne/Bradford
Bke Compo	Eastbourne/Birmingham
Third	
Third Bke	
Bke Compo	Eastbourne/Manchester
Dining	
Third	
Third Bke	
Bke Compo	Eastbourne/Liverpool
Third	
Third Bke	

To alternate with LMS stock.

Vehicle	Service
Third Bke	Brighton/Cardiff
Third	
Compo	
Dining	
Compo	
Third	
Third Bke	
Bke Compo	Brighton/Ilfracombe
Bke Compo	Brighton/Plymouth

Seven vehicles to work alternate days with GW stock and four for Ilfracombe and Plymouth (two each way per day).

The coaches for these services were built to four separate order numbers. No. 363 comprised Thirds 837–839, Third Brakes 3664/5, Composites 5585/6, Brake Composites 6575/6, and Dining Saloon 7939. Certain of these were used to form Set 458, Bournemouth to Newcastle. The Brake Composites were completed in June 1929, the remainder in July.

Order No. 364 comprised Thirds 840/1, Third Brakes with adaptors 3666–3669, Composites 5587–5589, and Dining Saloon 7940. Some of these were formed in Sets 427 and 459, used on the Bournemouth to Birkenhead/Manchester services. All 10 vehicles were completed by July 1929.

Order No. 365 comprised Thirds 842–844, Third Brakes (adaptor-fitted) 4095–4097, Brake Composites (adaptor-fitted) 6577–6580, and Dining Saloon 7941. All were dated August 1929; some may have found use on the Margate to Birkenhead through service.

Order No. 366 was for Thirds 1113/4, Third Brakes 3670/1 (adaptor-fitted), Composites 5590/1, Brake Composites 6581–6584, and Dining Saloon 7942. All were completed in December 1929. Certain coaches made Set 428, used on Brighton–Cardiff services.

All Third Brakes were of the four-compartment type. Composites 5585–91 were the only Maunsell ones ever built with three first and four third class compartments; however, they were structurally identical to the normal version, but the innermost wide compartment was narrowed by putting in extra walls, with a resultant gap of about five inches between the panels of this compartment and the panels of the adjacent one. Thirds and Brake Composites were as before, except for the high windows. The dining cars were also similar to earlier batches and did retain low windows; there were seats for 24 first class diners.

The Bournemouth/Newcastle set worked alternate days with LNER stock and was reduced in length during the winter, Set 458 being 3-coach only and working between Basingstoke and Newcastle, the rest of the train being four coaches – probably two Brake Composites, Third and dining car – which were joined to the 10.55 am Bournemouth West to Waterloo as far as Basingstoke, where they were detached; and on the return trip they were attached at Basingstoke to the 3.30 pm Waterloo to Bournemouth West. Southern stock worked outward on Mondays, Wednesdays and Fridays, and homeward on Tuesdays, Thursdays and Saturdays. In summer the whole train ran through, not being attached to a London train as in winter, but running separately.

Sets 459 and 427 alternated with Great Western stock. Only the Third Brakes (3666/7) and Composites (5587/9) were numbered as Set 459; the other vehicles, although formed inside the set, were officially loose. Set 427, with Third Brakes 3668/9 and Composite 5588, was the Manchester portion of the Bournemouth/Birkenhead train; it was detached at Wellington and ran via Market Drayton and Crewe.

Set 428 ran as five coaches in winter (Third Brake, Third, Dining Car, Composite, Third Brake). It alternated with Great Western stock, running from Brighton to Cardiff on Mondays, Wednesdays and Fridays and returning on Tuesdays, Thursdays and Saturdays. Of the loose Brake Composites, Nos. 6578, 6581 and 6582 were adaptor-fitted at *both* ends.

Destination board brackets on all 9 ft stock built from June 1929 were located immediately *above* the lower roof rainstrip, and earlier coaches had their brackets re-located to match. This stock also did not have the heavy cornice rail at cantrail level, a feature of the 1926-built stock. Third class seating had hammock-slung cushions instead of the bench-type seats found in the 1926 stock.

In April 1929, the following new carriage stock was authorised to be built: 20 Open Thirds, 50 Composite Brakes, 20 Nondescript Saloons, and 10 Kitchen/Dining Firsts.

The Open Third was an entirely new type. Body width was 9 ft with recessed doors for passenger access at the ends of the bodyside. There were three saloon compartments, arranged in seating bays of two plus three plus two; capacity was 56 passengers in two-and-two seating, with a central walkway. At each end of the vehicle was an entrance vestibule and a lavatory compartment. It was intended that the coaches should be employed largely as trailers to restaurant/kitchen cars. An unusual feature was that the seven large windows each side were opened by lowering the panes themselves, but no more than seven inches. The numbers of this first batch of Open Thirds were 1369 to 1388, completed in December 1930, to Order No. 461.

Corridor Third No. 805 (Diagram 2001) of 1928, painted in 'photographic grey'. *National Railway Museum, Eastleigh Collection*

Open Third, with drop windows, No. 1400 (Diagram 2005) built in 1930. Not only has the coach been photographed in works grey, but all the blinds have been drawn! *National Railway Museum, Eastleigh Collection*

The Composite Brakes, to Order No. 462, were the same as previous ones; numbers were 6585 to 6604 and 6643 to 6672. The jump in numbering was necessary because of the existence of former SEC stock numbered 6605–42. The first 20, plus 6643–8/50–3, were built in March 1930, followed by 6649/54–72 in April 1930. They were placed on Waterloo – West of England trains; from July 1930, these were formed almost entirely of the new Composite Brakes, of which one or sometimes two worked through to each of the western resorts.

Owing to the heavy building programme the Nondescripts were afforded low priority and so were not completed until June 1931. Numbered 7781 to 7800 (Order No. 463), they were similar to the earlier ones, with 42 seats arranged in seven bays.

The Kitchen/Dining Saloons, to Order No. 464, were numbered 7943 to 7952; 7943/5–7/9/50 were completed in May 1930, and 7944/8/51/2 in June. From 7th July, 1930, new dining cars worked in the 10.40 am Waterloo to Ilfracombe, 11.00 am, 12.40, 3.00 and 6.00 pm Waterloo to Exeter, and the 7.20, 10.30 am, 2.30 (TWThO), 4.30 and 5.55 pm (MFO) Exeter to Waterloo, and the 10.25 am Ilfracombe to Waterloo. A Nondescript, working as the kitchen car trailer, was formed in the 10.40 and 11.00 am Down, and the 10.25 am and 4.30 pm Up.

Even though by 1930 there was seemingly so much modern stock available, comparatively few train services had the benefit of it. There was still a very large number of non-corridor coaches, many of whose compartments had no lavatory access, running on mainline services; particularly those to Brighton, Portsmouth, Hastings and Ramsgate.

Thus, the abolition in 1929 of the Government Railway Passenger Duty was most welcome, as the SR then had the money available to build 200 additional corridor coaches, which were authorised on 26th June, 1929.

The 9 ft stock in this June order included four-compartment Third Brakes, Open Thirds, Composites, Composite Brakes, Firsts and Dining Saloons, all of the standard type previously detailed; and there were also further sets of 8 ft 6 in. and 8 ft 0¾ in. stock for the Eastern Section.

The Western Section stock was ordered as a 10-coach train and a 12-coach train intended for Waterloo, Bournemouth, Swanage and Weymouth services; and two 10-coach trains for Waterloo–Portsmouth services. Just to complicate the story, not all the coaches, when built, ended on their intended services. This was true of two 11-coach trains ordered for working Southampton boat trains; most of the vehicles, when built, were put on the Waterloo–Portsmouth line.

Order No. 487 comprised Open Third 1397, Third Brakes 3724–3727 plus six-compartment 3732, Composite 5634, Composite Brake 6673, First 7675 and Dining Saloon 7957; it was completed in September 1930 (No. 7957 in August).

Order No. 488 comprised Open Thirds 1398–1400, Third Brakes 3728–3731 plus six-compartment 3733, Composite 5635, Composite Brake 6674, First 7676 and Dining Saloon 7958. These vehicles were completed in October 1930 (Dining Car in September).

Corridor Third No. 1130 (Diagram 2001) of 1930.

National Railway Museum, Eastleigh Collection

Corridor Brake Composite No. 6597 (Diagram 2401) of 1930. These photographs appear to have been taken some time after the coaches entered service.

National Railway Museum, Eastleigh Collection

Order No. 489 comprised Thirds 1121–1130, Third Brakes 3716–3719, Firsts 7228–7231, and Dining Saloons 7953/4. All were completed in July 1930, except 7954 (June).

Order No. 490 comprised Open Thirds 1389–1396, Third Brakes 3720–3723, Firsts 7232, 7406–7412 and Dining Saloons 7955/6. The Dining Saloons were completed in July, half the remaining stock in August and the other half in September 1930. They entered service in September as two 8-coach un-numbered sets each formed Third Brake, Open Third, First, Dining Car, Open Third, First, Open Third and Third Brake.

By 1931 set formations had been settled as Third Brake, First, Third, Third Brake with numbers 204 to 209. Nos. 204 and 206 were allocated to the Bournemouth line and ran as 6-dining sets with a restaurant car and Open Third; while Nos. 205/7/8/9 ran as 7-dining sets with restaurant car, Open Third and Composite and were allocated to the Portsmouth line. Other sets made up from this 1930-built stock were 2-coach Nos. 179 and 180, for the Swanage portion of the 'Bournemouth Limited'; 3-coach 201, placed in the same link as sets 390–9 and 445–8; and 3-coach 202, which worked the Bournemouth portion of the 'Bournemouth Limited'.

Formations, as far as can be judged, were:

	Set 179	Set 180
Third Brake	3732	3733
Compo Brake	6673	6674

	Set 201		Set 202(?)
Third Brake	3730	Third Brake	3726
Compo	5635	First	7675
Third Brake	3731	Third Brake	3727

	Set 204	Set 205	Set 206	Set 207	Set 208	Set 209
Third Bke	3716	3718	3728	3724	3720	3722
First	7228	7229	7219	7218	7407	7411
Third	1122	1123	1124	1128	1129	1127
Third Bke	3717	3719	3729	3725	3721	3723

First Nos. 7218/9 were not part of this Order but were 1927-built vehicles transferred from loose stock.

In addition there was a 5-dining set, No. 203, whose formation was Third Brake, Dining Saloon, Open Third, Composite, Third Brake. It is believed that some coaches from Order No. 491 were used to supply part of Set 203, which was regularly used as the Weymouth portion of the 'Bournemouth Limited' train. Order No. 491 was for four 4-coach trains intended for London, Bognor and Portsmouth services; and Order No. 492 was for four similar sets intended for London, Worthing and Littlehampton services. The coaches were delivered as follows: Third Brakes 3734–3737 and Composites 5636–5639 in October 1930; 3738–3741 and 5640–5643 in November 1930 (Order 491); Third Brakes 3742–3749 and Composites 5644–5651 in November 1930 (Order 492).

Set 203 is thought to have been formed using Third Brakes 3734/5 and a Composite, either 5636 or 5637. Third Brakes 3736 and 3737 were used with Composite Brakes 6657 and 6588 to make 2-sets Nos. 199 and 200 respectively. These joined the link that included sets 381–385 and 179/80. Other coaches were formed as shown:

	Set 193	Set 194	Set 195	Set 464
Third Brake	3738	3740	3742	3744
Compo	5640	5642	5644	5646
Compo	5641	5643	5645	5647
Third Brake	3739	3741	3743	3745

	Set 426	Set 429
Third Brake	3746	3748
Compo	5649	5651
Third Brake	3747	3749

Set 193 worked the Brighton to Bournemouth service from 1931 and Nos. 194/5 and 464 ran on the Central Section as planned. Sets 426/9 ran as 4-coach, with an older-type restaurant car fitted with gangway adaptors, and worked the Brighton–Plymouth services from 1931, replacing the Composite Brakes built for this service in 1929. As one set was working to Plymouth the other would be working to Brighton. All 16 Third Brakes of this batch, 3734–49, were the six-compartment type.

The 9 ft coaches of the 1929 orders each had two rainstrips on each side of the roof, and the destination board brackets were located above the lower rainstrip. The allocation of set numbers was becoming more haphazard because the spaces originally allowed in the list were now filled, and a start had perforce to be made in using the numbers of sets now withdrawn, such as the ex-LSW 'bogie block' sets 181 to 244.

For the Eastern Section were orders for four 4-coach sets for London, Folkestone and Deal services; and two 8-coach sets for London and Ramsgate services (Order Nos. 493 and 494). Identical 8 ft 6 in. stock was ordered for the Eastbourne line: four 4-coach sets for London, Eastbourne and Hastings services, and two 8-coach trains to work between London and Eastbourne only (Order Nos. 495 and 496). The sets were sent into traffic with the following formations:

	Set 185	Set 187	Set 189	Set 191
Third Bke	3692	3696	3704	3708
Compo	5602	5606	5618	5622
Compo	5603	5607	5619	5623
Third Bke	3693	3697	3705	3709

	Set 186	Set 188	Set 190	Set 192
Third Bke	3694	3698	3706	3710
Compo	5604	5608	5620	5624
Compo	5605	5609	5621	5625
Third Bke	3695	3699	3707	3711

	Set 217	Set 218	Set 219	Set 220
Third Bke	3700	3702	3712	3714
Third	2356	2358	2360	2362
Compo	5610	5614	5626	5630
Compo	5611	5615	5627	5631
Compo	5612	5616	5628	5632
Compo	5613	5617	5629	5633
Third	2357	2359	2361	2363
Third Bke	3701	3703	3713	3715

Sets 185–8, for the Eastern Section, were built in February 1931, and Sets 217/8, also for the Eastern Section, came out in March. Sets 189–92 were completed in April, and Nos. 219 and 220 followed in May, all six being for the Central Section. They were the last 8 ft 6 in. sets built by the Southern Railway. As before, third class compartments seated four-a-side and first class two-a-side. Roof-board brackets were located below the rain-strip each side. Sets 189–192, 219 and 220 were soon reduced to 3-coach for the Eastbourne services, but after the electrification of the line in 1935 all became 4-coach and were transferred to the Eastern Section.

Twenty-two General Saloons, 8 ft 6 in. wide, were completed in June 1931, to the same design as the earlier ones and were numbered 7901 to 7911, 7959 to 7968, and 7994: Order No. 497.

The final order for June 1929 (No. 498) was for two 9-coach trains of 8 ft 0¾ in. stock for London, Bexhill and Hastings services; actually they were built as four 3-coach sets and six loose vehicles, coming out in January and February 1931.

	Set 213	**Set 214**	**Set 215**	**Set 216**
Third Bke	3684	3686	3688	3690
First	7404	7405	7416	7415
Third Bke	3685	3687	3689	3691

Loose Thirds were Nos. 1117, 1118. Loose Composites: 5598 to 5601. Clearly it had been decided that a Composite formed in a set provided insufficient first class accommodation with its two-a-side seating, and at some stage three of the earlier sets, Nos. 478–80, had their Composites replaced by Firsts, in order to match Sets 213–6 in seating capacity.

That completed the 1929 programme, which had been for no fewer than 300 corridor vehicles, including 16 restaurant cars; all had been finished in time for the 1931 summer season. In its June 1931 issue the *Southern Railway Magazine* stated that 10 Parlour Saloons (i.e. Nos. 7781–90), the first batch of 42 being built at Lancing and Eastleigh, were put into traffic in time for the Whitsun holiday. Seating was arranged two-and-one with off-centre walkway and the coach was divided into three saloon compartments.

An exhibition of new coaches was held at Wimbledon Station from 2nd to 7th November, 1931. The internal appointments of each were described by the *Southern Railway Magazine* the following month:

> Brake Composite No. 6666 – built April 1930: walls of first class compartments were polished walnut with sycamore panelling; upholstery was in 'Saladin' tapestry. Walls of third class compartments were polished mahogany, and upholstery in red, black and orange moquette. Lavatories had hot and cold water apparatus.
>
> General Saloon No. 7786 – built May 1931: interior in polished walnut and upholstery in tapestry. Hot and cold water apparatus.
>
> First Class No. 7412 – built September 1930: interior of polished walnut and sycamore panelling; upholstery in 'Saladin' tapestry; hot and cold water in lavatories.
>
> First Class Dining Saloon and Kitchen Car No. 7943 – built May 1930: interior in polished walnut, upholstery in moquette. Kitchen and pantry fitted with up-to-date cooking, refrigerating and storing applicances. Messrs Frederick Hotels, who

had just become refreshment caterers to the Southern, had staff in attendance.
Open Third No. 1382 – built December 1930: interior decor in polished mahogany, the upper panels being inlaid with white celuloid; upholstery in moquette. The floor was covered with linoleum, and gangways between the seats had sponge rubber mats laid. Hot and cold water in the lavatories.

No orders for new steam passenger stock were made in 1930, but in March 1931, 100 more coaches were authorised to be built: twenty 4-coach trains of 9 ft stock for general use on London, Portsmouth, Bournemouth and West of England services; one 10-coach train of 8 ft stock for London, Bexhill and Hastings services; and 10 Kitchen/Dining Saloons.

A small alteration to the 1929 design was made. Each lavatory ventilator was given two narrow bonnets, one above the other, instead of the single large one that had hitherto been provided. This 'two bonnets' feature was perpetuated in subsequent stock.

The first twelve sets were built as three-coach, and twelve loose Composites, Nos 5652 to 5663, were turned out somewhat ahead of them, 5652–6/9–61 being dated 1931 and 5657/8/62/3 following in early 1932. Third Brakes took the numbers of withdrawn stock, but there were not enough long runs of such stock so the new vehicles were unable to have consecutive numbers. Third Brakes were to Order No. 633A and Composites to Order No. 633B.

	Set 221	**Set 223**	**Set 225**	**Set 227**	**Set 229**	**Set 231**
Third Bke	3750	3754	3758	2757	2761	2765
Compo	5664	5666	5668	5670	5672	5674
Third Bke	3751	3755	2754	2758	2762	2766

	Set 222	**Set 224**	**Set 226**	**Set 228**	**Set 230**	**Set 232**
Third Bke	3752	3756	2755	2759	2763	2767
Compo	5665	5667	5669	5671	5673	5675
Third Bke	3753	3757	2756	2760	2764	2768

The eight remaining sets were completed as 4-coach, with Composites arranged in numerical pairs:

	Set 233	**Set 235**	**Set 237**	**Set 239**
Third Bke	2769	2794	2798	2802
Compo	5676	5680	5684	5688
Compo	5677	5681	5685	5689
Third Bke	2770	2795	2799	2803

	Set 234	**Set 236**	**Set 238**	**Set 240**
Third Bke	2771	2796	2800	2804
Compo	5678	5682	5686	5690
Compo	5679	5683	5687	5691
Third Bke	2793	2797	2801	2805

The trains were completed in April 1932, and the allocations in May that year were: Nos. 221, 222, 224: Waterloo–West of England; 223, 232: Plymouth–Portsmouth; 225 to 231, 233 to 237: London, Bognor and Portsmouth; and 238 to 240: Waterloo–Portsmouth. By 1935 Nos. 223, 224 and 238 had been transferred to the Central Section. Sets 233 to 237 each worked specific train services on the London to Bognor line and a Pullman car was placed between the two Composites in each 4-coach set in traffic. Sets 238, 239 and 240 were reduced to 3-coach by removing a Composite in each one. Set 223 had adaptor-fitted gangways at the brake-ends and later worked as the through portion from Hastings and Brighton to Birkenhead, alternating with GWR stock on this service.

At the opening of the new Hastings Station on 6th July, 1931, the SR chairman, Brigadier-General Baring, declared 'We have 10 trains of the best type running in each direction daily, and an order has just been given for a new train of 10 coaches of the most modern type.' This clearly refers to Order No. 634 and the train was completed in May 1932, as 7- and 3-coach sets of 8 ft 0¾ in. stock.

	Set 939		**Set 940**
Third Bke	3236	Third Bke	3234
Third	1119	First	7414
Compo	5579	Third Bke	3235
First	7418		
Compo	5578		
Third	1120		
Third Bke	3237		

No. 939 was placed on a regular working, but No. 940 joined the pool of general-use 3-coach sets on the SE Hastings line.

The Kitchen-Dining cars had different internal arrangements from the earlier ones but were similar externally. They were completed in May 1932, to Order No. 635, and took the numbers 7864 to 7871 and 7931, 7932. The original Nos. 7864–9, the Third Class dining cars of 1927, were being renumbered 1363 to 1368 as ordinary Open Thirds.

A large amount of loose vehicles was ordered in March 1932. There were to be 100 Corridor Thirds, 50 Open Thirds, and 30 Corridor Third Brakes, all 9 ft stock. Twenty Nondescript Brakes of a new design, 8 ft 6 in. wide, were also ordered. For London, Bexhill, Hastings, and Margate, Hastings, Brighton services, it was intended that 10 Thirds, 24 Brake Thirds, 12 Composites and 4 Firsts – all 8 ft stock – should be built. Finally there were to be 10 more restaurant cars.

The 100 Corridor Thirds were subdivided into three batches. Nos. 1131 to 1155 were to Order No. 686 and dated 1932, as were Nos. 1156 to 1180 which were to Order No. 687. Nos. 1181 to 1230 (Order No. 705) were turned out between September and November 1933. They were not built for any particular service but mainly as strengthening vehicles, though it does seem that there were far more than necessary because a few were later placed in permanent sets.

The Open Thirds, which were similar to the 1930 ones, were to Order No. 706 and were finished in May 1933. Numbers were 1312 to 1361; the number 1362 never was filled.

Nos. 3771 to 3800 were given to the 30 Third Brakes to Order No. 707, which were completed in August 1933. Externally they were the same as all previous six-compartment Third Brakes, but differed internally in one detail. At the point where the corridor led past the guard's compartment was a sliding door instead of the swing door hitherto standard. Most of the coaches

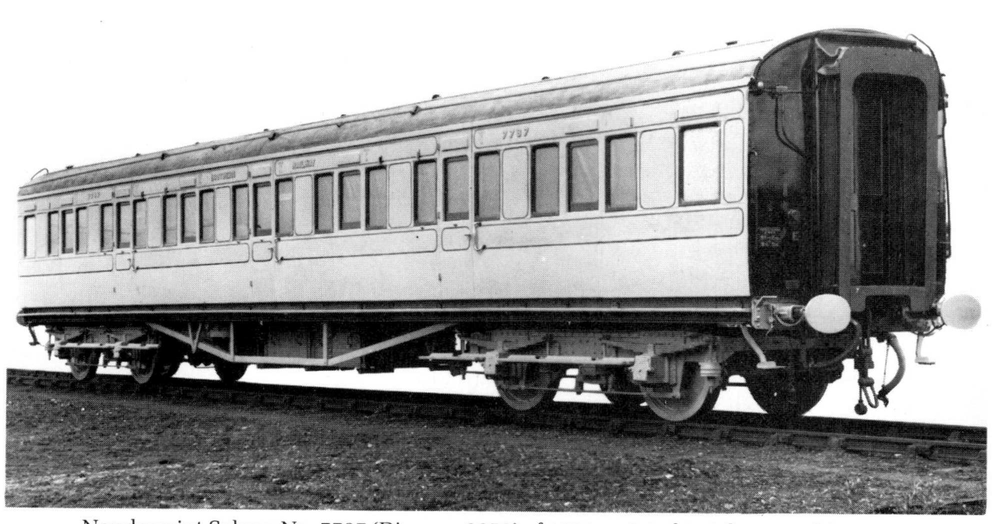

Nondescript Saloon No. 7787 (Diagram 2653) of 1931, painted in 'photographic grey'.
National Railway Museum, Eastleigh Collection

Corridor First No. 7230 (Diagram 2501) of 1930, photographed some time after it had gone into traffic.
National Railway Museum, Eastleigh Collection

were soon placed in sets, including Nos. 241 to 247 and 327 to 330, which were formed largely from loose stock.

The new Nondescript Brakes, intended mainly for Continental boat trains, were most interesting and unusual vehicles. Each had six seating bays with 36 seats, all having individual arms. Moving from the brake-end one observed that the first, fourth and sixth seating bays had a door leading into the space between the seats, and the second, third and fifth bays had a large fixed window, not extended up to the cantrail, with small sliding windows above it. There were two two-bay smoking compartments, and a two-bay non-smoking one at the inner end of the coach. One lavatory compartment was provided. Numbers were 4431 to 4450, to Order No. 708, built in June 1933.

The Depression years from 1931 had the effect of reducing the demand for first class accommodation because there were fewer people able to afford it. As compared with the earlier Hastings sets, with their seating capacity of 28 firsts and 72 thirds, the latest sets had only 16 firsts and 96 thirds. The 24 Third Brakes of the 1932 order were built as Composite Brakes, each seating eight first class and 24 third class passengers; and the 12 Composites emerged as 12 Thirds in addition to the 10 scheduled. Composite Brakes were numbered 6881 to 6904 (Order 710); Thirds were 1019 to 1040 (709); and the four Firsts were 7419 to 7422 (712). All were completed by May 1934, and were to be the last coaches built for the Hastings line for 23 years. Nos. 1019–26, 6887/8 and 7420–2 were loose coaches; the rest were formed into sets as follows:

	Set 941	**Set 944**	**Set 947**
Bke Compo	6881	6889	6895
Third	1038	1037	1040
Bke Compo	6882	6890	6896

	Set 942	**Set 945**	**Set 948**
Bke Compo	6883	6891	6897
Third	1028	1036	1032
Bke Compo	6884	6892	6898

	Set 943	**Set 946**	**Set 949**
Bke Compo	6903	6893	6899
Third	1033	1039	1035
Bke Compo	6904	6894	6900

	Set 950
Bke Compo	6901
Third	1034
Bke Compo	6902

	Set 951
Bke Compo	6885
Third	1031
Third	1030
First	7419
Third	1029
Third	1027
Bke Compo	6886

The 3-sets formed of two Brake Composites and one Third were referred to in the carriage working notices as 'O' sets; and the type formed of two Third Brakes and a First were 'F' sets. Most trains had one of each, plus a couple of loose coaches and a Pullman car, in the formation.

The 10 Kitchen/Dining Firsts, the last Maunsell ones to be built, were completed in July 1934, to Order No. 713. They took the numbers of withdrawn saloons but there were no long runs of consecutive numbers in the list so the numbering of the new cars was chaotic in the extreme. They were outshopped as Nos. 7878, 7880, 7933, 7934, 7969, 7995, and 7997 to 8000. Car No. 8000 was displayed at Wadebridge during a centenary exhibition of the Bodmin & Wadebridge Railway on 5th and 6th September, 1934.

Nondescript Brake No. 4448 of 1933 (Diagram 2654) photographed when new; blinds have been drawn, possibly to avoid unwanted reflections.
National Railway Museum, Eastleigh Collection

1934-built Restaurant Car No. 7998 to Diagram 2655. Earlier examples were lettered 'Dining Saloon'.
National Railway Museum, Eastleigh Collection

And so we come to the end of the 'middle period' of Southern Railway pre-War carriage design, in which a sizeable fleet of very standardised and perhaps rather traditional carriages had been built up. In the 'later period', which lasted only two years before construction of new steam-hauled carriages came to a stop, some 1930s-modern features were found.

WORKING OF CORRIDOR STOCK ON THE WESTERN SECTION, 1930–2

For the summer services of 1930 and 1931, two of the 3 P corridor sets were strengthened to six coaches by adding a loose Third between one Third Brake and the Composite, and a new Dining Saloon and Nondescript between the Composite and the other Third Brake. These worked on the 10.40 am Waterloo to Ilfracombe and 10.25 am Ilfracombe to Waterloo, both part of the summertime version of the 'Atlantic Coast Express'. Each set did the single trip on one day, returning on the next day. Another strengthened 3 P set was formed in the 'Bournemouth Limited', 7.32 am Weymouth to Waterloo and 4.30 pm return; it had a dining car and Open Third placed between the Composite and one of the Third Brakes. The other 3 P corridor sets worked various Bournemouth, Weymouth, Ilfracombe and Plymouth services in conjunction with other stock.

Working of 59 ft Dining Saloons on summer Saturdays in 1930 was as shown on page 56. In addition the 10.24 am (SO) Waterloo to Bude included one car and one Nondescript, and another pair was provided for the corresponding up service. The 5.40 am Waterloo to Weymouth and 11.15 am return also included a Maunsell dining car on Saturdays.

On the Portsmouth line modern stock replaced mixed LSW/'Ironclad' unnumbered dining sets on some services from 22nd September, 1930. These 7-dining sets Type 'C', Nos. 204 and 205, were formed Third Brake, Third, First, Dining Saloon, Third, Composite ('Ironclad' type) and Third Brake, and worked the following:

8.40 am Waterloo–Portsmouth Harbour, 11.50 am return
4.50 pm Waterloo–Portsmouth Harbour, 8.00 pm return
9.50 am Waterloo–Portsmouth Harbour, 1.00 pm return
3.50 pm Waterloo–Portsmouth Harbour, 6.35 pm return

There were also two 8-dining sets of loose stock, formed Third Brake, Open Third, First, Dining Saloon, Open Third, First, Open Third, Third Brake, and these worked as under:

11.50 am Waterloo–Portsmouth Harbour, 6.00 pm return
7.53 am (WX), 7.59 am (WO) Portsmouth Harbour–Waterloo, 12.50 pm return
3.48 pm Portsmouth Harbour–Waterloo, 6.50 pm return

From 6th July, 1931, the 'Bournemouth Limited' included new 5-dining set 203 and 3 P set 202 as the Weymouth and Bournemouth portions respectively. New Type 'A' 6-dining sets 204 and 206 were on the Bournemouth line while 7-dining sets Type 'C' Nos. 205, 207, 208 and 209 worked on the Portsmouth line.

Below are shown some set train workings as from 21st September, 1931:

Working No.

6 P dining sets Nos. 204 and 206

2. 9.30 am Waterloo–Bournemouth West and 3.30 pm return.
8. 7.30 am Bournemouth West–Waterloo and 3.30 pm return.

7 P dining sets Nos. 205, 207, 208 and 209

17. 8.50 am Waterloo–Portsmouth Harbour and 11.50 am return; 4.50 pm Waterloo–Portsmouth Harbour and 8.00 pm return.
18. 9.50 am Waterloo–Portsmouth Harbour and as shown for 22.9.30.
19. 11.50 am Waterloo–Portsmouth Harbour and as shown for 22.9.30.
20. 7.53 am (WX), 7.59 am (WO) Portsmouth Harbour and as shown for 22.9.30.

3 P sets Type 'F' Nos. 201, 390–399 and 445–448

21. 5.40 am Waterloo–Weymouth, 11.15 am Weymouth–Bournemouth Central. 12.34 pm (FSO), 1.28 pm (FSX) Bournemouth Central–Waterloo.
22. 8.30 am Waterloo–Weymouth and 1.20 pm return. On Saturdays worked 10.30 pm Waterloo–Dorchester, returning on the Sunday 7.20 am Dorchester –Waterloo.
23. 9.30 am Waterloo–Weymouth and 6.30 pm return.
24. 12.30 pm Waterloo–Weymouth and 5.25 pm return.
25. 4.45 pm Waterloo–Brockenhurst, 6.51 pm thence to Bournemouth Central.
26. (FSO): 1.28 pm Bournemouth Central–Waterloo. (FSX): 5.03 pm Bournemouth Central–Weymouth, 9.50 pm Weymouth–Southampton Terminus, 1.10 am thence to Waterloo.
27. (FSO): 2.30 pm Waterloo–Bournemouth Central, 5.03 pm thence to Weymouth, 9.50 pm Weymouth–Southampton Terminus, 1.10 am thence to Waterloo.
28. 9.15 am Weymouth–Waterloo and 6.30 pm return.
29. 6.15 am Plymouth–Bere Alston, 7.55 am return; 3.50 pm Plymouth–Waterloo.
30. 5.00 pm Waterloo–Yeovil Junction, 9.11 pm thence to Exeter.
31. 7.30 am Exeter–Plymouth; 2.10 pm Plymouth–Waterloo.
32. 6.00 pm Waterloo–Plymouth.

Three spare sets.

3 P set No. 202

58. 8.26 am Bournemouth West–Waterloo and 4.30 pm return.

5 P set No. 203 including Open Third and Restaurant Car

59. 7.32 am Weymouth–Waterloo and 4.30 pm return.

5-dining set No. 459 plus one Third in set

61. MWFO: 9.35 am Bournemouth West–Birkenhead. TThSO: 9.35 am Birkenhead–Bournemouth West.

3 P set No. 458

62. MWFO: 1.20 pm Basingstoke–York, empty to Newcastle. TThSO: 7.35 am Newcastle–York, thence 9.50 am to Basingstoke.

5 dining set No. 428

63. MWFO: 11.00 am Brighton–Cardiff via Portsmouth & Southsea. TThSO: 12.20 pm Cardiff–Brighton via Portsmouth & Southsea.

4 P dining sets Nos. 426 and 429 (alternate days)

64/65. 11.00 am Brighton–Plymouth via Portsmouth & Southsea.

65/64. 11.05 am Plymouth–Brighton via Portsmouth & Southsea.

3 P set No. 427

66. MWFO: 9.35 am Bournemouth West–Manchester.
TThSO: 10.10 am Manchester–Bournemouth West.

4 P set No. 193

67. 9.30 am Brighton–Bournemouth Central and 1.20 pm return.

2 P sets Type 'E' Nos. 179, 180, 199, 200

69. 5.45 am Bournemouth Central–Swanage, 7.20 am Swanage–Waterloo via Bournemouth West; 4.30 pm Waterloo–Swanage, 7.50 pm thence to Bournemouth Central.

Three spare sets.

WORKING OF RESTAURANT CARS ON OTHER SERVICES

1. 8.40 am Waterloo–Exeter and 5.55 pm return.
2. 12.40 pm Waterloo–Salisbury and 4.38 pm return.
3. 11.00 am* Waterloo–Exeter and 4.30 pm return.
4. 7.20 am Exeter–Waterloo and 3.00 pm return.
5. 10.30 am* Exeter–Waterloo and 6.00 pm* return.
6. 12.34 pm* Exeter–Waterloo.
7. 5.00 pm Waterloo–Yeovil Junction, thence 9.11 pm to Exeter.
30. MWFO: 10.55 am Bournemouth West–York, empty to Newcastle.
TThSO: 7.35 am Newcastle–York, 9.50 am thence to Bournemouth West.
32. MWFO: 9.14 am Margate–Birkenhead.
TThSO: 8.00 am Birkenhead–Margate.

*Working with 56-seat Open Third.

All trains from Bournemouth and the West of England, and most of those from Portsmouth, on arrival at Waterloo worked out empty to Clapham Yard for servicing and shunting, later working empty back to Waterloo for down departures. All sets starting in the morning and finishing in the evening at Waterloo were berthed at Clapham Yard, except the set on Working No. 17, which was kept at Wimbledon.

The workings stayed constant into 1932, and by June of that year three of the new '221' class 3-sets had workings, including local services such as the 5.47 pm Waterloo to Farnham and 8.41 am Farnham to Waterloo. One was on the 6.50 am Waterloo to Salisbury as well.

WORKING OF CORRIDOR STOCK ON THE CENTRAL SECTION, 1931

From 5th July, 1931, sets 387 and 456 worked the 7.20 am Bognor to Victoria, 10.05 am Victoria to Brighton and 12.05 pm return, and 3.20 pm Victoria to Bognor, one set being detached at Barnham and continuing to Chichester.

Set 465 worked the 8.10 am Eastbourne to London Bridge and 4.05 pm return, and Set 466 the 8.33 am Eastbourne to London Bridge and 5.05 pm return. Sets 469 and 470 worked the same services as in 1928, between Worthing and London.

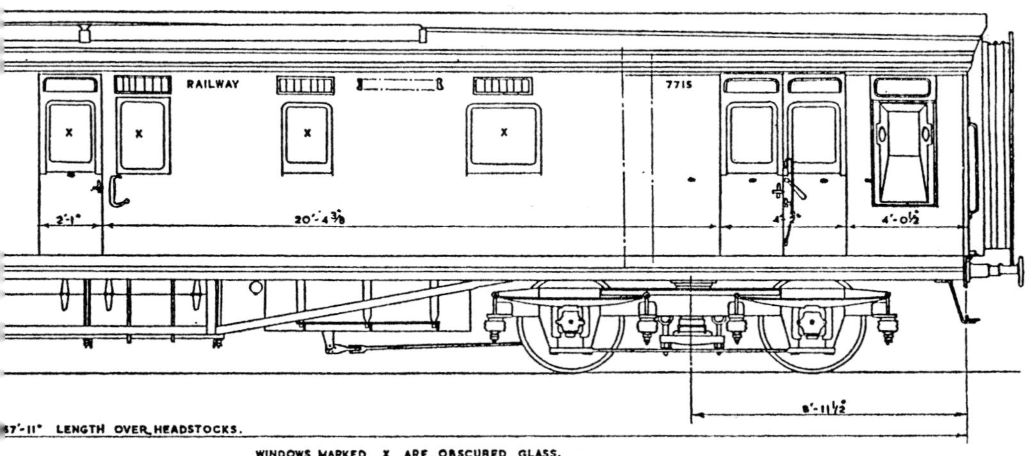

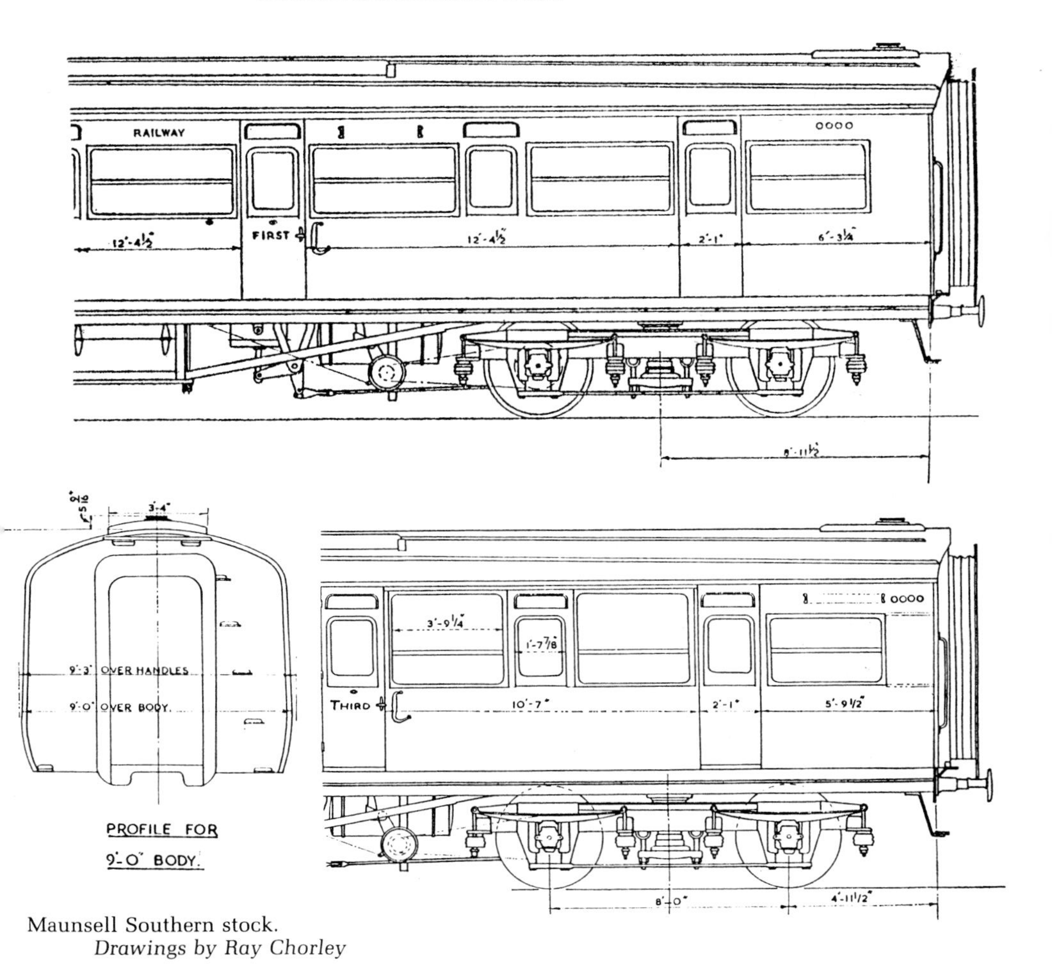

Maunsell Southern stock.
Drawings by Ray Chorley

Open Third with sliding ventilators (Diagram 2007), built in 1935; this example is No. 1311.
National Railway Museum, Eastleigh Collection

Corridor Brake Composite No. 6695, for 2-set 168, built in 1935 (Diagram 2403). Note the frameless droplights on passenger doors and the simplified lining-out. *National Railway Museum, Eastleigh Collection*

Chapter Six

Later 59 ft Corridor Stock

At the start of 1933 the *Southern Railway Magazine* announced that since Grouping 1,085 steam-hauled carriages had been built. If the 114 'Ironclads', 67 'Continentals', 77 'Thanets', 10 LBSC Composites built in 1924, and eight 10-compartment SEC Thirds built in 1923 are added to the Maunsell coaches built since 1926, the total comes to 1,065. An error, or are 20 unaccounted for?

Orders placed in April 1933 were for 100 Corridor Thirds and 30 Open Thirds. Actually, only 90 Corridor Thirds were built and they were to the same design as Nos. 1131–1230 of 1932/3. The new Thirds, to Order No. 760, were built between May and September 1934 (Nos. 1231 to 1280) and late 1934 (Nos. 1801 to 1840).

The Open Thirds, Nos. 1282 to 1311, Order No. 761, had very different body styling. The windows were virtually flush with the bodysides, which exhibited large quantities of screw-heads. There were seven seating bays, each with a large window equipped with two sliding ventilator glasses. The top quarters of these windows were square-cornered but the lower quarters had large-radius rounded corners. Each lavatory window had two ventilator bonnets above it. Entry to the vehicle was by end doors, which were slightly recessed. The whole massive construction looked modern to 1930s eyes but was not really very attractive on close inspection. The coaches were completed in July 1935.

In about 1933 several sets were assembled from examples of recently-built coaching stock plus some Corridor Firsts of 1927/30. These were Set 203 (Type 'K') for the 'Bournemouth Limited'; Sets 241–7 (Type 'N'), which could be made up to 6-dining sets as required for Waterloo–Bournemouth services; Sets 327/8 (Type 'B' for special traffic) and Sets 329/30 (Type 'D' for special traffic). Set 203 replaced the 1930 Set 203.

	Set 203
Third Bke	3781
Compo	5653
Third Bke	3784

	Set 241	**Set 243**	**Set 245**	**Set 247**
Third Bke	3799	3778	3785	3777
Third	?	1224	1197	1187
First	7676	7412	7211	7212
Third Bke	3800	3779	3796	3794

	Set 242	**Set 244**	**Set 246**
Third Bke	3790	3786	3771
Third	?	1218	1193
First	7675	7215	7213
Third Bke	3791	3787	3788

	Set 327	**Set 328**
Third Bke	3773	3797
Third	1208	1215
First	7223	7406
Third	1209	1216
Third Bke	3774	3798

	Set 329	**Set 330**
Third Bke	3793	3782
Third	1227	1221
First	7230	7231
Third	1226	1222
Third	1225	1223
Third Bke	3792	3783

For Waterloo–Southampton Docks trains an 8 P dining set, No. 308, was made up with the formation Third Brake (four-compartment), two Thirds, Open Third, Dining Saloon, two Firsts, and Third Brake (four-compartment).

Further examples of flush-sided stock were ordered in March, 1934: 60 Corridor Thirds to Order No. 798, 25 Corridor Brake Composites to Order No. 799, and 25 Corridor Third Brakes to Order No. 800. Although having the same compartment layout as earlier designs they looked very different externally, with their heavily-rivetted steel sheeting, large-radius corners to the windows, and frameless droplights on the doors. Each of these droplights was equipped with a locking lever labelled 'Free' and 'Secure', with the instruction inside 'To Open Window. Put Handle in Free Position and Pull Down Window.' At long last the 'dummy doors' on the corridor side were done away with, being replaced by fixed windows which extended up to the cantrail. Roofs, however, continued to be of the traditional wooden construction, canvas-covered.

The Thirds were numbered 1841 to 1900, Nos. 1841–63 being turned out in the latter part of 1935, Nos. 1864–76 in January 1936, Nos. 1877–95 in February and Nos. 1895–1900 in March 1936.

Composite Brakes, numbered 6675 to 6699, were constructed between August and October 1935, and most were allocated to the Eastern Section, which was now able to accept 9 ft stock, at least on the Ramsgate and Dover lines.

The Third Brakes, whose numbers had to be split because of the deficiency of blanks in the list, were numbered 2776 to 2792 (built October 1935) and 2831 to 2838 (completed in December 1935).

Some more sets were made up from certain of these 1935-built coaches, plus a few older ones: six 2-coach sets for Waterloo–Swanage/Lymington and Waterloo–West of England services; four additional Type 'N' sets, which were made up to 6-dining sets as required for Waterloo–Bournemouth services; and a further 3-coach set Type 'K'.

	Set 168	**Set 172**	**Set 178**	**Set 196**	**Set 197**	**Set 198**
Third Bke	2776	2777	2836	2778	2779	2780
Compo Bke	6695	6696	6690	6697	6698	6699

	Set 202	**Set 248**	**Set 249**	**Set 250**
Third Bke	2837	2781	2783	2785
Third	1827	1199	1848	1884
First	7672	7216	7222	7674
Third Bke	2838	2782	2784	2786

	Set 400
Third Bke	2787
Compo	5654
Third Bke	2788

The lining-out on the bodies of these 1935-built carriages was simplified. All that was done was to represent 'panelling' on the waist only, and on the doors under the droplights. Lettering style was unchanged, 'First' and 'Third' still being written in full.

In March 1935, there came orders for what proved to be the last new steam carriage stock to be constructed for nine years. The Southern's carriage-building programme seemed to be running out of steam, for quite a few of the vehicles ordered in 1935 were not built. These were fourteen 4-coach

Open Third No. 1450 of 1936 (Diagram 2007); perhaps the most elegant of all Maunsell coach designs.
National Railway Museum, Eastleigh Collection

Corridor Third No. 802, a replacement body built in 1936 (Diagram 2008) on the original underframe of 1928. There are flush quarter-lights with large-radius corners; frameless droplights; two bonnets over lavatory windows; and simplified lining-out.
National Railway Museum, Eastleigh Collection

sets, each to be formed of two four-compartment Third Brakes, a First and a Third; nine restaurant cars; and four buffet cars – an innovation. In addition, of twenty 4-coach sets ordered, to be formed of two six-compartment Third Brakes, a Composite and Third, 10 never appeared.

Possibly it had been decided that there was now no requirement for additional sets because of the forthcoming electrification to Portsmouth. Should any further sets be required they could be assembled from the large stock of loose coaches now available.

Ten Corridor Thirds, in the same style as Nos. 1841–1900, were completed in April 1936, to Order No. 862; their numbers were 1901 to 1910. Additionally, two bodies of this type were built as replacements, on existing underframes, for Thirds Nos. 802 and 1834 which had been destroyed by a fire at Dover Marine in July 1935. The replacements were dated May 1936.

For the final batches of steam stock a different method of construction was employed. The 'heavily-rivetted' look had seemingly lost favour rather quickly – it is thought because of corrosion problems – and the fixed windows were framed with wooden mouldings (according to Mr Denis Cullum) or Alpax aluminium window frames (according to Mr Lawrence Mack). This meant that on the compartment side the coaches looked similar to the 1932 series, except that they had frameless droplights. On the corridor side, however, the appearance was quite different. The windows were very large, two being between each entry door with only a narrow space between them. Doors were no longer placed opposite alternate compartments but *between* alternate compartments, so that passengers entering the coach this side had to turn right or left into the corridor before a compartment could be entered. Guard's compartments were still flat-sided and fitted with standard duckets.

Forty-one Open Thirds with this much neater styling, and fitted with airstream sliding ventilators, were completed in 1936 to Order No. 861, and received the numbers 1410 to 1450. Seating capacity was 56 in seven bays. Nos. 1410–24 were dated April, 1425–49 May, and 1450 June, 1936. Of the whole range of Maunsell/Lynes coaches these were quite the most handsome. Unlike the other 1936-built coaches they did have wooden-framed droplights. The body style was later seen on the Portsmouth electric motor coaches.

Of the twenty 4-coach trains ordered, only 10 were actually built and they entered traffic as 3-coach sets and 10 loose Corridor Thirds. Initially all ran on the Western Section, but soon all were transferred to the Eastern Section. All the vehicles were 9 ft over body. Third Brakes (Order No. 869) each had six compartments, Composites (Order No. 870) had four first and three third class compartments, and the Thirds (Order No. 871) had eight compartments. The running numbers of the Thirds were 1911 to 1920 and they were dated June 1936. Giving up the struggle to find blank numbers within the Third Brakes range, the Southern's rolling stock clerks started a new series in the 4200s, originally allocated to Second Class coaches and so still vacant. Composites Nos. 5695–8 were dated July 1936, and the sets were completed in August. They were placed on Folkestone and Ramsgate services, and often a Pullman car was marshalled between the Composite and a Third

Brake. The Thirds were used as strengthening vehicles on boat train and Kent Coast services.

	Set 952	**Set 954**	**Set 956**	**Set 958**	**Set 960**
Third Bke	4231	4235	4239	4243	4247
Compo	5692	5694	5696	5698	5700
Third Bke	4232	4236	4240	4244	4248
	Set 953	**Set 955**	**Set 957**	**Set 959**	**Set 961**
Third Bke	4233	4237	4241	4245	4249
Compo	5693	5695	5697	5699	5701
Third Bke	4234	4238	4242	4246	4250

No more steam examples of the final Maunsell/Lynes design were to appear but it was perpetuated in the 4-COR and 2-BIL electric stock of 1937 and 1938.

'IMPROVED' BOURNEMOUTH LINE STOCK, 1938

Maunsell retired in 1937, by which time both his coaches and their livery of dark green with full lining-out were beginning to look a little old-fashioned. His successor, Oliver Bulleid, experimented with various shades of green, some more vivid than others. The Directors, naturally enough, wanted their railway to look up-to-date so, in an attempt to bring the appearance of its trains in line with contemporary ideas of styling, the Southern Railway decided to refurbish two 11-coach trains for the Bournemouth line service. Externally the coaches were painted in light green, known officially as Bulleid Green, without any lining-out, and with class designations shown on the doors in large numerals instead of being spelt out. The title 'Southern' was painted on the waist instead of under the cantrail, but coach numbers remained in their old position.

The coaches were ready in time for the start of summer services in July 1938, and were well publicised. The August issue of the *Southern Railway Magazine* gave detailed descriptions in enthusiastic tones, but irresponsibly gave the impression that the improved vehicles were entirely new. Very smart they may have been, but 'new' they were not.

The inside walls and ceilings were covered in Rexine, coloured pale yellow in first class compartments and stone in the thirds. All compartments had individual seat-backs with 'scalloped' tops. In the first class compartments were tubular lamps, fitted over the seats and in the ceilings; and heaters were placed on *both* sides instead of on only one side as hitherto. Upholstery was pale green. In the third class compartments were framed pictures by Donald Maxwell in place of the usual maps and advertisements; and there were actually floor rugs! Upholstery was pale pink.

Two Kitchen/Dining Firsts were also converted: the dining section was fitted with individual armchair seats and green Wilton carpet. In the roof were electric extractor fans, and the walls were hung with original water-colour paintings.

Each 11-coach train weighed 352 tons and had a seating capacity of 102 first and 408 third class passengers. 'The scheme of decoration gives a pleasing suggestion of coolness and cleanliness,' said the *Southern Railway Magazine*.

The sets actually involved in the scheme were 2-coach Type 'E' Nos. 180 and 199; 3-coach Type 'K' Nos. 221 and 232; and 6-dining sets Nos. 241 and 242. These became Type 'O' and, with their formations altered to include two Open Thirds (both of which could be used as dining cars), they were to be kept rigidly to the booked workings. Formation of these sets was:

	Set 241	**Set 242**
Third Bke	3799	3790
First	7676	7675
Dining Sal.	7940 or 7943	7940 or 7943
Open Third	1419	1412
Open Third	1410	1413
Third Bke	3800	3791

In addition, four loose coaches were 'improved'; clearly the Southern was determined that nothing should spoil the effect of a complete light-green train and, if it needed to be strengthened at busy times, nothing else but one of these four (which were Thirds Nos. 1802/3 and Composites Nos. 5637/9) could be used. Actually they spent much of their time sitting around at Clapham Yard or Bournemouth West.

The improved stock began work at the start of the summer timetable in July 1938, on the following services:

Up: 7.15 am from Swanage (2-set); 7.42 am from Weymouth (3-set); 8.20 am from Bournemouth West (6-dining set). These portions ran as 11 coach train from Bournemouth Central to Waterloo.

Down: 4.30 pm – Front, Weymouth (3-set); Middle, Swanage (Composite F O, 2-set); rear, Bournemouth West (6-dining set). The Composite returned Up on Saturdays. These services were the 'Bournemouth Limited'.

Down, Saturdays excepted: 12.30 pm – Front, Weymouth (3-set); Middle, Swanage (2-set); Rear, Bournemouth West (6-dining set).

Up: 5.37 pm from Weymouth, 5.41 pm from Swanage, 6.21 pm from Bournemouth West to Waterloo.

Down, Saturdays until 3rd September: All 11 coaches, plus loose Third, worked 12.30 pm Waterloo to Weymouth and 5.37 pm return. From 10th September the dining set ran to and from Weymouth, the 2-set to and from Swanage and the 3-set to and from Bournemouth.

The winter services were similar to the 'Saturdays excepted' summer services. One of the loose Thirds was attached to the 8.20 am up on Wednesdays and the 4.30 pm down on Fridays; the other was on the 12.30 pm down and 6.21 pm up on Fridays and Saturdays. From 1st January, 1939, only one loose Third had a regular working: 12.30 pm Waterloo to Weymouth and 5.37 pm return on Fridays and Saturdays only.

Workings of the light-green sets were maintained until 11th September, 1939, when the 'panic' timetable was introduced; from October they could be used on any working. By 1941 the dining cars had been removed and replaced by Thirds, presumably Nos. 1802/3. Meanwhile the dining cars had been placed on Waterloo–Exeter–Plymouth services, No. 7940 being booked to work with a 2-set 'E' on the 10.59 am (MWFO) Waterloo to Padstow and 8.30 am (TThSO) Padstow to Waterloo from October 1941. By May 1944, all restaurant car working was suspended and the cars were stored, Nos. 7940/3 remaining out of use up to mid-1947.

Dining saloon No. 7955 was also converted in a similar manner to the other two, probably in 1939. During 1941 it had a regular duty in a 6-dining set on the 8.30 am Waterloo–Bournemouth and 2.20 pm return; in 1943 it was booked to work the 7.30 am Exeter–Waterloo and 5.00 pm return. It spent the next few years out of use. All three were noted in lists as having 'special interior fittings' and each was equipped with a geyser.

WORKING OF MAUNSELL STOCK ON THE CENTRAL AND EASTERN SECTIONS, 1935 to 1947

Corridor sets generally stayed on the lines to which they had been originally allocated, until displaced by electrification. Thus, major upheavals were caused by the successive electrification of the Brighton, Eastbourne and Bognor lines.

Following the Brighton and Worthing electrification, 8-set 469 was reduced by two coaches and transferred to the Kent Coast line, where it was for a year or two one of the only two sets of 9 ft stock operating on the Eastern Section. Its formation when in traffic (regularly on the 3.15 pm Victoria to Ramsgate) was now: Third Brake 4048, Thirds 2349/50, First 7665, Composite Pullman, Third 2351 and Third Brake 4049.

Set 470 was reduced to three coaches in about 1933 (Third Brake 4050, Composite 5656, Third Brake 4051) and ran on Bognor and Portsmouth services; when they were electrified in 1938 it went to the Eastern Section, where it was employed on general workings.

In 1935, until electrification, the Eastbourne services were being operated by 3-sets 189 to 192, 219, 220; three un-numbered 3-sets each formed of two ex-LSW Corridor Third Brakes and one Maunsell 8 ft 6 in. Composite; 5-set 466; and 6-sets 465 and 467. In traffic each of these three 'long' sets included in the formation a First Pullman and a Third Pullman car. Three examples of Eastbourne 3-set workings from January 1935, are shown below.

Working No.

600. 7.30 am Eastbourne–London Bridge and 12.05 pm return.
8.50 pm Eastbourne–Brighton, 10.10 pm Brighton–Hastings.

601. 9.10 am Victoria–Eastbourne and 12.20 pm return.
3.10 pm Victoria–Eastbourne and 5.25 pm return.

602. 11.10 am Victoria–Eastbourne and 2.25 pm return (attached at Polegate to portion from Hastings).
4.30 pm (SX), 4.32 pm (SO) Victoria–Hastings.

The 5.06 pm London Bridge to Eastbourne was still worked by Set 466, with the reduced formation of Third Brake 4081, Third 835, First Pullman, Third Pullman, Firsts 7397/4 and Third Brake 4082.

After July 1935, all the 8 ft 6 in. stock was transferred to the Eastern Section, Sets 189–92 and 219/20 being made up to four coaches to match Nos. 181–8 and 449–54 already on the ex-South Eastern main line; Nos. 465–7 went to the Kent Coast main line. The un-numbered 3-sets were disbanded.

Stock allocated for use on London, Bognor, Portsmouth and associated services in 1935 comprised 3-sets 193, 224–31, 238, 387, 456, 464 and 470; and 4-sets 194, 195, 233–7. Certain of the 4-sets operated with one or two Pullmans formed in. After the electrification of these lines in July 1938, they were dispersed somewhat; some went to the Eastern Section but others remained on the Central to work a group of lines that up to now seldom had enjoyed the luxury of corridor stock – the Oxted, East Grinstead and Tunbridge Wells West routes. The *Railway Magazine* noted (Vol. 83, p.385) that the 3.55 pm Victoria to Brighton and Eastbourne via Eridge was composed of six or seven standard corridors from July 1938; and that the 5.09 pm London Bridge to Forest Row via Three Bridges and 8.29 am Forest Row to Victoria via Oxted also had corridor stock at that time.

The only other Central Section 3-set in 1935 was No. 223, which had standard gangways (adaptor-fitted) at the brake-ends; this set was used for the through service from Hastings, Eastbourne and Brighton to Birkenhead.

On the Eastern Section the position was more stable; in 1935 the Hastings line had 3-sets 213–6, 475, 476, 478–80, 940–50 and 7-sets 939 and 951. 4-sets 181–8, 449–54 worked the best Folkestone trains, while on the Kent Coast line 6-set 469, 7-sets 217, 218, 468 and a new 8-set, No. 430, were found on the better services along with the 'Thanet' stock. Each ran with a Composite Pullman formed in the set.

Set 430 had been made up in about 1933 from newly-built Open Thirds and Third Brakes plus older stock. Its formation in 1935 was: Third Brake 3775, Third 776, Open Third 1343, Firsts 7409 and 7225, Open Third 1351, Composite Pullman, First 7667 and Third Brake 3776.

For the Folkestone, Dover and Gravesend boat trains certain Maunsell stock was allocated in addition to the SE-style 'Continental' coaches. There were 10 Open Thirds Nos. 1315/8/24/5/7/32/9/47/53/9, four Third Brakes Nos. 3772/80/9/95, and four Firsts Nos. 7210, 7410, 7671/3. Newhaven boat trains still employed the 1927 stock built for them.

In 1938/9 some of the Maunsell stock allocated to boat train services was 'improved' in the same manner as the Bournemouth sets, being painted in Bulleid green. The vehicles concerned were Open Thirds 1434, 1449, Nondescript Brakes 4439, 4442 (which were redesignated Second Brakes), Second Brakes 4481/2, Firsts 7232, 7410; and seven Nondescript Saloons which were classed as Seconds and renumbered as shown:

Old No.	*New No.*	*Old No.*	*New No.*	*Old No.*	*New No.*	*Old No.*	*New No.*
7793	4391	7902	4393	7905	4395	7911	4397
7800	4392	7904	4394	7906	4396		

The *Southern Railway Magazine* (Vol. 17, p.165) noted that a new coach put into one of the Continental boat trains on 3rd April, 1939, was decorated with original drawings of Italian subjects by Helen McKie. They were drawn on tinted paper to tone with the panelling and upholstery. Once again, on closer inspection, this 'new' coach turns out to be one of the 'improved' vehicles. Some of them were in use by February 1939. No. 4393 had a short life in its new form as it was destroyed by enemy action in November 1940.

The Carriage Working Notice for 5th May, 1941, shows that despite war-

Corridor Third No. 1244, built in 1934 (Diagram 2001). The coach is fully lined-out although this is invisible in the photograph. *Lens of Sutton*

4-coach set No. 236 plus Pullman on a Victoria to Portsmouth service at Sutton c.1937. *F.M. Gates*

time conditions a reasonable number of trains on the Eastern and Central Sections was still running, and Pullman cars were still formed in some Folkestone and Ramsgate via Chatham services. On the Central, 3-sets 223–30, 238 and 387 were allocated to London, East Grinstead, Tunbridge Wells West, Brighton and Eastbourne services, two sets being spare at Eardley carriage sidings. 4-sets 194/5 were at Eardley, 4-set 237 at Hove, and 6-sets 465/6 were at Victoria; none of these had any booked workings. Sets 465/6 were sent to the Western Section as 8-coach in 1945, returning in mid-1947.

On the Eastern Section, the Hastings line had 3-sets Type 'F' Nos. 213–6, 478–80, 940; and 3-sets Type 'O' Nos. 476, 941–50, which had more third class accommodation than the 'F' sets. A typical Hastings line diagram, employing two 'F' sets with a Pullman marshalled between them, took in the 8.28 am Hastings to Charing Cross and 5.06 pm Cannon Street to Hastings, with a visit to Rotherhithe Road carriage shed in the middle of the day. Only the 4.20 pm from Charing Cross now had a through portion for Bexhill West; it was detached at Tonbridge, ran as a stopping service to Bexhill, thence empty to Hastings via Crowhurst.

The 'O' sets tended to wander round other Eastern Section lines and in 1941 were working some very obscure night-time services, such as the 1.35 am Cannon Street to Charlton, 4.00 am Barnehurst to Charing Cross; and the 3.45 am Erith to Charing Cross; the two sets being joined in the platform at the London terminus to form the 8.25 am to Hastings.

The only two 'long' corridor sets on the Hastings line were Nos. 939 and 951, and they worked as under:

7-set 939 SX: 7.40 am Hastings–Cannon Street and 6.22 pm Charing Cross–Hastings.
SO: 7.40 am Hastings–Tonbridge, 10.55 am Tonbridge–Cannon St, 12.14 pm CS–Hastings.

7-set 951 SX: 2.55 pm Hastings–Charing Cross, 5.31 pm return.
SO: 7.27 am Hastings–Cannon Street, 2.25 pm Charing Cross–Hastings.

Three-coach sets of 9 ft stock – Nos. 193, 231, 456, 464, 470 and 952–961 – were allocated to London, Ashford, Maidstone East, Minster and Ramsgate services; one being on the 6.51 am Ramsgate to Cannon Street and 11.15 am Charing Cross to Margate. Another was in the 8.35 am Victoria to Dover via Chatham and 1.10 pm return. A spare set stood at Ramsgate and another at Stewarts Lane.

Four-coach sets of 8 ft 6 in. stock – Nos. 181–192, 219, 220, 449–454 – also worked a great variety of train services in Kent. Third Brake No. 3714 in Set 220 had been damaged by fire at Swanley in March 1938, and replaced by 'Thanet' Third Brake No. 3574.

Other workings of 'long' sets on the Eastern Section were as follows:

7-set 217: Spare at Margate.
7-set 218: Spare at Ramsgate.

6-set 233: SX: 3.25 pm Ramsgate–Victoria, 7.15 pm return.
SO, with Composite and Third: 11.32 am Ramsgate–Victoria and 3.35 pm return.

5-set 234: SX: 8.15 am Herne Bay–Cannon St, 12.35 pm Victoria–Ramsgate; empty to Herne Bay except Fridays.
SO, with four Thirds: 1.15 pm Ramsgate–Victoria, 6.06 Victoria–Ramsgate, empty to Herne Bay.

5-set 235, plus one Third (SX), three Thirds (SO): 10.35 am Victoria–Ramsgate, 4.15 pm (SX), 3.43 pm (SO) Ramsgate–Victoria.

7-set 236, plus two Thirds: 6.15 am Ramsgate–Cannon Street, 12.45 pm (SO), 5.46 pm (SX) return.

9-set 430, less one First on Saturdays: 7.10 am Ramsgate–Cannon Street, 1.15 pm (SO), 4.45 pm (SX) return. (Pullman car)

7-set 467: Spare at Margate.

7-set 468: Spare at Maze Hill.

7-set 469: 9.55 am Ramsgate–Victoria and 2.10 pm (SO), 3.35 pm (SX) Victoria –Ramsgate. (Pullman car)

In 1943 two three-coach sets were made from existing 9 ft vehicles: No. 760, to replace non-corridor stock on a Maidstone West–Paddock Wood –London service, and No. 962, for general use on the Eastern Section. They were formed:

	Set 760			**Set 962**	
Third Brake	2833	ex Loose	Third Brake	3734	ex Loose
First	7673	"	Compo	5645	ex Set 195
Third	1114	"	Third Brake	3735	ex Loose

A rather odd set of eight coaches, No. 194, was made up in about 1947 for London–Tunbridge Wells West services. A real break with tradition, it was formed with a Corridor Third at each end, and the Third Brakes, whose brake-ends faced inwards, were the second and seventh coaches. Most platforms on the Oxted lines could accommodate only six coaches, so this arrangement ensured that the guard was always alongside the platform when the train stopped. It foreshadowed the present-day practice of marshalling the brake coaches absolutely anywhere in the train except at the ends. Special dispensation had to be obtained from the Ministry of Transport to form Set 194 like this, its view having been that the end coach ought to be a brake without passenger accommodation to minimise injuries in the event of a collision. Many trains had been running with loose Thirds at the ends anyway!

In June 1947, the final year of the Southern Railway's existence, the allocation of Maunsell sets to the Central and Eastern Sections was as follows:

3-sets 193, 387, 456, 464, 470, 952 to 962: London, Margate, Ramsgate, Dover, Stewarts Lane.

3-sets 195, 223 to 231, 238: London, East Grinstead, Tunbridge Wells West, Brighton, Lewes, Eastbourne.

3-set 760: London, Paddock Wood, Maidstone West.

3-sets 'F': 213 to 216, 478 to 480, 940: London–Hastings.

3-sets 'O': 476, 941 to 950: London, Tonbridge, Hastings.

4-sets 181 to 192, 219, 220, 449 to 454: London, Margate, Ramsgate, Dover, Tonbridge, East Grinstead, Tunbridge Wells West, Brighton.
5-set 235: London–Ashford.
6-set 469: London–Ramsgate.
7-sets 217, 218, 233, 234, 467: London–Ramsgate.
7-set 468: Rotherhithe Road for special traffic.
7-sets 939, 951: London–Hastings.
8-set 194: London–Tunbridge Wells West.
8-sets 236, 237: London–Ramsgate.
8-sets 430, 465, 466: Eardley for special traffic.

The formation of Set 430 had been almost entirely altered since 1941. It now had Third Brake 2834, Third 1914, Open Third 1424, Firsts 7225, 7666, 7221, Open Third 1425 and Third Brake 2835.

Set Nos. 217, 218, 237 and 467 operated with a restaurant car each, normally Nos. 7869, 7870, 7871 and 7948. Use of Pullman cars had ceased in May 1942, and when refreshment facilities were restored after the War it was with SR restaurant cars instead of Pullmans.

WORKING AND DISPOSITION OF CORRIDOR STOCK ON THE WESTERN SECTION, 1936 to 1947

Western Section set workings remained fairly stable, and only the electrification of the Portsmouth line in July 1937 caused any upset. A selection of workings of set trains from 1st May to 4th June, 1936, is given below.

Working No.

6-dining sets Type 'N' Nos. 241 to 250

12. 12.30 pm Waterloo–Bournemouth West and 6.19 pm return.
17. 8.35 am Bournemouth West–Waterloo and 4.45 pm return.
19. 10.50 am Bournemouth West–Waterloo and 6.30 pm return.

5-dining set No. 202 ('Bournemouth Limited' stock)

21. 8.20 am Bournemouth West–Waterloo and 4.30 pm return.

7-dining sets Type 'C' Nos. 204 to 209

22. 8.50 am Waterloo–Portsmouth Harbour and 11.53 am return.
4.50 pm Waterloo–Portsmouth Harbour and 8.05 pm return.
23. WThX, 24 WThO. 9.50 am Waterloo–Portsmouth Harbour and 1.02 pm return.
3.50 pm Waterloo–Portsmouth Harbour and 6.34 pm return.
24. WThX, 23 WThO. 11.50 am Waterloo–Portsmouth Harbour and 5.40 pm return.
26. FO. 1.50 pm Waterloo–Portsmouth Harbour and 4.56 pm return.
SO. 1.50 pm Waterloo–Portsmouth Harbour (returning on Sunday 8.05 pm Portsmouth Harbour–Waterloo).
27. 7.12 am Portsmouth Harbour–Waterloo and 5.53 pm (SX), 5.50 pm (SO) return.

5-dining set No. 459: Bournemouth West–Birkenhead.
4-dining sets Nos. 427/8: Brighton–Plymouth.
4-set No. 234: Brighton–Bournemouth West.
2-sets Nos. 168, 172, 178–180, 196–200: Waterloo–Swanage/Lymington Pier; Bournemouth West–Manchester.
3-sets Type 'K', Nos. 203, 221, 222, 232, 239, 240, 400: Waterloo–Weymouth, Waterloo–Plymouth.

3-sets Type 'K' Nos. 426 and 429: Portsmouth–Plymouth.
3-sets Type 'F' Nos. 201, 390–399, 445–448 and 458: Waterloo–Bournemouth–Weymouth, Waterloo–Plymouth, Basingstoke–York–Newcastle.

Special traffic sets: No. 327 was berthed at Eastleigh, No. 328 at Bournemouth West, and Nos. 329/30 at Wimbledon Park.

The dining sets displaced from the Portsmouth services from July 1937 were transferred to Waterloo–Bournemouth services replacing the 'Iron-clad' sets, which were relegated to secondary and high-season services. Saturday workings for the 'C'-type dining sets, from 9th July to 24th September, 1938, were:

30. 5.40 am Waterloo–Weymouth and 11.26 am return.
31. 9.32 am Waterloo–Bournemouth West and 3.20 pm return.
32. 11.38 am Waterloo–Lymington Pier and 4.04 pm return.
33. 7.25 am Bournemouth West–Waterloo and 2.30 pm return.
34. 10.12 am Bournemouth West–Waterloo and 1.30 pm return.
35. 12.15 pm Bournemouth West–Waterloo and 5.30 pm return.

Working of 6-dining sets Type 'N' on Saturdays in summer 1938 was:

29. 11.2/11.8 am Bournemouth West–Waterloo and 6.30 pm return.
41/42. 9.20 am Swanage–Waterloo and 1.22 pm return.
43. 7.35 am Bournemouth West–Waterloo and 3.30/3.35 pm return.
44. 8.35 am Bournemouth West–Waterloo and 4.45 pm return.
45. 8.30 am Waterloo–Weymouth and 1.35 pm return.
46. 8.38 am Waterloo–Sidmouth and 2.20 pm return.
These two workings employed 10-dining sets 'N':
47. 11.30 am Waterloo–Bournemouth West and 3.30 pm return.
48. 12.24 pm Waterloo–Bournemouth West and 5.05 pm return.

Many other sets were temporarily made up with restaurant cars for the summer Saturday services; virtually everything was diagrammed, including loose stock. On the West of England line every dining car ran with a 56-seat Open Third as restaurant trailer. The four special traffic sets each did a single trip on Saturdays:

7-dining sets 'B' Nos. 327 and 328
53 or 54. 10.24 am Waterloo–Ilfracombe.
54 or 53. 10.10 am Ilfracombe–Waterloo.

8-dining sets 'D' Nos. 329 and 330
55 or 56. 10.35 am Waterloo–Ilfracombe.
56 or 55. 10.30 am Ilfracombe–Waterloo.

Such were the demands of summer Saturday holidaymakers and the lengths taken by the Southern to satisfy them!

The service in summer 1939 was virtually the same, but it was not allowed to run its full length; on 3rd September War was declared with Germany and from 11th September the carriage working notice was withdrawn and skeleton services substituted. There was some improvement in services from 16th October and Sets 202, 204–9 and 241–50 resumed working with restaurant cars; but from 5th February, 1940, the use of Open Thirds as restaurant car trailers ceased.

By 1st March, 1941, dining cars Nos. 7859/66, 7933/4/45/58 had been 'temporarily' withdrawn from traffic, and Maunsell Pantry Brake Firsts Nos. 7715/6 were in use with the pantries closed off. The carriage working notice of 6th October, 1941, was the last to show the use in traffic of dining sets, and from 1st June, 1942, all restaurant facilities were withdrawn from the Bournemouth line. Sets 202, 204–9 and 243–50 then ran with a Third in place of the restaurant car and Sets 241/2 had an extra First instead. Dining cars were still provided on the Exeter trains until 1944, the complete workings being:

1/2. 9.00 am Waterloo–Exeter.
2/1. 12.50 pm Exeter–Waterloo.
3. 10.50 am Waterloo–Exeter and 5.55 pm return.
4. 7.30 am Exeter–Waterloo and 5.00 pm return.
5. Spare loaded car at Clapham Yard.
6. Spare loaded car at Clapham Yard.
7. Spare loaded car at Exeter Central.

All restaurant car working was completely suspended by Government order from 4th April, 1944. Wartime travel was becoming increasingly unpleasant – not that passengers were encouraged to make journeys – with overcrowding, despite the great length of many of the trains on the Exeter run. Here the record was held by the 10.37 am up from Exeter, which had no fewer than 16 coaches, an unheard-of thing in peacetime. This was formed of two 2-sets from Exeter, a Composite, a 3-set and 2-set from Ilfracombe and Torrington respectively, and a 2-set and 4-set ('Ironclad') from Plymouth. This train had to be divided at Clapham Junction because no platform at Waterloo could accommodate 16 coaches. The six Plymouth vehicles forming the rear portion followed on five minutes after the main train had left. Not surprisingly with such loads schedules were very much slower than in peacetime.

Restaurant cars were restored to this route in 1945, operating on the same trains as in 1942/3 except that the 6.00 pm Waterloo to Exeter replaced the 5.00 pm. The only cars in use were Nos. 7862, 7866, 7871, 7932, 7939, 7941, 7950, 7954, 7957 and 7969. Four were in traffic, two available for Jersey boat trains and four spare.

In 1945 3-sets 203, 221, 222, 232, 239 and 240 were strengthened to five coaches, each with extra Composite and Third; and nine additional 5-sets, Nos. 265 to 273, were formed entirely from loose stock. They were allocated to West of England services, including two for Brighton–Plymouth services and one for the Brighton–Bournemouth train. The nine 'new' sets were formed:

	Set 265	**Set 266**	**Set 267**
Third Bke	2790	2832	2831
Third	1201	1210	1206
First	7209	7220	7669
Third	1211	1240	1207
Third Bke	2792	3780	3775

	Set 268	Set 269	Set 270	Set 271	Set 272	Set 273
Compo Bke	6676	6675	6687	6682	6663	6571
Third	1870	1806	1838	1873	1894	771
Compo	5640	5634	5646	5650	5657	5636
Third	1841	1807	1847	1891	1897	787
Compo Bke	6678	6680	6693	6689	6668	6574

In 1947 Thirds Nos. 1211, 1240 and 1207 were removed from Sets 265–7, which then went to the Weymouth line where they were used as 6-dining sets by the addition of a restaurant car and Open Third; the same thing occurred with Sets 232–50.

Eight-coach sets Nos. 465 and 466 were temporarily transferred from the Eastern to the Western Section in 1945. Each worked regular Basingstoke–Waterloo services. One of the sets, while working the 4.54 pm Waterloo to Basingstoke on 10th November, 1945, was involved in a smash at Woking. Both sets were returned to the Eastern Section in mid-1947.

By May 1946, a few Bournemouth trains included restaurant cars but they were not formed inside the sets. The services were the 8.30 am down and 2.20 pm up; 11.30 am down and 6.20 pm up; and 8.20 am up and 6.30 pm down. All the cars operated with Open Thirds. Gradually the post-War services were improving, and by October 1946, 6-dining sets were again to be seen on the Bournemouth line.

The allocation of Maunsell corridor sets working on the Western Section in 1947 was as shown below.

2-sets 'P' – 168/72/8–80/96/8–200:	Waterloo–West of England. Waterloo–Swanage.
3-sets 'M' – 201, 390–9, 427/8, 445–8, 458:	Waterloo–Weymouth. Waterloo–Salisbury.
4-sets 'H' – 202/43–50/65–7, 327–30, 400:	Waterloo–Bournemouth–Weymouth.
5-sets 'G' – 203/21/2/32/9/40/68–73, 426/9:	Waterloo–Southampton. Waterloo–Salisbury.
6-sets 'E' – 204–9, 308:	Waterloo–Bournemouth–Weymouth.
6-dining sets 'D' – 241/2:	Waterloo–Bournemouth.
8-set 'B' – 459:	Bournemouth–Birkenhead.

Kitchen/Dining cars still out of use at the start of 1947 were Nos. 7861, 7864, 7865, 7867, 7878, 7934, 7940, 7943, 7953, 7998 and 7999. Cars noted as having 'special interior fittings' were Nos. 7858, 7940, 7943, 7946, 7949, 7952 and 7955.

Kitchen cars were still supplied with gas made from oil at an oil-gas plant located at Eastleigh. It had been intended to equip each car with calor gas from 1937, but in fact only one car, No. 7934, had been converted and in 1947 it was still the only example.

A post-war West of England train of mixed stock. The front coach is an 'Ironclad' Corridor First; next comes a Maunsell 2-set, a Corridor Third, Open Third and Dining Car. *W.N. Lockett*

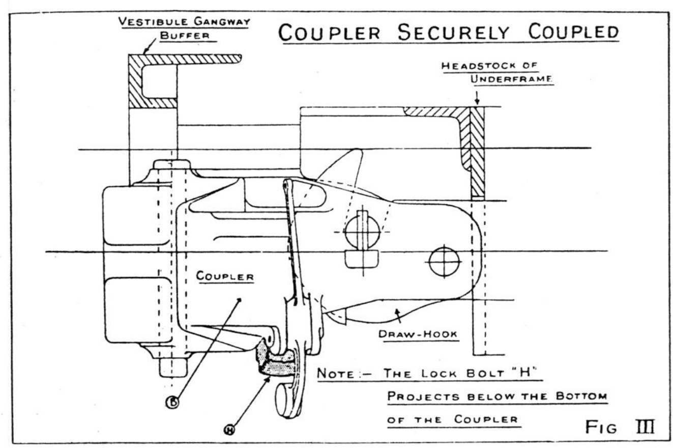

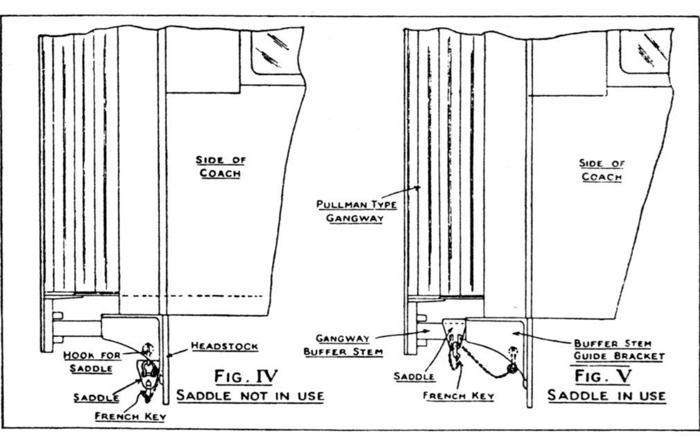

Chapter Seven

Minor alterations to coaches

These in most cases were carried out in the 1930s, and included the removal of intermediate buffers from certain vehicles, the re-location of destination board brackets, and the fitting of metal roller shutters at the gangways of some other coaches.

With Pullman-gangwayed stock, side-buffers are unnecessary as the buffing forces are taken by the gangway buffer stems in conjunction with the Buckeye automatic coupler. Retractable side buffers were retained, however, for use when the coach was coupled to one fitted with screw couplings. With permanently-coupled set trains it was found that buffers of the intermediate coaches could safely be removed, and several of the 3-coach sets had been so modified by 1934. Those identified include Nos. 392, 395 to 399 and 446.

The gangways of all coaches in 8-set 220 were equipped when new in 1931 with metal roller shutters, which obviated the use of the normal gangway shields. Coaches Nos. 3680 (Set 479) and 6659 (loose) were each fitted with a metal roller shutter at one end. Each shutter, which was similar to those used for some shop-fronts, was held by a spring in the open or closed position, and it was possible to close it from either inside or outside the coach. Gangway shields for protecting Pullman gangways were 4 ft by 6 ft 9 in. and those for British Standard gangways were 3 ft 2½ in. by 6 ft 10½ in. From July 1933, end gangway doors on all new corridor coaches were faced on the exterior with metal and fitted with a special fastening on the outside. With these doors no gangway shield was necessary. It was intended to fit the metal-faced doors on certain pre-1933 corridor coaches. These doors were supposed to be waterproof.

When the 'Ironclad' and earliest Maunsell coaches appeared they carried their destination boards in brackets immediately above the cornice rail; there was only one rainstrip on the roof each side. The brackets were moved to a position immediately above the rainstrip some time in the 1930s. Later 9 ft stock had two rainstrips each side, with brackets immediately above the lower one; 8 ft 6 in. stock carried the brackets below the rainstrip, and 8 ft stock above it. From 1952 many coaches had their upper rainstrips removed, presumably when the roof needed re-canvassing.

Composite Brakes Nos. 6656 and 6660 were altered to First/Second Composite Brakes in 1947 for Dover boat train services and renumbered 6905 and 6906. In 1949 they were altered back to First/Third Brakes but kept their new numbers.

PULLMAN CARS AND CORRIDOR COACHES FITTED WITH PULLMAN TYPE GANGWAYS AND COMBINED AUTOMATIC COUPLINGS AND ORDINARY DRAWGEAR.

The diagram in figure I represents the drawgear and buffers in position for use when a coach equipped with the automatic coupling is to be attached to a vehicle not so equipped.

The diagram in figure II represents the drawgear and buffers in position for use when two coaches, each equipped with the automatic coupling, are to be coupled together.

To convert from the ordinary and emergency arrangement (Fig. I) to automatic coupling arrangement (Fig. II) :—Remove the loose saddles A (Fig. II) between the buffer heads and guides and place them on hooks F; push buffers home against the guides G (Fig. I). Extract drop-ended pin C (Fig. I) from coupler, raise coupler B to working position, then replace pin, care to be taken that the tail piece of the pin falls downwards.

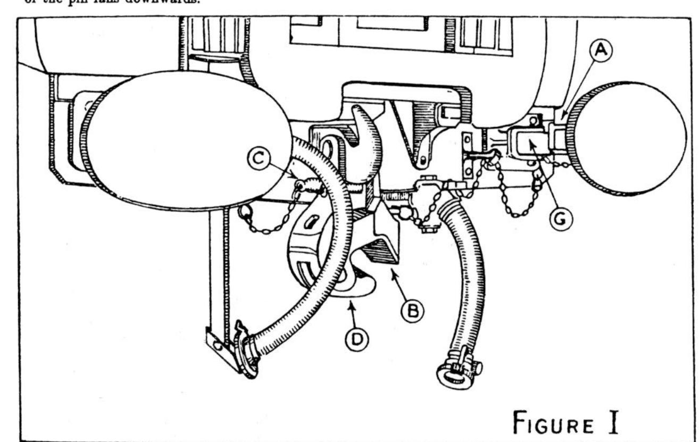

FIGURE I

To couple automatic couplings.—Pull the release lever chain E (Fig. II) to open the coupler knuckle D and bring the coaches together with sufficient pressure to automatically lock the couplers.

Lock bolt H (Fig. III) should drop below the coupler B and be visible to the extent of about 1½ inches. Shunters must satisfy themselves that the bolt has actually dropped.

After bringing the coaches together the Driver should be instructed to ease forward before the gangway curtains, lighting, etc. cables, brake and steam pipes are placed in position, in order that it may be ascertained that the automatic couplings have actually locked.

To uncouple automatic couplings.—Slightly compress the couplers, pull chain E to release the knuckle, and then draw apart.

To revert from automatic coupling to ordinary and emergency arrangement.—Close coupler knuckle, support coupler and withdraw drop-ended pin, then lower the coupler and replace the pin. Extend buffers and insert loose saddles.

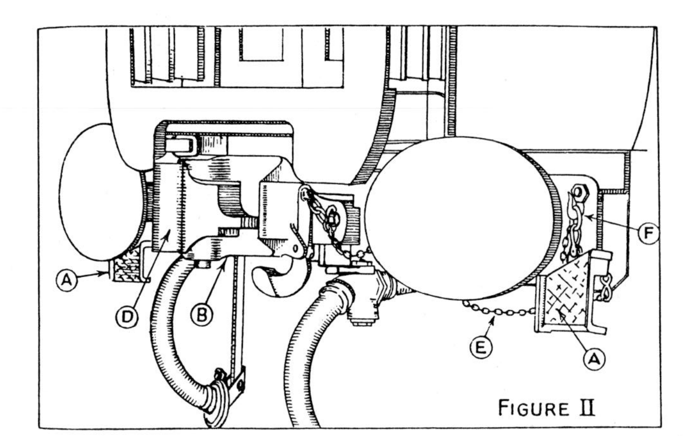

FIGURE II

Failure of automatic couplings.—In the case of certain 3-coach sets, where the intermediate side buffers have been removed, two removable saddles for placing on the gangway stems are provided.

Normally these saddles are carried out of use in the position shown in figure IV.

In the event of a failure with the automatic coupling and it being necessary to resort to the use of the screw coupling, these saddles are to be placed over the gangway buffer stems as shown in figure V before the coaches are coupled together by the screw coupling.

These saddles are not to be used when coaches are coupled together by means of the automatic couplings.

NOTE.—Coaches without buffers should not be connected to engines or coaches which have ordinary buffers. For example, in the event of the leading or rear vehicle of such 3-coach sets being stopped for repairs at a station en route, arrangements should be made for all three coaches to be withdrawn from traffic.

When the automatic coupling is out of use and side buffers are extended the gangways of two adjacent coaches will not come together, nor is there sufficient clearance for gangway shields to be used without the risk of their being forced off, and in such cases shields should be left off and the gangway doors must be locked to prevent passengers passing from one coach to the other.

Emergency screw couplings.—Each coach with automatic couplings is provided with one loose screw coupling for use when such coach is formed next to a vehicle not provided with automatic couplings, and this should be used in preference to the coupling of the adjacent coach. These loose couplings are marked with the number of the coach to which they belong and they must be considered to be part of the coach equipment. Special hooks are provided at one end only of each coach and screw couplings when not in use must be placed on these hooks.

Coupling or uncoupling vehicles fitted with automatic couplings.—Every precaution should be taken when vehicles fitted with automatic couplings have to be parted or joined together, and a clear understanding as to what is required to be done must be arrived at between the Shunter and the Enginemen before a commencement is made to adjust the automatic coupling equipment.

When the work is performed on running lines, two men must be employed, one to give the necessary hand signal to the Enginemen and the other to attend to the adjustment of the automatic coupling equipment; whenever practicable this procedure must be adopted when the work is carried out in sidings.

INSTRUCTIONS FOR AUTOMATIC COUPLINGS

Chapter Eight

Accidents involving SR-built coaches, 1927–1947

SEVENOAKS On 24th August, 1927, the 5.00 pm Cannon Street to Deal train came to grief at Shoreham Lane bridge, near Sevenoaks; four vehicles were damaged beyond repair. Apart from the Pullman car the train was formed entirely of Eastern Section 57 ft stock built in 1924/5; the Pullman had been converted in 1920 from a former South Eastern 'American Car' built in 1891.

Formation of the train from front to rear was:

Third Brake 3564. Extensively damaged and broken up on the spot.
Composite 5541. Two bogies and underframe badly damaged; vehicle later returned to traffic.
Composite 5520. Extensively damaged and broken up on the spot.
Composite 5518. Extensively damaged and broken up on the spot.
Pullman *Carmen*. Extensively damaged and broken up on the spot.
Third 988. End smashed where it had hit *Carmen* and underframe damaged. Repaired and returned to traffic.
Composite 5533. Buffer rods bent, both gangways broken. Repaired and returned to traffic.
Third Brake 3575. Buffer rods bent, one gangway broken, damage to cornice. Repaired and returned to traffic.

DOVER MARINE Four coaches had their bodies destroyed by fire in July 1935; the cause is unknown. The vehicles involved were:

'Continental' Third 779. Underframe re-used for electric Trailer Third No. 9078, December 1935.
1928-built Third 802. Returned to traffic with new body to 1935 design, May 1936.
1934-built Third 1834. New body as above, May 1936.
'Continental' First 7372. Underframe re-used for electric Trailer Third No. 9298, August 1937.

MICHELDEVER On 15th August, 1936, fire broke out on the 4.58 pm Channel Islands boat train from Southampton to Waterloo between Winchester and Micheldever. The train was formed of ex-LSW corridor bogie Guard's Van No. 330 (originally built as a corridor Third in 1908); Maunsell First No. 7227; 'Ironclad' Firsts Nos. 7180 and 7169; Pullman car *Rainbow*; Maunsell Thirds Nos. 1899, 808, 1906 and 876; and ex-LSW non-gangwayed bogie Guard's Van No. 242, built in 1895.

The fire was believed to have started at the trailing end of coach 7180 or the leading end of coach 7169; smoke was observed by passengers and the train was brought quickly to a halt. Several passengers jumped out. A down train then passed at reduced speed but even so the flames were fanned by its passage and, because the staff had been unable to uncouple the burning coaches, soon spread from No. 7180 to No. 7227 and from No. 7169 to *Rainbow*. Eventually the four stricken coaches were detached, shunted to a siding at Micheldever and allowed to burn themselves out.

The Inspecting Officer, Colonel A.C. Trench, believed the cause of the fire was an electrical short circuit near the trailing end of No. 7180 but he also considered the possibility that a spark from the engine (class 'H15' No. 482) might have landed on the canvas covers of the gangways between coaches 7180 and 7169 and ignited them. The Inspector recommended the substitution of leather covers for this type of gangway (British Standard) and he also indicated his dislike of non fire-resistant wooden roofs.

In the Inspecting Officer's report on the accident there were some details of the construction of the 'Ironclad' Firsts, which had heavy steel underframes; body framing of teak and oak, covered with No. 16 SWG steel sheets; interiors panelled with mahogany and plywood; roofs of deal panelled inside by asbestos millboard; and 'decolite' flooring on corrugated sheets.

SWANLEY JUNCTION Coach 3714 (Set 220) and 'Thanet' Composite 5537 were both fire-damaged in an incident in March 1938. They were shunted into Bournewood Crossing Siding (west of Swanley Junction) where they remained under tarpaulins for a month or so.

HAYWARDS HEATH On 2nd September, 1945, a special empty coaching stock train, 3.03 am Streatham to Newhaven, was diverted to the Down Siding at Haywards Heath to reverse to the up road, on which single line working was in force owing to engineers' possession on the down line. Presumably the locomotive crew had forgotten this as the train entered the siding quite fast and the locomotive, class 'N' No. 1811, smashed into the tunnel buttress at which the siding terminated, killing both enginemen. Both bogies of the leading coach and the leading bogie of the second coach were piled underneath the locomotive tender. The left-hand solebar of the front coach was torn off and thrown to one side, and the roof was driven forward over the locomotive; the rest of the underframe was distorted and crumpled. The rear part of the second coach's body was practically destroyed.

Of the 13 coaches forming the train 11 were undamaged. Numbers were not quoted in Col Trench's report on the accident, but the two smashed vehicles are presumed to have been Third Brake No. 4065 and Composite No. 5156, both of Set 468.

WOKING On 10th November, 1945, the 4.54 pm Waterloo to Basingstoke train, formed of eight Maunsell coaches, was struck by the 5.00 pm Waterloo to Exeter train, worked by class 'N15' locomotive No. 452, opposite the Southern Railway orphanage at Woking. The end Third Brake of the Basingstoke train was telescoped for about half its length. Almost certainly it was No. 4081 of Set 466, which was 'on loan' from the Eastern Section at this time.

CATFORD The 2.10 pm Victoria to Ramsgate train, hauled by class 'V' locomotive No. 917, became derailed at about 40 mph on a curve between Bridges 468 and 469 near Catford on 20th September, 1946. The derailment was caused by irregular cant and alignment. Seven of the nine coaches left the rails; the second and third fell into a car park at the bottom of the 20 ft embankment and the first and fourth fell on their sides on the bank, with one end of each vehicle resting at ground level. A passenger in the first coach was killed and several others injured.

The body of the front coach, Third No. 801, was severely damaged by a rail torn up by the locomotive, and the second coach – a Third Brake – had its bodywork badly crushed at the leading end. All the front four coaches lost their bogies.

Lt Col E. Woodhouse's report on the accident did not quote coach numbers, but the train certainly comprised Eastern Section 1925 stock, which as a class seems to have been singularly unlucky. Three vehicles were written off after the Catford accident: Third Brake 3563 and Thirds 977 and 991, all from Set 460. The Maunsell Third, No. 801, seems not to have disappeared from the lists until after 1947.

FARNBOROUGH On 26th November, 1947, the signalling power supply failed near Farnborough and the 3.05 pm Bournemouth West to Waterloo train was halted. Its driver tried to obtain instructions by telephone but was unable to do so. The following passenger train, the 12.15 pm Ilfracombe to Waterloo, was incorrectly admitted into the section by the signalman at the rear and it collided at about 20 mph with the stationary train. One passenger was killed.

The Bournemouth train had nine Maunsell coaches, of which the eighth and ninth were demolished and the seventh was seriously damaged. Third Brake No. 3796 and Thirds Nos. 807 and 1881 were all written off. It is presumed that the train included in its formation 4-set No. 245 at the rear running as a 6-set with the two loose Thirds formed inside the set. The locomotive that did the damage was class 'N15' No. 453, and it overturned; but the coaches of the Ilfracombe train were not damaged.

SR-BUILT COACHES DAMAGED OR DESTROYED IN WARTIME

Records of vehicles damaged or destroyed between 1940 and 1944 seem to be very incomplete. Although every air raid was written up in some detail in the Southern's Air Raid Log Books, describing damage and destruction to the Company's property, the identity of any coach that was damaged was not always recorded.

It seems that 16 SR-built coaches were destroyed, or at least damaged beyond repair, by enemy action. These were:

Thirds: 1014–c.1941. U'frame to 1875S, 9/43: Yard Wagon, Lancing Works.
1145–Beighton, LNER, 3/42. U'frame to Dover shunting truck 61328 in 1947.
1146–Beighton, LNER, 3/42.
1255–28/5/41.
1263–Newington, 16/8/44.
1836–Newington, 16/8/44.

Third Brakes: 2782–Clapham Junction, 8/9/40.
4049–9/9/44.
4077–pre 12/40. U'frame to Dover shunting truck 61329 in 1947.

Second: 4393–11/40.

Composites: 5513–27/11/40.
5514–25/12/40.

Compo Brakes: 6698–1/41.
6884–c.1944.

Firsts: 7382–Clapham Junction, 8/9/40.
7395–12/40.

A great many more were damaged, several very severely; but every one of them was repaired and returned to traffic. Many coaches were set alight by incendiaries but usually the fires were extinguished before too much damage was caused. Countless window glasses were broken by bomb blast, but damage of this sort was the least the Southern had to contend with.

On 8th September, 1940, a high-explosive bomb fell on the carriage cleaning shed at Clapham Junction, causing a great deal of damage to stock, including Thirds 1193, 1199 (body lifted off bogie and bolster finished up resting on top of bogie frame), 1200, 1346 (body lifted off bogie and damage to brakework), 1895 (roof and interior badly damaged); Third Brakes 2782 (half of body demolished), 3771, 3788; Firsts 7185, 7216, 7382 (body off bogies and extensive damage to interior); First Brake 7751; and Dining Saloons 7863, 7948 and 7956. All were later repaired except Nos. 2782 and 7382.

First No. 7403 suffered fire damage through enemy action at Cannon Street on 28th May, 1941. A new body was constructed and the vehicle re-instated in December 1941.

The Maunsell coaches damaged at Beighton, Sheffield, in 1942 are presumed to have been in the Ashford–Newcastle leave train that ran during the War, SR and LNER stock running on alternate days in each direction. Mr Edward G. Dott wrote in 1980: 'I saw the rake at Nottingham Victoria during this period, and several of the coaches had been very much shot-up, with lots of windows boarded over, but nevertheless the stock even then looked extremely clean.'

On 16th August, 1944, a flying bomb destroyed an underline bridge near Newington and the 3.35 pm Victoria to Ramsgate train, drawn by class 'N15' locomotive No. 806, which was unable to stop in time, partly fell into the hole. Two coaches were telescoped and destroyed (Thirds Nos. 1263 and 1836), and two others were badly damaged.

Corridor First No. 7669 (Diagram 2501), built in 1927. The vehicle is painted in malachite green livery, unlined; '1' numerals on doors. *Lens of Sutton*

Corridor Brake Third, No. 3799, built 1933.
National Railway Museum, Eastleigh Collection

Corridor brake third

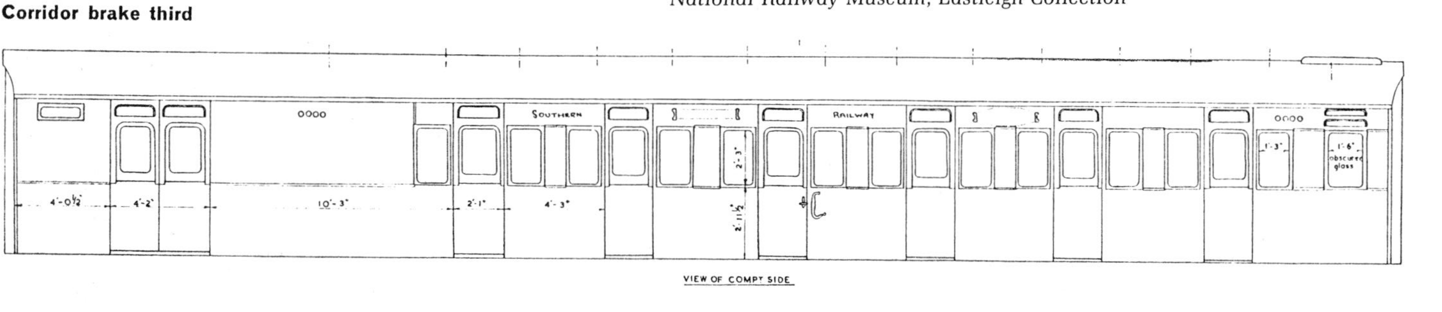

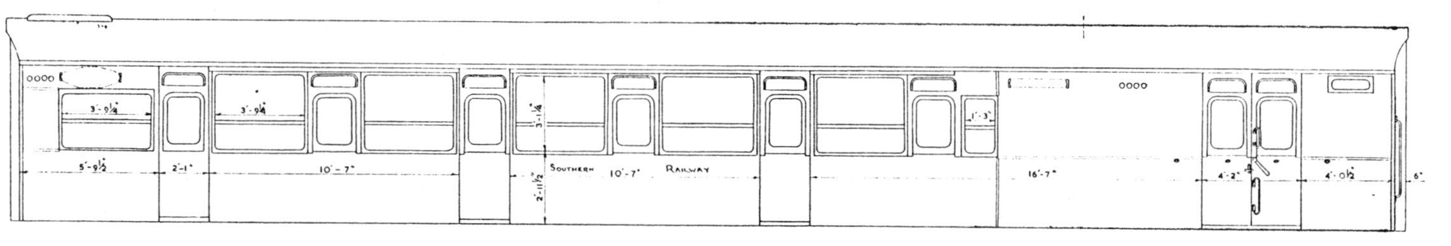

Drawing by Ray Chorley

Coach numbers: R0: 3672—3683
R1: 3692—3715
R4: 3732—3749, 3799

Alterations to set formations

The following list shows all known permanent alterations to sets comprising Maunsell standard coaches down to 1947 inclusive. Temporary alterations are not shown, nor are wartime formations where many sets contained extra coaches that were not even marked with set numbers. For example, when dining cars and trailers were removed from the 6-dining sets their place was taken by two unspecified Thirds. Sets that remained unaltered are also not included here.

Set
189 : Reduced to 3-set ; 5618 to Loose. Reverted c. 1935.
190 : Reduced to 3-set ; 5620 to un-numbered 3-set with Third Bkes 3096 and 3102. Reverted c.1935.
191 : Reduced to 3-set ; 5622 to Loose. Reverted c. 1935.
192 : 5624 to Loose, 5625 to un-numbered 3-set with Third Bkes 3104 and 3110 ; replaced by 5629 ex Set 219. 5625 reverted c.1935 ; formation now 3710, 5625, 5629, 3711.
193 : Reduced to 3-set ; 5640 to Loose pre 1935.
194 : Strengthened to 8-set, 1947. Formed 1231, 3740, 5642, 7226, 5643, 1232, 3741, 1233.
195 : Reduced to 3-set, 1943. 5645 to new Set 962, 1943.
197 : 6698 destroyed by enemy action c.1941; 2779 to Set 248. Set deleted.
202 : 3726/7 to Set 308, 7675 to Set 242, 1933 ; set deleted. Replaced by new Set 202 in 1935, formed 2837, 1827, 7672, 2838.
203 : Deleted by 1933. New Set 203 formed c.1933 : 3781, 5653, 3784. 5691, 1840 added by 10/45.
204 : Strengthened to 6-set : 3716, 1122, 7228, 1134, 1389, 3717 from 1947.
205 : Strengthened to 6-set : 3718, 1123, 7229, 1867, 1358, 3719 from 1947.
206 : Strengthened to 6-set : 3728, 1124, 7219, 1236, 1313, 3729 from 1947.
207 : Strengthened to 6-set : 3724, 1128, 7218, 778, 1287, 3725 from 1947.
208 : Strengthened to 6-set : 3720, 1129, 7407, 1186, 1360, 3721 from 1947.
209 : Strengthened to 6-set : 3723, 1127, 7411, 1140, 1338, 3722 from 1947.
217 : Reduced to 7-set ; 5610 to Loose.
218 : Reduced to 7-set ; 5617 to un-numbered 3-set with Third Bkes 3100 and 3118. To Loose c.1935.
219 : Reduced to 3-set ; 2360/1, 5626/7 to Loose, 5629 to Set 192. 5627 reverted to Set 219 c.1935 so now 4-set. 2360/1 to Set 466, c.1945.
220 : Reduced to 3-set ; 2362/3, 5630/1/2 to Loose. 5632 reverted c.1935 so now 4-set. 2362/3 to Set 465 c.1945. 3714 wdn fire damage 3/38 ; replaced by "Thanet" 3574 by 5/38.
221 : Strengthened to 5-set, 1945: 3750, 5664, 5637, 1243, 3751.
222 : Strengthened to 5-set, 1945: 3752, 5665, 5652, 1862, 3753.
232 : Strengthened to 5-set, 1945: 2767, 5675, 5639, 1817, 2768.
233 : Strengthened to 5-set with 1175, c.1941. 1157/8 added, c.1942 ; now 7-set.
234 : Strengthened to 5-set with 1183, c.1941. 1180/1 added, 1945; now 7-set.
235 : Strengthened to 5-set with 1159, c.1941.
236 : Strengthened to 7-set with 1170/1/2 c.1941. 5688 added, ex Loose, 1944.

Set

237 : Strengthened to 7-set with 1161/2/3 c.1942. 5686 ex Loose added 1944.

238 : Reduced to 3-set ; 5686 to Loose by 1935.

239 : Reduced to 3-set ; 5688 to Loose by 1935. Strengthened to 5-set, 1945 : 2802, 5689, 5638, 1824, 2803.

240 : Reduced to 3-set ; 5691 to Loose by 1935. Strengthened to 5-set, 1945 : 2804, 5690, 5658, 1813, 2805.

241 : Formation, 1944 : 3799, 1419, 7676, 1252, 1410, 3800. 1252 replaced by 1802 in 1945. 1419 removed in 1947 ; became 6-dining set.

242 : Formation, 1944 : 3790, 1412, 7675, Third, 1413, 3791. Third replaced by 1803, in 1945. 1412 removed in 1947 ; became 6-dining set.

245 : 3796 accident damage Farnborough 11/47 ; later replaced by 3789 ex Loose.

248 : 2782 destroyed in air raid at Clapham Jn 9/40 ; replaced by 2779 ex Set 197.

308 : Formation in 1944-7 : 3726, 1151, 1164, 7398, 1283, 3727.

327 : Formation in 1945 : 3773, 1208, 1121, 7223, 1209, 3774. Reduced to 4-set by 1947 ; 1208, 1121 to Loose.

328 : Formation in 1945 : 3797, 1215, 1267, 7406, 1216, 3798. Reduced to 4-set by 1947 ; 1267, 1216 to Loose.

329 : 10-set with unspecified Thirds from 10/41 ; reduced to 4-set by 1947. Formation : 3792, 1226, 7230, 3793.

330 : 10-set with unspecified Thirds from 10/41 ; reduced to 4-set by 1947. Formation : 3782, 1221, 7231, 3783.

400 : Strengthened to 8-set with four Thirds and one First, 10/41. 5654 to Loose, 1947. Formation now 2787, 1849, 7217, 2788.

426 : Reduced to 3-set ; 5648 to Loose. Strengthened to 5-set with 823 and 5659 in 1947.

428 : Reduced to 3-set by 1938 ; 3670, 5590, 3671.

429 : Reduced to 3-set ; 5650 to Loose. Strengthened to 5-set with 783 and 5662 in 1947.

430 : Formation in 1947 : 2834, 1914, 1424, 7225, 7666, 7221, 1425, 2835. Formed probably c.1942.

454 : 4077 destroyed by enemy action c.1940. Replaced by 4079 ex Set 465.

458 : Altered to 3-set by 1936 : 3664, 5660, 3665.

459 : Altered to 8-set, 10/39. Formation from 1945 : 3666, 1242, 5587, 5589, 5648, 1816, 1818, 3667.

464 : Reduced to 3-set ; 5646 to Loose by 1935.

465 : Reduced to 6-set ; 833 and 7392 to Loose pre 1935. 833 reverted, 7393 to Loose by 1941. 4079 to Set 454, replaced by LSW 3rd Bke 3110 c.1941. Strengthened to 8-set, 1945 ; 3110 replaced by 2791 ex Loose ; 2362/3 added. 4080 to Set 466, 1947 ; replaced by 4043 ex Set 471.

466 : Reduced to 5-set ; 836, 7395/6 to Loose pre 1935. 836 reverted by 1941, so now 6-set. Strengthened to 8-set, 1945 ; 2360/1 added. 4081 wdn accident damage ; replaced by 4080 ex Set 465, 1947. 7394 replaced by 7392.

467 : Reduced to 6-set ; 765 to Set 468, 5152 to Loose pre 1935. 5152 reverted by 1941, so now 7-set.

468 : Reduced to 7-set ; 5157/8 to Loose, 765 ex Set 467 added pre 1935. 4065, 5156 wdn accident damage ; 5155 to Loose ; replaced by 4095, 5157/8 ex Loose, 1946. Formation now 4095, 765, 767, 5158, 5157, 768, 4066.

469 : Reduced to 6-set ; 7666 to Loose, 7667 to Set 430, c.1933. 4049 damaged by enemy action c. 9/44 ; replaced by 2789 ex Loose, c.1945.

Set

470 : 2354/5, 7671/2/3/4 to Loose ; 5656 ex Loose added c.1933. Now 3-set. 7672 to Set 202, 7674 to Set 250 in 1935. 7673 to Set 760 formed in 1943.

475 : 3672/3, 5592 to Loose after 1935. Set deleted.

476 : 3674/5, 5593 to Loose after 1935. Set deleted. Replaced by new Set 476, formed 6887, 1026, 6888 ex Loose by 1941.

477 : 3676/7, 5594 to Loose pre 1935. Set deleted.

478 : 5595 to Loose, replaced by 7403 ex Loose pre 1935.

479 : 5596 to Loose, replaced by 7402 ex Loose pre 1935.

480 : 5597 to Loose, replaced by 7400 ex Loose pre 1935.

942 : 6884 withdrawn ; replaced by 6886 ex Set 951, 1944.

951 : 6886 to Set 942 ; replaced by 3674 ex Loose, 1944.

Victoria to Ramsgate train passing Bromley South on 9th September, 1933; 7-set No. 218 plus Pullman. *H.C. Casserley*

Waterloo to Southampton Docks train passes Vauxhall on 27th August, 1932; 3-coach set No. 427, with 'standard' gangways, adaptor-fitted, at the brake ends. *H.C. Casserley*

Chapter Nine

Maunsell stock under British Railways

The policy of operating set trains was continued on what became the Southern Region of British Railways, although changes of formation were made more frequently than before the War. It would make reading too tedious to attempt to detail every change made between 1948 and 1963, but the introduction of 'new' sets of Maunsell stock – and some of the train services which they were intended to work – will now be described.

In 1948 Sets Nos. 203, 221, 222, 232, 239 and 240 reverted to 3-coach with their original coaches. Sets 426 and 429 were also reduced to 3-coach as running before the War. Sets 265, 266, 267 and 400 were disbanded and the Third Brakes used with loose Composite Brakes to form eight 'new' 2-coach sets for Waterloo–West of England services. They were formed thus:

	Set 22	**Set 24**	**Set 26**	**Set 28**
Third Bke	2790	2832	2831	2787
Compo Bke	6691	6602	6586	6569
	Set 23	**Set 25**	**Set 27**	**Set 29**
Third Bke	2792	3780	3775	2788
Compo Bke	6575	6665	6603	6567

By 1959 they had been demoted to local train workings in the Western District, referred to as 2-sets 'P'. Normally they were not seen east of Honiton, but were the mainstay of the Bude and Padstow branches. Composite Brake No. 6575 later achieved fame by being the first Maunsell coach ever to be preserved as a historic vehicle when the new-born Bluebell Railway purchased it in 1960.

8-set 237 was chosen in 1948 to wear one of the new experimental liveries that BR was trying – in this case chocolate and cream. The formation was Third Brake 2798, Thirds 1161/2, Composite 5684, loose Composite 5637, Kitchen/Dining car 7934, loose Third 1252, Composites 5685/6, Third 1163 and Third Brake 2799. Services worked were the 7.20 am Ramsgate to Cannon Street and 5.15 pm return. Unfortunately this attractive livery proved very difficult to keep clean and so it was replaced in 1953. Another experimental livery, 'plum and spilt milk', was carried by Thirds 1200 and 1254 and First 7224. After some time in service the colours looked quite ghastly!

In 1950 an untidy-looking set of nine vehicles, No. 263, was assembled for special traffic on the Eastern Section, being berthed at Stewarts Lane in summer and Eardley in winter. It included 'Continental' Third Brakes, new Bulleid Composites, and Maunsell Thirds. Formation was 3552, 819, 818, 5885, 5884, 5883, 1177, 1176 and 3558. In 1953 the 'Continentals' were replaced by Maunsell Composite Brakes 6565/6; in 1955 the Composites were replaced by 'Thanets' 5531/2 and Maunsell 5591; and by June 1959, two more Bulleid Composites, Nos. 5868/9, had replaced the 'Thanets'. Summer Saturday workings in the 1950s were the 9.08 am Victoria to Ramsgate and 2.24 pm Herne Bay to Victoria. Set 263 was withdrawn in the summer of 1959, the Composite Brakes being condemned and the other vehicles re-deployed.

Sets 202, 241–50 and 327–30 were reduced to 3-coach in mid-1951. This involved removing the First and Third from each one and substituting a Composite, sometimes a Bulleid one. Sets 248 (green) and 328 (crimson and cream), when photographed in 1951, each contained a temporary Bulleid vehicle in the centre; but there is no reference to them in the official lists. The permanent formations were:

	Set 202	**Set 243**	**Set 246**	**Set 249**	**Set 328**
Third Bke	2837	3778	3771	2783	3797
Compo	5638	5662	5654	5688	5637
Third Bke	2838	3779	3788	2784	3798
	Set 241	**Set 244**	**Set 247**	**Set 250**	**Set 329**
Third Bke	3799	3786	3777	2785	3792
Compo	5639	5659	5691	5655	5686
Third Bke	3800	3787	3794	2786	3793
	Set 242	**Set 245**	**Set 248**	**Set 327**	**Set 330**
Third Bke	3790	3785	2779	3773	3782
Compo	5663	5658	5661	5652	5634
Third Bke	3791	3789	2781	3774	3783

They were allocated to Waterloo–Bournemouth–Weymouth and other services on the Western Section. By 1956 they were down-graded to local services. Late in 1959 Set 241 was transferred to the Central Section for working the Oxted and Redhill groups of services and by 1962 No. 327 had arrived there too.

Alterations to sets and disposals follow:

202: 5638 replaced by 5641 June, 1961; set withdrawn December 1961.
241: Composite replaced by Bulleid Composite 5814 c.October 1961; set withdrawn mid-1962.
242: Composite replaced by Bulleid Composite 5799 in 1961, later 5902; set withdrawn mid-1962.
243: Set withdrawn by November, 1959. 3778/9 to Set 443.
244: ran as 7-buffet set from 1954 to 1957; Composite then 5785; replaced by 5660 ex Set 458 in 1958; set withdrawn June 1962.
245: Composite replaced by Bulleid Composite 5873 early 1962; set withdrawn later that year.
246: withdrawn early 1962; 3771 to Set 271, 3788 to Set 30.
247: 5691 replaced by 5659 ex-Set 244, 1955; replaced by Bulleid Composite 5889 c.November 1961; set withdrawn 1962.
248: withdrawn December 1961.
249: 5688 withdrawn December, 1961; set strengthened to eight coaches formed 2783, 1236, 1887, 5803/4, 1870, 1838 and 2784. Withdrawn at end of 1962.
250: Composite replaced by Bulleid Composite 5800 mid-1961; set strengthened to eight coaches in 1962 formed 2785, 1893/4, 5800, 5814, 1827, 1880, 2786. Withdrawn at end of 1962.
327: Composite replaced by Bulleid Composite 5808, 1962; set disbanded June 1962. 3773/4 to Set 443.
328: withdrawn 1959; 3797/8 to Set 432, 1960.
329: disbanded March 1962; 3792/3 to Set 428.
330: withdrawn 1958; 3782 to Set 434.

Set 212 had quite an involved history, starting as a Maunsell set in 1953 and ending up with Bulleid coaches in 1965. Its formation when introduced was Composite Brake 6604, Third 1839, Composites 5630, 5586, Third 1861, Composite Brake 6661. It was a special traffic set, kept at Margate in the summer and Eardley in winter. In 1956 Seconds 780/1/2 were added and its summer stabling point until 1958 was Blackheath. As a 6-set from 1953 it worked on alternate Saturdays in summer the 10.35 am Margate to Redhill and Reading, making the return seven days later with the 10.50 am to Redhill and Margate. As a 9-set from 1956 it worked (SX) 8.58 am Blackheath to Ramsgate and 6.26 pm return; (SO) 10.26 am Victoria to Ramsgate and 7.00 pm Ramsgate to Blackheath. From September 1958, it became the Central Section's special traffic set, stabled at Hassocks. A BR-built Open First appeared in the formation in 1960; Maunsell Open Brake Seconds 4442 and 4450 replaced the end coaches; during 1963 the middle coaches were all BR standard stock; and in 1964 it was entirely re-formed with Bulleid coaches. Its most frequent use was on enthusiasts' railtours.

Set 211 had long been formed of ex-LSW corridor vehicles and as these were withdrawn more modern stock replaced them. From 1953 'Continental' Third Brake 3559, Maunsell Third 1131 and 'Thanet' Composite 5526 were put in; 'Thanet' Third 989 joined them a year later. Three Maunsell Firsts, Nos. 7393/4/6 (8 ft 6 in. stock) were downrated to Thirds in 1954 and renumbered 656–658 in the same order. No. 656 was placed in Set 262 and No. 658 went to Set 211 by 1955. After many other changes the set was withdrawn in mid-1959, by which time its formation was 3587, 1131, 989, 5524/6/7, 786, 658 and 3588. During the summer Set 211 was berthed at Blackheath sidings and in winter was at Maze Hill for special traffic. During the 1954 summer season it worked a Saturday 'rounder': 11.26 am Victoria to Ramsgate, empty to Deal, 3.48 pm Deal to Charing Cross.

Also renumbered in 1954 were the Seconds and Second Brakes built in 1927 for the Newhaven boat train. They were downrated to Thirds.

Old No.	*New No.*	*Old No.*	*New No.*	*Old No.*	*New No.*
4483	1921 1.55	4485	1923 10.54	4481	2772 12.54
4484	1922 10.54	4486	1924 10.54	4482	2773 12.54

Third Brake 2772 was placed in Set 234 in 1957 as a replacement for 2793 but was withdrawn in December 1958; the other five were loose coaches until their withdrawal.

A 10-coach set, No. 938, was formed in 1954 for Hastings line business services. All the coaches were formerly loose, several being 'Continental' former Seconds. From 1956 the set ran with four of the Seconds outside the Second Brakes, viz: 1012/3, 3676, 5592/3/4, 1016, 3677, 1017/8. No doubt there had been problems with short platforms on the Hastings line. The set was berthed at Tonbridge; running empty to Wadhurst it formed the 7.54 am from there to Charing Cross; 9.25 am Charing Cross to Hastings and 2.10 pm return; 4.20 pm Charing Cross to Hastings and 6.55 pm to Sevenoaks, empty to Tonbridge. On being displaced by diesel-electric multiple units in June 1958, it was transferred to the Brighton–Cardiff through service, returning to the Eastern Section (Maze Hill) in September until its withdrawal in June 1959.

Allocations of sets formed of Maunsell stock as from 8th June, 1953, according to the Appendices to Carriage Working Notice, follow:

2-sets 'R' 22–9, 168/72/8–80/96/8–200: Waterloo–West of England.
3-sets 'B' 193/5, 221–32/8–40, 387, 429, 456, 464, 470, 952–62: London–Margate–Ramsgate–Dover–East Grinstead–Tunbridge Wells West–Brighton–Lewes–Eastbourne.
3-set 'B' 760: London–Paddock Wood–Maidstone West.
3-sets 'F' 213–6, 478–80, 940: London–Tonbridge–Hastings.
3-sets 'M' 201–3/41–3/5–50, 327–30, 390/6–9, 426, 445–8, 458: Waterloo–Bournemouth–Weymouth, Waterloo–Basingstoke–Salisbury, Waterloo–West of England.
3-sets 'N' 391–5: Bournemouth West–Bath.
3-sets 'O' 476, 941–50: London–Tonbridge–Hastings.
4-sets 'E' 181–92, 219/20, 449–54, 467: London–Margate–Ramsgate–Dover–Tonbridge–East Grinstead–Tunbridge Wells West–Brighton.
5-set 951: London–Tonbridge–Hastings.
6-set 212: Margate–Reading.
6-set 428: Reading–Margate.
6-set 459: Portsmouth–Salisbury–Bristol W.R.
6-set 469: London–Ramsgate.
7 Pullman dining set 271: Waterloo–Southampton Docks.
7-set 939: London–Hastings.
8-sets 204–9, 308: Waterloo–Bournemouth–Weymouth. Waterloo–Salisbury.
8-set 194: London–Tunbridge Wells West.
8-set 235: London–Ramsgate.
8-set 236: Birchington for special traffic.
8-set 430: Stewarts Lane for special traffic.
8-set 465: Grove Park for special traffic.
8-set 466: Herne Hill Sorting Sidings for special traffic.
8-set 468: Hastings–London Midland Region.
9-sets 217/8: Deal or Grove Park for special traffic.
9-set 263: Stewarts Lane for special traffic.
10-sets 233/4: Margate–Birmingham services.
10-set 237: London–Ramsgate.
10 dining sets 268–70: Waterloo–Bournemouth–Weymouth.
10 Pullman dining sets 272/3: Waterloo–Southampton Docks.

Note: Sets 268–73 were reduced to 5-sets during the winter.

8-set 194, which for several years had regularly worked the 7.49 am Tunbridge Wells West to London Bridge and 5.50 pm back from Victoria, was replaced in June 1955 by an equivalent set of Bulleid coaches. Set 194 was reduced to three coaches – 3740, 5642, 3741 – for general working on the Central and Eastern Sections.

Since 1949 the official livery for all main-line coaches had been crimson and cream with yellow and black lining. In seven years it should have been possible to repaint the whole Southern Region fleet, but by 1956 there were some coaches still in green; they had been re-varnished to put off the evil day when they must be repainted. Set 458 was still in SR malachite green in April 1953. Maunsell coaches in BR livery normally had the cream area taken up to the cantrail, but some, including Sets 214, 453 and Third 1168, had a broad crimson band on the compartment side between the cantrail and

4-set No. 453 in crimson and cream livery with a broad band of crimson above windows. The train is the Stephenson Locomotive Society's 'South London Junctions' special at West Brompton, 15th April, 1950. *E.R. Wethersett*

Open Third No. 1313 (Diagram 2005) of 1933. It is in crimson and cream livery with cream taken up to cantrail. *Lens of Sutton*

Open Second with '2' numerals on doors, No. 4397, formerly Nondescript No. 7911, built in 1931 and withdrawn July 1959. *Lens of Sutton*

the tops of the windows. The vehicle number was displayed at waist level at the left-hand end of the body until early 1951, when it was decided to place it at the right-hand end so that it could be read in conjunction with the weight and restriction plates on the coach end. From a study of photographs here is a record of some of the sets and coaches that appeared in crimson and cream:

Left-hand numerals	*Right-hand numerals*
2-set 23	3-set 396
2-set 178	3-set 397
4-set 185	3-set 446
3-set 193	3-set 941
3-set 214	3-set 945
3-set 231	3-set 946
3-set 240	
3-set 328	
4-set 453	
3-set 464	
Coaches 1168, 5680.	Coaches 1313/57, 1447, 4397, 7421, 7860.

Probably most of the Hastings sets (which had had their interiors extensively rebuilt to BR standards in the Eastleigh 'new stock' shops in 1952/3) were reliveried, as well as any coach expected to run in Continental boat trains. Uniformity was never achieved, and many trains ran with mixed liveries; even some *sets* were formed with both green and crimson/cream coaches. In April 1956, it was announced that green would henceforth be used for all Southern Region coaches. It was not a restoration of the Bulleid malachite green, being rather darker; it was applied without lining. Eastleigh started to use the green in July 1956. All sets were green by about 1960.

Also in 1956, from 3rd June, third class was renamed second class although not with any outward visible change since '3' had not been indicated on doors etc. since about 1948.

In 1957 a 9-coach set, No. 455, was assembled to replace the original No. 455 which had been formed mainly of ex-LSW corridor stock. It used the vehicles from 3-set 223, plus Composite 5617, and five former Nondescript Saloons now classed as Open Seconds – Nos. 7981, 7909, 7982/4/7. It was kept at Eardley for special traffic. Composite 5666, formerly in Set 223, was withdrawn in February 1959, and replaced by Second 656 from Set 262; and the whole set was withdrawn in July 1959.

Also in 1957 3-sets 456, 464 and 470 were each strengthened to eight coaches, as shown below:

	Set 456	**Set 464**	**Set 470**
Second Bke	4083	3744	4050
Open Second	4394	7992	7977
Open Second	7965	7991	7985
Composite	5172	5647	5656
Composite	5610	5626	5635
Open Second	7968	7993	7988
Open Second	7975	7986	4392
Second Bke	4084	3745	4051

Set 456 was berthed at Bellingham or Walmer in summer and Eardley in Winter; 464 at Blackheath or Martin Mill in summer and Maze Hill in winter; and 470 at Bellingham or Walmer in summer and Bellingham in winter from June 1957, until June 1959. The latter two were then withdrawn; Set 456 was strengthened to ten coaches and transferred to the Western Section where it was retained for special traffic until its withdrawal in December 1961.

A 9-coach set, No. 696, again for special traffic on the Eastern Section, was made up by June 1957 to replace a non-corridor set. It was formed of Composite Brake 6578, Open Seconds 4395/6/7, Composite 5155, Open Seconds 4391, 7967, Second 978 (from Set 460) and 'Continental' Second Brake 3589. Its berthing station until withdrawal in July 1959 was Broadstairs.

Yet another set, No. 917, was created in 1957 to replace a non-corridor set and included the 8 ft 6 in. Open Seconds, these being Nos. 7963/6/74/6/9/80; with 'Continental' brakes 3553 and 6642, and 'Thanet' Composite 5545, it was a real hotchpotch. It was berthed at Blackheath for special traffic until withdrawal in July 1959.

The reason for the increase in sets was that the old SEC non-corridor stock kept for working many of the summer Saturday Ramsgate services was being withdrawn, and corridor stock was needed to replace it.

3-set 760, the special 'Maidstone West' set, was altered to standard formation in 1957. Nos. 7673 and 1223 went to loose stock, being replaced by Second Brake 2793 from Set 234 and Composite 5678 from loose stock. It continued to work on the Maidstone West branch until June 1961, then went to the Oxted group of lines until withdrawal in August 1961.

The final special traffic set made up for the Eastern Section was No. 937 in 1958, and it lasted only a year, displaced by electrification. Formed entirely of 8 ft stock, it comprised Second Brake 3673, Seconds 1020/1, Composite 5595, 'Continental' six-compartment First 7367, Composite 5596, Seconds 1022/3 and Second Brake 3675, all being former loose stock. It was berthed at Maze Hill for special traffic from mid-1958 to mid-1959, when it was withdrawn.

Sets 340 and 341 were introduced for the Western Section in 1958. Formations were:

	Set 340		**Set 341**
Compo Bke	6570	Second Bke	3668
Second	827	Second	823
Composite	5541	Composite	5136
Second	1278	Second	824
Second	1843	Composite	5522
Compo Bke	6651	Second Bke	3669

Alterations: 6570 replaced by 6644 in 1959 and 5541 replaced by Second 810 in 1959. No. 5522 was replaced by Second 829 in 1959 and 5136 ('Ironclad') replaced by 5633 (8 ft 6 in.) in 1960.

Booked workings in 1960 were:

1. 6.22 am Eastleigh–Fawley, 8.06 am thence to Southampton Terminus; 5.05 pm Southampton Terminus–Wimborne (all SX).

2. 5.17 am Wimborne–Eastleigh. On Fridays empty to Southampton Terminus for 4.53 pm to Winchester. On Saturdays 6.42 am Winchester–Southampton Terminus, thence 12.47 pm to Wimborne.

Set 340 was disbanded in June 1961, Nos. 810/27 being withdrawn and the remainder becoming loose; and Set 341 was withdrawn in September 1961, No. 5633 alone being transferred to Set 428 for further use.

Eleven additional 2-coach sets for local services in the Western District were made up in 1958, differing from the earlier ones in having a Corridor Brake Composite and an ex-SEC 10-compartment non-corridor Second. Numbered 100–110, they ran thus until late 1959 when the Second was replaced by a Maunsell Open Second; these formations were maintained until 1962.

	Set 100	**Set 102**	**Set 104**	**Set 106**	**Set 108**	**Set 110**
Compo Bke	6599	6577	6589	6573	6590	6595
Open Second	1303	1306	1314	1370	1310	1325
	Set 101	**Set 103**	**Set 105**	**Set 107**	**Set 109**	
Compo Bke	6906	6905	6589	6592	6594	
Open Second	1300	1304	1327	1399	1339	

These 2-sets 'W' worked on the Bere Alston to Callington line, also the Sidmouth/Exmouth branches. On the Lyme Regis branch normally only the Brake Composite of the set was used, the Open Second being held at Lyme Regis for strengthening as required.

The year 1958 saw the first withdrawals of Maunsell sets apart from war or accident damage, these being Nos. 183, 184, 391, 393, 445 and 448. Second Brake 4092 from Set 183 went to the West London line Set 156, then to Set 453 late in 1959; Second Brake 4062 from Set 448 went to Set 436 in 1959; but all the other coaches were condemned. A trickle of withdrawals would very soon become a torrent.

8 ft Corridor Brake Composite No. 6881, built in 1934 (Diagram 2402), seen at Hastings in crimson and cream livery. *Lens of Sutton*

Chapter Ten

Maunsell carriage stock on the decline

Completion of the first stage of the so-called Kent Coast Electrification scheme (the 'Chatham' lines to Sheerness, Dover and Ramsgate) in June 1959 resulted in the withdrawal from service of a huge amount of steam-hauled coaching stock, including a great many Maunsell sets. The former South Eastern lines in Kent were in the second stage of electrification and remained steam-worked for two more years, but there was sufficient modern stock – Bulleid and BR Standard – to work most of these services and so nearly all the older sets, particularly those used for summer weekend services, were no longer required. Nearly all the Restriction 'O' Hastings sets were withdrawn at the same time; they had been retained for a year or two after the Hastings line had gone over to diesel-electric working (partial services from 6th May, 1957, complete service from 9th June, 1958) because having been renovated they were in good condition; they had been given employment on Brighton/Eastbourne–Tonbridge–Redhill services. A certain amount of Western Section stock was withdrawn at the same time.

The following sets were withdrawn in 1959, the stock in almost all cases being condemned: 193, 211, 215, 220, 225, 237, 240, 243, 262, 263, 273 to 276, 308, 328, 392, 447, 452, 453, 455, 464, 470, 476, 478, 480, 696, 937 to 951.

Sets 217 and 218 were reduced to four coaches (3700, 5611/2, 3701 and 3702, 5615/6, 3703 respectively), 5151/2 being condemned and the remaining vehicles becoming loose stock. Sets 221, 231 and 954 were deleted, but most of the stock from them was used in other sets. Set 453 was replaced by a 'new' 453, formed Second Brake 4092 from Set 156 (previously in 183), Composites 5617 from Set 455 and 5626 from Set 464, and Second Brake 4080 from Set 466. As all these Restriction '1' vehicles had high corridor windows the set was now identical in appearance to Nos. 181–92.

Much of the condemned stock was sent to the Ardingly branch, one line of which was used as a much-elongated carriage siding. The vehicles stood there for several months, gradually being cleared out for cutting up at Newhaven and other places.

In 1959 four Open Second Brakes (formerly Nondescripts) Nos. 4438/44/5/9 were rebuilt into Ambulance Ward Cars and renumbered 7920 to 7923 (Order No. 4559). Each car had 11 seats and 24 cots. They were used by pilgrims on the first stage of their journey to Lourdes. The cars were stored at Stewarts Lane during 1966 and later withdrawn. No. 7920 became DB 975279 in about 1973 and No. 7923 became DB 975406 in October 1974. The former was acquired by the Kent & East Sussex Railway in June 1980; the latter by the Mid Hants Railway in November 1978. No. 7921 went to the Bluebell Railway in August 1980.

Later in 1959 a start was made on converting 20 Maunsell Brake Composites and Open Seconds into push-and-pull sets to replace the many overage ones still running. Initially 10 sets were made up, Nos. 600 to 609, to Order No. 4634. The Brake Composite in each set had the lavatory sealed off and the gangway at the brake-end was removed. Here a driving end was provided, with two small windows ('4-EPB' size) overlooking the track, and a droplight on each side replaced the guard's duckets. All these vehicles were the 1935 type. The Open Seconds were the 1930 type with drop windows; the lavatories were closed off and the gangway at the locomotive end of the set was removed. The first 10 sets were in traffic by November 1959, and another 10, Nos. 610 to 619, were completed by June the following year. Formations were:

	Set 600	**Set 604**	**Set 608**	**Set 612**	**Set 616**
Compo Bke	6693	6676	6689	6683	6695
Open Second	1338	1360	1330	1356	1359
	Set 601	**Set 605**	**Set 609**	**Set 613**	**Set 617**
Compo Bke	6687	6677	6694	6688	6696
Open Second	1351	1349	1353	1347	1361
	Set 602	**Set 606**	**Set 610**	**Set 614**	**Set 618**
Compo Bke	6681	6678	6679	6690	6697
Open Second	1318	1328	1317	1354	1342
	Set 603	**Set 607**	**Set 611**	**Set 615**	**Set 619**
Compo Bke	6675	6682	6680	6691	6699
Open Second	1320	1343	1323	1341	1331

Initial allocations were: London Central District Nos. 600–7/16–9; Western 608/9/12–5; South Eastern Division 610/1. By June 1960, No. 603 had been transferred to the Western and No. 609 to the Eastern. Compared with what they replaced they were very comfortable; but unfortunately many of the branch lines for which they were provided were closed within a year or two. Until then they could be seen on the Allhallows, Hawkhurst and Westerham branches; on Tunbridge Wells–Oxted, Three Bridges–East Grinstead and Horsham–Brighton/Guildford services; and on the Lymington, Swanage, Seaton and Yeovil Town branches. By September 1961, No. 611 had gone to the Western Section and No. 614 to the SE Division.

Nos. 600/1/2/5/7 were withdrawn in 1963 and Nos. 611/2 in May 1964. By then all surviving sets were on the South Western Division, plus three loose push-and-pull-fitted Open Seconds 1331/42/3. Sets 618 and 619 had been disbanded in 1963, but the Composite Brakes worked as loose coaches on the Hayling Island branch until its closure in November of that year. The last sets, Nos. 604/6/9/13/5/7, were withdrawn in November 1964, bringing to an end on the Southern the long era of traditional (as opposed to the later high-speed main-line) push-and-pull working.

It was in 1959 that the now-notorious directive was issued by the British Transport Commission that any coach over 30 years old must be withdrawn; until then the Southern had cheerfully operated coaches 40 or even 50 years old. The aim was to reduce the Southern's fleet of some 2,900 locomotive-hauled coaches to 1,700 by 1962, and of these only about 400 would be Maunsell vehicles. The directive was taken so literally that the Southern landed itself with a severe stock shortage, and several vehicles were hastily re-instated. In particular there was a shortage of Restriction '1' vehicles necessary to work the Tonbridge–Brighton services. Some trains from Brighton had to be terminated at Tunbridge Wells West and passengers required to change into a train of 8 ft 6 in. stock for the rest of the journey.

8 ft Corridor Third Brake No. 3687 (Diagram 2105) of 1931, rebuilt 1952; lavatory window position altered. *Lens of Sutton*

Push-and-pull set No. 603 on the Seaton Branch train at Seaton Junction. Corridor Brake Composite No. 6675 was converted in 1959 and withdrawn in October 1964. *Lens of Sutton*

Corridor First No. 7666 after condemnation in July 1959. The coach was built in 1927 to Diagram 2501. *Lens of Sutton*

There was a lull in 1960, and hardly anything was withdrawn. The former Hastings 3-sets that had not been withdrawn in 1959 were re-formed with a Composite in place of the First and kept on for a while longer. These were Nos. 213 (5598 replacing 7404), 214 (5601 replacing 7405), 216 (5599 replacing 7415) and 479 (5592 replacing 7402). Sets 216 and 479 were withdrawn in 1960, all the stock becoming loose; Set 214 went in 1961 and Set 213 in June 1962 – the last survivor of the Maunsell 8 ft stock.

Allocations of Maunsell sets from 13th June, 1960, were:

2-sets 'P' 22–9, 168/72/8–80/96/8–200: Western District.
2-sets 'W' 100–110: Western District.
3-sets 'M' 242/4–50, 327/9: Western Section local services.
3-sets 'O' 213/4: London–Tonbridge–Hastings–Ashford.
3-sets 'SD' 390/4–9, 446: Bournemouth West–Bath.
3-sets 'T' 202/3: Ramsgate/Hastings–Wolverhampton.
3-sets 'T' 194/5, 222/4/6–30/2/8/9/41, 387, 760, 952/3/5–62: London–East Grinstead –Forest Row–Tunbridge Wells West–Brighton–Eastbourne; Reading South–Redhill–Tonbridge.
4-sets 'E' 181/2/5–92, 217–9, 449–51/3/4, 467: Tonbridge–Tunbridge Wells West –Brighton–Redhill–Reading South.
6-sets 340/1: Eastleigh–Wimborne.
6-sets 428, 459: Woking–Basingstoke.
6-set 465: Margate miners' train.
8-sets 201/4–9, 235/6, 269/71/2, 426, 431–4/6/42–4, 469: Waterloo–Salisbury; Waterloo–Bournemouth–Weymouth; Through services to other Regions.
8-sets 466/8: Hastings–Walsall, Hastings–Leicester (Saturdays).
9-set 212: Hassocks–special traffic.
10 Buffet sets: 268/70: Waterloo–Bournemouth.
10-sets 233/4: Margate–Birmingham.
10-set 429: Brighton–Cardiff (Saturdays).
10-sets 430, 440, 456: Western Section–special traffic.

Sets 268/70 were reduced to 8-sets during the winter.

The 9.15 am Margate to Wolverhampton was a very special sort of train by 1960. It provided Redhill station with the delicious aromas that only a dining car can provide. The formation was Composite Brake, Buffet Car, Open Second, Corridor Second and Second Brake. At Ashford a 3-set was added on the front; it had worked from Ramsgate via Dover. At Redhill another 3-set, this time from Hastings via Eastbourne and Brighton, was added on the rear and all 11 coaches continued on their journey via Guildford and Reading, the front of the train now being the rear. This train, which alternated with Western Region stock, was virtually the only 'good' train still being worked regularly by Maunsell stock. The 10.42 am from Wolverhampton arrived at Redhill with the Ramsgate and Margate section at the south end so that it could depart first, and the Hastings portion was at the north end.

Only two trains on the Hastings line were still steam-hauled: the early-morning news train, which included a loose Restriction 'O' Second Brake, and the 5.45 am London Bridge to Hastings, with one 3-set No. 213 or 214. This continued to Ashford, leaving there at 9.30 am for Tonbridge, thence empty to Rotherhithe Road. But the retention of these trains could not be tolerated by the operating people beyond mid-June 1961, when partial electric services began on the South Eastern Dover line; and so the first train of the morning from Charing Cross to Hastings was now not until 8.40 am.

An enormous quantity of Maunsell stock was withdrawn in 1961. Not only did the second stage of the electrification of the Kent lines render a great deal of steam stock redundant, but there was now a deliberate policy of reducing the amount of carriages in circulation anyway, as BR began to look askance at the old practice of maintaining special traffic sets for perhaps a dozen trips a year. At this stage it often happened that stock was withdrawn at district level in response to a general directive that the batch was life-expired or nearly so and if something went wrong with a carriage it was to be condemned. Withdrawals proceeded faster than they could be recorded; for example, a certain quantity might be consigned to one of the many 'dumps', such as Ardingly, Hassocks, Micheldever or Worthy Down. From time to time the Southern had a check-up and any carriages that could not be found were regarded as withdrawn and a date recorded – which might be two or three months after the actual date!

Withdrawal of Sets 194, 195, 201, 204, 205, 209, 214, 222, 224, 226 to 228, 233 to 236, 238, 340, 341, 390, 394 to 399, 426, 429, 431, 434, 440, 444, 446, 456, 459, 465, 466, 468, 469, 760 and 962 was effected during 1961 and the stock in most cases condemned. Most sets were withdrawn intact, but some that had been formed of both old and more recently-built coaches had the former replaced and as sets lasted a few years longer.

A survey of standing vehicles between Horsted Keynes and Ardingly in December 1961 found 130 Maunsell coaches there, almost all of which had been withdrawn that year. They included complete sets Nos. 195, 222, 227, 228, 394 and 962, and portions of others such as Nos. 204, 209, 233, 236, 426, 444 and 459. Other coaches were to be found at Gatwick Airport sidings during autumn 1961. Nine coaches of 10-set 440 were there: 804, 828, 795, 5588, 5585, 816, 793, 802 (with replacement 1936-built body) and 3665. Apparently the tenth coach, 3664, had been withdrawn slightly later and was sent to Ardingly. Set 397 also was at Gatwick. It is worth noting that, apart from temporary strengthening, Sets 390–9 were kept intact with all their original coaches during their entire existence.

Allocations of Maunsell sets from 11th September, 1961, were:

2-sets 'P' As 1960: Western District.
2-sets 'W' As 1960: Western District.
3-sets 'M' 242/4–50, 327/9: South Western Section local services.
3-set 'O' 213: London–Tonbridge–Hastings.
3-sets 'T' 229/30/2/9/41, 387, 952/3/5–61, 202/3: London–East Grinstead–Forest Row–Tunbridge Wells West–Brighton–Eastbourne; Reading South–Redhill–Tonbridge–Brighton–Horsham.
4-sets 'E' As 1960.
6-set 428: Andover Junction–Basingstoke.
8-sets 206/7/8, 268–71, 432/3/6/42/3: Waterloo–Salisbury; Waterloo–Bournemouth –Weymouth; Through services to other Regions.
8-set 272: Waterloo–Basingstoke.
9-set 212: Hassocks–special traffic.
10-set 430: Western Section–special traffic.

The Restriction '1' 4-sets survived almost unscathed – they were indispensable so long as involved carriage diagrams were in force, which required through journeys such as the 7.55 am Brighton to Reading via Tonbridge and Redhill. Two re-formations were made in 1961. Set 182: 4089 withdrawn 6.61 and replaced by 3715 from loose stock. Set 453: 4092 withdrawn 6.61 and replaced by 4082 from Set 466. Of the nineteen 4-sets 'E', 15 were diagrammed and were worked quite intensively.

Elimination of all the remaining Maunsell Restriction '4' 3-sets and most of the special traffic sets was completed in 1962. This was made possible by the introduction of diesel-electric multiple units on the Oxted line in June of that year. Most special traffic sets still existing were by now made up largely of Bulleid or BR standard stock, and after 1962 the only Maunsell vehicles surviving in these were mainly Seconds of 1935 and 1936 vintage. Restriction '1' stock was still required for Reading–Tonbridge–Brighton/Eastbourne services as only 19 diesel units had been built. On 31st December, 1962, the Southern got rid of all its Western District 2-sets and several loose Brake Composites by the simple measure of handing over all its lines west of Wilton to the Western Region. The Western promptly painted out all the set numbers, while vehicle numbers had their 'S' prefixes altered to 'W'.

Sets withdrawn during 1962 were: 22–29, 100–10, 168/72/8–80, 196/8–200, 202/3/6/7/8/13, 229/30/2/9/41/2/4–50, 268–70/2, 327/9, 387, 434/6/42, 953/6/7/9/60/1.

Some of the withdrawn stock was used to make some 'new' 2-coach sets in about February 1962 (former set number in brackets):

	Set 30	**Set 31**		**Set 77**	**Set 78**
Second Bke	3788 (246)	2838 (202)	Compo Bke	6596 (268)	6597 (268)
Compo Bke	6668 (272)	6662 –	Second	1841 (268)	1846 (803)

Sets 30 and 31 were withdrawn or transferred to the Western Region at the end of 1962, and Sets 77/8 – which were used as Victoria–Eridge–Eastbourne through portions (previously provided by loose Brake Composites and Seconds) – were withdrawn also at the end of 1962.

Sets 271, 432, 433, 443, 952, 955 and 958 were kept for special traffic during 1962, mostly eight or nine coaches each and including some Bulleid examples. Re-formations occurred annually or even more frequently; Mr Denis Cullum has remarked that 'As the earlier coaches had to be withdrawn this led to wholesale splitting up of sets and caused a great deal of work and much cussing.' Quite possibly the actual formations did not always agree with what was laid down in the Appendix to Carriage Working Notices, especially taking into account the expected short life of the sets.

Of the Restriction '1' 4-sets, No. 181 was entirely re-formed: 4087/8, 5173/4 withdrawn January 1962, replaced by Open Brake Seconds 4439/41 and Composites 5624/31 all ex-'Loose'. Set 182 – 5175/6 withdrawn December 1961, replaced by 5613/4 ex-'Loose'. Set 450 was also completely re-formed: 4069/70, 5161/2 withdrawn January 1962, replaced by Open Brake Seconds 4447/8 and Composites 5630/2 all ex-'Loose'. An additional set, No. 452, was created at the same time from Open Brake Seconds 4432/43 ex-'Loose', 5610 ex-Set 456 and 5633 ex-Set 428.

Despite this it was felt that there were still not quite enough sets for the services, taking into account maintenance and overhaul, and it occasionally happened that the sets were split, half a 4-set 'E' turning up on a working booked for push-and-pull, such as Tonbridge to Oxted or Three Bridges to East Grinstead. So it was decided to split all the sets into permanent halves to provide twice as many sets, 4-coach trains being run normally, but certain services (perhaps lightly-loaded) being diagrammed for a single set. One of the first, Set 449, was split into 2-sets 449 and 460, and left Lancing Works on 21st August, 1962; the remainder were split and renumbered probably in time for the winter 1962/3 timetable. Here is the list of these 2-sets 'E', of which half kept their original numbers and the other half were given new numbers from the many blanks that were now in the list (original set number in brackets):

	Set 180	**Set 188**	**Set 444**	**Set 452**	**Set 460**
Second Bke	4439 (181)	3698 (188)	3695 (186)	4432 (452)	4068 (449)
Compo	5624 (181)	5608 (188)	5605 (186)	5610 (452)	5160 (449)
	Set 181	**Set 189**	**Set 445**	**Set 453**	**Set 461**
Second Bke	4441 (181)	3704 (189)	3697 (187)	4082 (453)	4448 (450)
Compo	5631 (181)	5618 (189)	5607 (187)	5617 (453)	5632 (450)
	Set 182	**Set 190**	**Set 446**	**Set 454**	**Set 462**
Second Bke	3715 (182)	3706 (190)	3697 (188)	4079 (454)	4443 (452)
Compo	5613 (182)	5620 (190)	5609 (188)	5169 (454)	5633 (452)
	Set 183	**Set 191**	**Set 447**	**Set 455**	**Set 463**
Second Bke	4090 (182)	3708 (191)	3705 (189)	3709 (191)	4072 (451)
Compo	5614 (182)	5622 (191)	5619 (189)	5623 (191)	5163 (451)
	Set 184	**Set 192**	**Set 448**	**Set 456**	**Set 464**
Second Bke	3692 (185)	3710 (192)	3707 (190)	3711 (192)	4080 (453)
Compo	5602 (185)	5625 (192)	5621 (190)	5629 (192)	5626 (453)
	Set 185	**Set 217**	**Set 449**	**Set 457**	**Set 465**
Second Bke	3693 (185)	3700 (217)	4067 (449)	3701 (217)	4078 (454)
Compo	5603 (185)	5611 (217)	5159 (449)	5612 (217)	5170 (454)
	Set 186	**Set 218**	**Set 450**	**Set 458**	**Set 466**
Second Bke	3694 (186)	3702 (218)	4447 (450)	3703 (218)	4063 (467)
Compo	5604 (186)	5615 (218)	5630 (450)	5616 (218)	5153 (467)
	Set 187	**Set 219**	**Set 451**	**Set 459**	**Set 467**
Second Bke	3696 (187)	3712 (219)	4071 (451)	3713 (219)	4064 (467)
Compo	5606 (187)	5627 (219)	5164 (451)	5628 (219)	5154 (467)

These continued working on Reading–Redhill–Tonbridge services as well as certain Tonbridge–Brighton and Eastbourne services not covered by diesel units. Sets 454 and 465 were withdrawn in December 1963, and Sets 217, 451, 457 and 463 in May 1964. By March 1964, coach 4439 in Set 180 had been replaced by 4442 and coach 4448 in Set 461 by 4450. When at last the Tonbridge–Reading line became diesel-operated in January 1965, all but two sets were condemned, these being Nos. 190 and 192, and Composite 5627 from Set 219, which were kept on until the closure of the line between Eridge and Hailsham in June 1965. And that really was the end of the long-lived Restriction '1' stock on BR. Four were purchased for preservation by the Kent & East Sussex Railway in November 1965: Open Brake Seconds 4432 and 4443, and Composites 5153 and 5618.

During 1963, special traffic sets Nos. 432, 433, 443, 271, 952, 955 and 958 were withdrawn. Seconds Nos. 1183, 1205, 1210, 1215 and 1221 were formed in the Bertram Mills circus train but after sustaining accident damage at Ascot on 4th November, 1963, were withdrawn. For the 1964 season the Bertram Mills circus train included Maunsell Seconds 1808, 1822, 1878, 1901, 1904 and 1914; all were withdrawn at the end of that year. Other Seconds still extant in 1964 were formed in special traffic sets with Bulleid Second Brakes and Composites. These were 8-sets 769, 964, 980, 981 and 984, each of which contained three or four Maunsell Seconds; 6-sets 854 and 855 (three Seconds each), allocated to the Ramsgate–Wolverhampton service; and 10-set 952 (seven Seconds), used on the Margate–Wolverhampton summer service. The last of these were withdrawn at the end of 1964.

What happened to the condemned stock? After lengthy storage in sidings it was eventually sent away to breakers' yards. Some of the stock movements are known, and examples are given:

22nd May, 1962: Hassocks to Newhaven – 5176, 5175, 1842, 766, 1357, 1218, 7955.
12th November, 1963: Micheldever to Newhaven – 1882, 6573.
15th February, 1964: Ardingly to Newhaven – 4051, 1139, 1167, 3747, 7962, 7209, 3746.
7th April, 1964: Hassocks to Llanelly – 1351, 1429, 4078, 4439, 5170, 6687, 7875.
11th April, 1964: Gatwick Airport to Queenborough – 785, 810, 1114, 3206, 3666, 3667, 3671, 5587, 5589, 5590, 4448.
5th May, 1964: Lancing to Llanelly – 2836, 6650.
30th January, 1965: Polegate to Queenborough – 1813, 1865, 1212, 3715, 5632.
8th May, 1965: Micheldever to Queenborough – 3684, 4434, 4435, 5626, 3685, 5598.

In time for the winter 1959/60 train service four Maunsell coaches had been fitted with electric heaters, these being Open Brake Seconds 4434 and 4435 and Composite Brakes 6685 and 6686. The only electrically-hauled passenger trains on the South Eastern Division were the 'Golden Arrow', the 'Night Ferry', and the early-morning newspaper train; a few Bulleid and BR standard coaches were converted to electric heating at the same time. Both Composite Brakes were allocated for use in the 'Night Ferry'. The Open Brake Seconds were withdrawn at the end of 1964, and Composite Brake 6685 in January 1967; so it was this coach that had the distinction of being the very last survivor, not rebuilt in any way, of the Southern Railway's pre-War steam carriage stock on BR. Companion coach No. 6686, withdrawn in September 1966, was purchased in January 1967, by the Southern Locomotive Preservation Co. and delivered to Droxford. To see it when it was later stored at Fareham in pristine BR green livery, long after all other Maunsell coaches had disappeared, was rather like experiencing a time-slip; was this really 1969?

Chapter Eleven

Conversion of restaurant cars into buffet cars

All the Southern's restaurant cars had been built as Kitchen/Dining vehicles with seats for 24 first class diners; third class diners being accommodated in restaurant car 'trailers', i.e. 56-seat Open Thirds. Where these were not provided, passengers could enjoy the first class dining facilities, presumably.

It was felt that for some services a buffet car might be more suitable, so in March 1935, four were authorised to be built; but they never were. They were not forgotten; as late as 1942 and 1943 it was optimistically stated in a report that, along with 697 other passenger vehicles ordered, they would 'be proceeded with according to availability of materials and labour.' Instead, the cheaper expedient of converting existing cars was undertaken, particularly as there was in the post-War period a surplus of restaurant cars anyway.

Four cars, Nos. 7864, 7865, 7867 and 7999, were converted in 1947 into Kitchen/Buffet cars; all had been out of use during the War and after. The kitchen and pantry compartments in each car were unchanged structurally, but all the seating was removed and part of the area used for a large counter for the sale of snacks and drinks. Opposite the counter was a narrow seat rest, and at the end of the car were two narrow tables next to the car walls, each with four stools.

To work with the Kitchen/Buffet cars were four Refreshment Saloons, converted in 1947 from Open Thirds Nos. 1365–1368 and re-numbered 7841–7844. Each of these, which had originally had three saloon compartments seating in total 64 passengers, had the partitions removed and a new one put in to divide the car equally. The first class saloon – at the lavatory end of the vehicle – was given 24 loose chairs, and the third class saloon at the other end had 31 fixed seats, all with tables; seating was exclusively for passengers taking refreshments. The first class end of this car was adjacent to the kitchen end of the other car.

The four 'pairs' were allocated to the Western Section. In summer 1951 Nos. 7864 with 7841 ran on the Bournemouth–Newcastle service, 7865 with 7842 worked the Saturday 8.27 am Waterloo–Exeter and 1.10 pm return, 7867 with 7844 ran on the Bournemouth–Birkenhead service, and 7999 with 7843 was scheduled for the Saturday 11.35 am Waterloo–Exmouth, returning on Sunday with the 11.50 am Exeter–Waterloo. The 'pairs' did not remain constant, and in the following summer two sets were allocated to the Brighton–Plymouth services, one to Bournemouth–Newcastle and the fourth to Bournemouth–Birkenhead.

In later years the four 'pairs' were employed only during the peak summer season, standing spare between September and June. By 1959 all four Kitchen/Buffet cars had been fitted for propane gas. Saloon No. 7844 had been withdrawn, leaving No. 7999 to work with an Open Second. Upon withdrawal of Nos. 7864 in January 1962, and 7841 in September 1961, the two cars were sold to the Bluebell Railway.

For the Dover portion of the Dunkirk Ferry service – resumed after wartime suspension – two restaurant cars and two Open Thirds were converted in 1947. Nos. 7878 (which had been out of use for some years) and 7969 became Kitchen/Buffet cars with similar internal arrangements to Nos. 7864/5/7 and 7999 but with a different window layout. The two Open Thirds, 1363 and 1364, were rebuilt into Saloon Firsts, with all dividing partitions removed and with 48 loose chairs, eight wide tables on one side of an off-centre walkway and eight narrow tables on the other side. Each of the cars, which were renumbered 7846 and 7847, had a Continental gangway fitted at one end for coupling to Wagon-Lits ferry coaches. Later the seating became unclassed. The four cars were allocated to the 'Night Ferry' for many years, one Kitchen/Buffet and one Saloon being in traffic and the other pair spare at Stewarts Lane. The Kitchen/Buffets were fitted for propane gas about 1957, and in 1959 all four cars were given electric heaters, the 'Night Ferry' being electrically-hauled from 8th June of that year. By the mid-1960s the cars were replaced by BR vehicles, except that No. 7969 was retained until 1966 as spare car. In that year, most surprisingly, it was on the list of coaches 'scheduled for re-deployment' after the electrification of the Bournemouth line and was to be placed in a Waterloo–Exeter set of steam-heated coaches. This was not done, but the vehicle lasted all through 1967, even turning up on 7th October in the 12.15 Exeter–Brighton train in place of the usual BR Buffet/Restaurant car. By a long way it was the last survivor on BR of the pre-War catering cars, even though rebuilt. It was *not* painted blue and grey!

In 1946 cars 7858, 7946, 7949 and 7952, although retained as 24-seat Kitchen/Dining Firsts, received special interior fittings, for example loose chairs. From June 1951, they were paired with Open Thirds Nos. 1444, 1447, 1448 and 1450. Workings were:

7946 with 1447: SO 7.40 am Waterloo–Ilfracombe, empty to Exeter.
Sunday 12.02 pm Exeter–Waterloo.
7949 with 1448: SO 7.36 am Waterloo–Padstow, empty to Exeter.
SO 10.18 am/12.55 pm Exeter–Waterloo.
7952 with 1450: SO 10.18 am/12.55 pm Exeter–Waterloo.
SO 7.36 am Waterloo–Padstow, empty to Exeter.
7858 with 1444: SX 7.30 am Exeter–Waterloo and 3.00 pm return. Extended to Ilfracombe on Fridays. SO 10.40 am Ilfracombe–Waterloo. Sundays: not staffed, Waterloo–Exeter.

All were spare during the winter timetable; workings for summer 1952 were similar to those of 1951. By 1959 the Kitchen/Diners had been fitted for propane gas.

Kitchen/Dining Firsts 7940 and 7943, internally modified in 1938, had been stored out of use in the War, and in 1947 were at Stewarts Lane for 'special purposes'. In July 1948, they were renumbered 98 S and 99 S and reserved for official duties, running with the new Bulleid sleeping car and giving BR's recently appointed officers a tour of the system. The cars reverted to their original numbers in 1951 and two years later No. 7940 was altered to a Kitchen/Buffet car (*see later*).

In 1952 cars 7939 and 7954 were converted into Cafeteria cars. The interiors were completely stripped, a small counter was put in where the kitchen had been, and the rest of the car was given 48 fixed seats arranged 'two-and-two' with a central walkway. Seating was unclassed. The work was carried out partly to keep Eastleigh employed, since the Government had restricted supplies of sheet steel for new stock. After the completion of two conversions, an official Cancellation Order (dated 19th September, 1952) was made and that was the end of the Cafeteria programme ('Ironclad' restaurant car 7853 had been converted in about 1950).

Just to confuse historians, the diagram of the Cafeteria conversion in the SR Diagram Book is dated March 1959. Mr Lawrence Mack believes that someone felt compelled to make the Cafeterias' existence legitimate by endorsing the diagram with a date – any date! The Cafeterias were painted crimson and cream on conversion and revarnished at intervals until their withdrawal in about 1962/3. No. 7954's dates were: 8.52, V12.53, V2.55, V1.56, 4.57 (green), V4.58, V12.58 and V2.60. No. 7939 was noted on 26th August, 1952, on a Bournemouth to Wolverhampton train. Once converted, the Cafeterias did not lead very strenuous lives; in winter they were spare for excursion or special traffic. For a while one ran in the Margate–Birkenhead service, and a long-standing duty was the 8.55 am Reading to Brighton excursion (which ran on four weekdays and five Sundays each summer) formed inside an 8-set of the 204–9 series. There was also a Reading –Margate excursion on two Sundays each summer. By 1959 the cars were fitted for propane gas.

On the Eastern Section the working of Pullman cars, which had ceased on 22nd May, 1942, was never reinstated in ordinary train services (except for the all-Pullman 'Thanet Belle') and the practice began of working SR restaurant cars on the Ramsgate and Dover services staffed by the Pullman Car Co. The cars could not work on the Hastings line, whose passengers had to make do with a mere three 'refreshment cars' converted from Pullmans, which worked two up and two down trains only. Ten restaurant cars were allocated to the Eastern Section in 1947: Nos. 7859/60/3/6/9/70/1, 7948/57/8. They were serviced at Margate, Ramsgate and Stewarts Lane. In 1948 they were joined by Nos. 7862 and 7934, the latter being repainted in chocolate and cream, and in 1949 Nos. 7951 and 7995 were added.

Workings of restaurant cars on the Eastern Section in 1949 were:

Formed in Set 233/4: 6.29 am Ramsgate–Cannon St, 5.45 pm return.
Formed in Set 237: 7.20 am Ramsgate–Cannon St, 5.15 pm return.
Formed in Set 235: 7.35 am Ramsgate–Cannon St, 4.45 pm return.
Formed in Set 233/4: 8.25 am Ramsgate–Victoria, 12.35 pm return.
Formed in Set 469: 9.25 am Ramsgate–Victoria, 3.35 pm return.
Formed in Set 217/8: 3.20 pm Ramsgate–Victoria, 7.15 pm return.
With loose stock: 6.44 am Ramsgate–Cannon St, 5.00 pm return.
With loose stock: 7.30 am Margate–Charing Cross, 11.15 am CX–Folkestone, 4.55 pm Folkestone–CX, 7.15 pm Charing Cross–Margate.
With loose stock: 9.35 am Margate–Charing Cross, 1.15 pm return.
With loose stock: 12.36 pm Margate–Charing Cross, 4.15 pm return.

These workings were maintained for several years, even when Bulleid sets replaced the Maunsell ones on the City services and BR standard stock appeared on the Victoria services.

During 1953 and 1954 these 14 cars were rebuilt into Buffet cars; at the same time a further eight on the Western Section were similarly altered. In each one the kitchen, pantry and one seating bay were stripped. The area formerly occupied by the kitchen was given a small stand on which passengers could place drinks etc; next came a small counter; and roughly in the centre of the car a new small kitchen was located for making up snacks and hot drinks. Eighteen of the original 24 seats at the other end of the car were retained.

For the Pullman Car Company's operation on the Eastern Section were 14 Buffet cars to Order No. 3966:

7859	1953	7863	1953	7870	1954	7948	1954	7958	1954
7860	1953	7866	1954	7871	1954	7951	1954	7995	1954
7862	1954	7869	1954	7934	1953	7957	1954		

And for operation by the Hotels Executive on the Western Section were the remaining eight, to Order No. 3972:

7941	1953	7944	1953	7947	1953	7953	1954
7942	1953	7945	1953	7950	1954	7956	1954

Seating capacity was now 18, and the cars were fitted for calor gas at the time of conversion. The Eastern Section batch worked in the same services as before, 10 being in traffic and four spare. From June 1959, they were allocated jointly to London Central District and South Eastern Division, having been refitted for propane gas. Nos. 7869 and 7957 were electrically heated in 1959 for use in the 'Night Ferry'.

The Western Section cars also began to be re-equipped for propane gas, although by 1961 Nos. 7942/7/50 still retained calor gas equipment. Workings of this series of Buffet cars from 12th September, 1960, were:

15 (7944): 9.00 am Waterloo–Exeter and 2.30 pm return.
16 (7941 – in set 517): 3.00 pm Bournemouth West–Waterloo, 9.30 pm Waterloo –Bournemouth Central.
17 (7947): 8.30 am Waterloo–Bournemouth West and 1.00 pm return.
18 (7956 – in Set 272): Spare, Clapham Yard.
19/20 (7945 – in Set 515 or 516): 11.10 am Plymouth–Brighton.
19/20 (7953 – in Set 515 or 516): 11.30 am Brighton–Plymouth.
21 (7950): Spare.
22 (7942): Spare.

In 1953 two further cars were altered to Kitchen/Buffet vehicles to Order No. 3971, these being Nos. 7940 and 7955 for the Western Section. Kitchen and pantry were retained, but all seating was removed and a counter 12 ft 4½in. long was built next to the pantry. The rest of the area was given a few stands and shelves for passengers' use. Both were fitted for calor gas, and painted crimson and cream. Green again by 1960, they were formed in the sets of BR stock allocated to the Bournemouth–York and Bournemouth –Birkenhead trains.

Fourteen cars were not converted and were retained as Kitchen/Dining Firsts. All remained on the Western Section, either for Bournemouth or Exeter services at peak times, few being used during the winter timetable.

For example, the workings from 12th September, 1960, show only three in use:

23 (7997): 7.30 am Exeter–Waterloo and 3.00 pm return.
28 (7858): (Fridays) 9.30 am Waterloo–Bournemouth West and 2.20 pm return. 5.30 pm Waterloo–Bournemouth West.
(Saturdays) 8.35 am Bournemouth West–Waterloo and 3.20 pm return.
(Mondays) 1.00 pm Bournemouth–Waterloo (not staffed).
29 (7998): (Sundays) 4.00 pm Waterloo–Exeter.
(Mondays) 8.53 am Exeter–Salisbury (not staffed) thence Clapham Junction.

All the others stood spare at Clapham Yard, Exeter Central or Bournemouth West.

The following cars were officially recorded as having been painted in crimson and cream: 7862/70, 7948 by 6.50; 7945/55 by 6.51; 7940 by 9.51; 7951 by 6.52; 8000 by 9.52; and 7934 by 9.53. In addition No. 7860 was so painted, probably in 1953. All were green by 1960. Withdrawal of the Maunsell catering cars began in 1960 and with the one exception already noted was completed by the end of 1963.

Buffet Car No. 7951 at Stewarts Lane. It was altered from Kitchen/First in 1954 and used on the Eastern Section: the car was originally built in 1930. *Lens of Sutton*

Kitchen/Buffet Car No. 7999 at Clapham Junction, 19th May, 1957; rebuilt from Kitchen/First in 1947 it was originally built in 1934. *H.C. Casserley*

Chapter Twelve

Maunsell carriages as museum-pieces

Maunsell corridor coaches were not in the early days of railway preservation seen as items of particular historic interest and in consequence few were purchased at the time when there were still plenty to be had in running order. In contrast, several have been acquired in more recent years as 'departmental' vehicles, but these have tended to be in poor condition and have usually been gutted. To restore such a vehicle to passenger train service is a long and expensive operation, but it has been done. Pre-War SR coaches may be found on at least six private railways; details of some of them under their new owners will now be given.

Bluebell Railway

The Bluebell Railway was the first to acquire an SR-built coach: Composite Brake No. 6575 of 1929. It was worked from Brighton via Horsted Keynes to Sheffield Park on 17th May, 1960, in company with an SR reframed LSW coach. They were purchased because they were serviceable and, with opening day three months away, stock in good mechanical order was required for that first season's traffic. Both were painted blue with no numbers or lettering, except that the prominent set number 23 on the Composite Brake was retained; and both vehicles worked all passenger trains in 1960.

In the summer of 1965 No. 6575 received a second coat of blue – of a different shade – and this time the set number was painted out. In 1967/8 No. 6575 was regularly formed in the 'Blue Belle' limited train and now had class figures on the doors.

It was found to be in rather bad condition and the roof was recovered to prevent leaking. In 1970 the coach was painted in a sickly green and ran thus until 1972, when a plan to effect a structural rebuild was announced, the vehicle being 'in a poor state both mechanically and structurally'. On its last legs, it was withdrawn from service in 1974, serious work on it not being started for another five years.

New wood and steel were used where necessary, although most of the body framing was sound. All the old interior varnish was stripped, revealing excellent walnut in the first class compartments and mahogany in the third class. All ceiling panels were replaced by new hardboard. External mouldings for the windows were made new from teak. The roof was re-canvassed. The coach was then painted in SR olive green, fully lined and lettered; there were 14 undercoats, two topcoats and two varnishes. After two years' work No. 6575 was sent into traffic on 13th September, 1981: a superb spectacle and highly popular with discerning passengers.

A Buffet Car, No. 7864, built in 1932 and rebuilt in 1947, arrived on the Bluebell on 28th March, 1962, being followed by a Composite Dining Saloon, No. 7841 (formerly 1365 and 7866), on 24th February, 1963. The Buffet was put to use as a static refreshment car at Sheffield Park, and the Saloon was later coupled to it to provide additional seating for passengers (the two cars had been altered in 1947 to work together). In 1965 a large awning was erected alongside the Buffet Car and a large double door was cut into the coach side for ease of access.

For 19 years No. 7864 never turned a wheel; but in 1981, on being replaced by a temporary buffet, it made the journey northwards to Horsted Keynes for a further lengthy period of slumber in the carriage sidings there, still in BR green (paint dates 4.56, V12.57, 2.59, 11.60).

Saloon No. 7841, now officially 1365 again, entered into traffic in 1970. There was some minor tinkering with the interior in connection with a scheme to provide light refreshments from a servery occupying the site of the lavatory compartment. Loose chairs were retained in the former first class half of the saloon. Externally, No. 1365 was painted in the same sickly green as No. 6575, and the two coaches ran together with two Bulleid vehicles as 4-coach set No. 23. This was disbanded after 1972, and three years later No. 1365 was said to be requiring a complete overhaul. Since then it has remained out of use.

The fourth Maunsell coach to arrive on the Bluebell Railway was actually the property of the Southern Locomotive Preservation Company, which acquired the vehicle, Composite Brake No. 6686, on 28th January, 1967, when it was delivered to Droxford (home of the exotic Sadler Rail Coach). The SLP and its stock led a Romany existence: No. 6686 was moved to Fareham in July 1969, and to Liss on 30th May, 1970. When, owing to local opposition, the Liss preservation scheme fell through, the SLP, in a massive transfer of stock, moved its coach to Haywards Heath on the night of 26th/27th September, 1971, final arrival at Sheffield Park (by road) being on 2nd October. In May 1974, No. 6686 was painted in a magnificent SR 1935 livery, lined-out and lettered absolutely accurately.

The coach saw regular service in the coming years, being for some time the only Maunsell vehicle in use. Gradually the green turned khaki and, to arrest further deterioration, a coat of BR coach green was applied in February 1984, complete with BR-style number S 6686 S. By then the SLP had sold the coach to the Bluebell.

Three further coaches were acquired in 1973, all having become service vehicles: Open Third No. 1309 (BR No. 081642), which arrived on 1st March; Corridor Third No. 2356 (BR 081315) and Nondescript Brake No. 4441 (BR 082444), both from Streatham Common and delivered in October, 1973.

No. 1309 was at first used by the Bluebell's Carriage and Wagon Department, but in September 1981, work began on the three-year task of restoring it to passenger service. Some interior fittings and seats were taken from withdrawn 4-COR electric units, the motor coaches having been very similar in layout; other fittings came from sister coach No. 1306 (DS 70267) about to be cut up at Briton Ferry. One lavatory partition came from this vehicle; the other was newly constructed. Six new steam-heating radiators were made. Exterior cladding was new, and upon this were applied 12 coats of paint and two of varnish. No. 1309, in all its 1935 glory of olive green and full lining and lettering, was outshopped from Horsted Keynes on 19th September, 1984, justifiably winning the Association of Railway Preservation Societies' Coach of the Year competition.

No. 2356 was used as a mess coach and Carriage Electric Lighting Section workshop. Its roof was re-canvassed in 1977, and the body received olive green livery in January 1978. No. 4441 was used as a stores coach for Carriage and Wagon Department materials.

Ambulance Car 7921 (formerly Nondescript 4444) arrived on 29th August, 1980. It had been located at Bramley (Ministry of Defence) as AD 777; the MOD examiner had condemned it on the spot after falling through the roof. On the Bluebell the roof was renewed and in May 1981, the coach was employed as temporary static buffet car to replace No. 7864. The opening, in July 1986, of a newly-built buffet block rendered No. 4444 redundant in its turn.

In 1987 came Third Brake No. 3724 of 1930, still in Chipman Chemical Company colours (red and white) as spraying coach CWT 7. It joined the ever-lengthening queue of coaches awaiting restoration.

Kent & East Sussex Railway

On the Kent & East Sussex Railway there are now nine Maunsell coaches. The first four were acquired in November 1965, all 8 ft 6 in. stock straight out of BR capital stock: Composites 5153 and 5618 and Open Brake Seconds 4432 and 4443. They were run down the Hastings line for storage at Robertsbridge; being out of gauge they first had to have all handles and roofboard brackets removed before being allowed on this line. On 11th April, 1966, one of the Brakes and one of the Composites were moved from Robertsbridge to Rolvenden, the track then still being down; the other two followed six weeks later. By 1968 Nos. 5618 and 4443 were in the KES livery of brown and cream and renumbered 26 and 27 respectively; the others were similarly repainted later. By 1972 it had been decided to number coaches in a series starting at 51, and so 4432 became 53, 4443 (27) became 54, 5153 became 55 and 5618 (26) became 56. When the first part of the line opened to passengers in 1974 these four coaches were regularly used. Since then it has been an unending fight to arrest deterioration.

No. 53 had its roof re-canvassed in 1977; the following year it was withdrawn for a complete overhaul, when the seats were re-upholstered in a rich maroon moquette, the interior woodwork was french polished and the floor carpeted. The restoration was completed and the vehicle sent into traffic on 26th April, 1980, exclusively on the 'Wealden Pullman'. It is now officially a Brake First. In 1987 it was fitted for table lamps.

No. 54 was re-upholstered in May 1976, and its roof re-canvassed in October that year. It re-entered traffic at Easter 1977, being used mainly on Wine and Dine trains until replaced in that capacity by No. 53. Withdrawn in September 1982 with a leaking roof it went in shops for a prolonged heavy overhaul, during which parts of the interior have been renewed where rotten or corroded, exterior panels below the waistline have been replaced by new material, and the vehicle has been rewired.

No. 55 was re-canvassed in 1977 but was out of use by January 1981. No. 56 was the 'spare' vehicle in later years (re-canvassed in October 1976) but was in poor condition by 1986 when it too was withdrawn for a heavy overhaul.

On 6th November, 1971, three further vehicles were delivered, all ex-departmental and gutted: 081621, formerly First No. 7400 of 1929; DS

70109, formerly Saloon No. 7798 of 1931; and DS 70134, formerly Second No. 1020 of 1934. The KES gave them theoretical numbers 57, 58 and 59, but none has entered passenger service. At first all three stood at Northiam: No. 57 went to Tenterden where it was used by the Signals & Telegraph Department as a mess and sleeping coach, and No. 58 followed later to be employed as Carriage and Wagon Stores at Tenterden. No. 59 remains at Northiam in a very poor state; it appeared briefly in the TV play '1984'.

Yet another former Nondescript Brake was acquired: No. 4438, later Ambulance 7920, later DB 975279. Located at Dover Marine, it was delivered by road to Rolvenden on 19th June, 1980, and sent for storage at Northiam, officially KES No. 72.

Tenterden saw the arrival on 1st September, 1982, of one of the very attractive Open Seconds with drop windows: No. 1346 of 1933, which had been BR DS 70201, then 083181. All partitions and lavatories and some seats were still in place. Although its allocated KES number is 78, it has in fact been painted in SR livery as No. 1346, with the lettering 'Ambulance Car' and complete with red crosses. It is the only Restriction '4' Maunsell coach on the line and, just to be on the safe side, it has been lettered 'Not to work between Tonbridge and Hastings'.

Mid Hants Railway

The Mid Hants has several examples of both 'Ironclad' and Maunsell coaches, but all are out of BR departmental stock and continue to be used, if at all, in that capacity by their new owners. The vehicles are:

Third Brake 3187 of 1921 (ADS 179), acquired January, 1980;
Third Brake 3190 of 1923 (DW 70016); acquired November, 1978;
Third Brake 3719 of 1930 (DS 70168), acquired March, 1976;
Ambulance 7923 (formerly 4449 of 1933 and BR ADB 975406 since October, 1974), acquired November, 1978;
Composite Brake 6601 of 1930 (DW 150386), acquired November, 1978;
Composite Brake 6699 of 1935 (Chipman Chemical Co CWT 11), acquired about 1983;
Dining Saloon 7851 of 1923 (DS 625), acquired December, 1980.

No. 3719 was converted into a refreshment coach for MHR workers at Ropley, and was then used as a mess coach for the gang employed on tracklaying between there and Alton.

No. 4449 was owned by the Maunsell 4449 Group, who began work on reconverting the vehicle to its original state externally, but adapting the interior for the use of handicapped persons. Unfortunately in 1984 the coach was involved in an accident, which was rather a set-back to the work done by then.

No. 6699 had already been altered by BR as a push and pull driving trailer before it was sold to Chipmans as a weedkilling spray coach, when the interior was largely stripped.

Swanage Railway

Only two Maunsell coaches are known to have been sold to this concern: Open Third No. 1381 of 1930 (DS 70175) in October, 1979, and Third Brake No. 2768 of 1932 (DS 70172) in November, 1981.

West Somerset Railway

Although 'Ironclad' Third Brake No. 3204 (DS 70085) was reported as being at Cranmore on the East Somerset Railway, another published source states that it is on the *West* Somerset Railway. It was sold by BR in June 1973 to the Somerset & Dorset Railway Museum Trust.

Keighley & Worth Valley Railway

'Continental' Third Brake No. 3554, originally purchased by Mr Roy Edwards in 1961, was sold to the northern railway four years later and has remained there. It has worked in passenger trains at various times.

It can be seen that in recent years a great many coaches have been rescued from the scrapman, but owing to shortage of funds and manpower little or nothing has been done to them by their new owners. So many of the vehicles acquired had lost seats, compartments, gangways and much else; very few Maunsell coaches can be ridden in by fare-paying passengers, but what a joy it is that the opportunity is there to experience the delights of even those few! Yes, the Maunsell coach was a pleasing, friendly sort of vehicle; not hopelessly old-fashioned in its later life but comfortable if perhaps a little uninspired. It was very much part of the 'image' of the old Southern Railway and for that reason alone is well worth preserving.

Kent & East Sussex Railway coach No. 54, ex-SR Nondescript Brake No. 4443 of 1933. Painted brown and cream, lined in gold and black, it is seen here at Tenterden on 4th October, 1975. *Author*

Appendix

Disposition and withdrawal dates of Maunsell Corridor Coaches

The following list shows coach numbers and the sets in which each vehicle was placed from inception until final withdrawal. The date following each set number is that of the vehicle's first appearance in the set concerned, according to the Carriage Working Notices or their appendices, but in many cases the actual date of transfer may have been some months earlier than shown. 'L' indicates a loose coach.

THIRDS

No		Wdn
	Restriction "1"	
765	467, 468 c.33, 218 6.50, L 1959	8.61
6	467, 468 5.49, 217 6.50, L 1959	10.61
7	468	10.59
768	468	1.60
	Restriction "4"	
769	L, 243 1945, L 1.47, 434 6.57	10.59
770	L, 444 6.52	10.61
1	L, 273 1945	8.59
2	L, 234 6.50	10.59
3	L	7.58
4	L, 439 1948, 434 11.59	12.61
5	L, 444 6.52	10.61
6	L, 430 1933, L 1942, 433 6.57	11.61
7	L, 432 6.57	9.61
778	L, 207 1.47	12.59
783	L, 429 1.47, 432 6.57	9.61
4	L, 462 6.52, L 1959	7.61
5	L, 432 6.57	9.61
6	L, 237 6.53, L 1957, 211 6.59, L 11.59	6.61
7	L, 273 1945	8.59
8	L, 201 6.57	12.59
9	L, 433 6.58	11.61
790	L, 201 6.57	12.59
1	L, 234 6.55	11.59
2	L, 433 6.58	11.61
3	L, 440 6.58	7.61
4	L, 236 6.55	9.61
5	L, 440 11.59	7.61
6	L, 308 9.49, 201 11.59	11.61
7	L, 309 10.47, L 1948, 462 6.52, 469 11.59	6.61
8	L, 431 6.57	10.61
9	L, 201 6.57	12.59
800	L, 235 6.50	4.61
1	L. Accident damage 9.46	c.48
2	L, 440 11.59	7.61
3	L, 426 6.59	10.61
4	L, 440 6.58	7.61
5	L, 201 6.57, 272 11.59	12.61
6	L, 431 6.57	8.61
807	L. Accident Farnborough	11.47

No		Wdn
808	L, 456 11.59	12.61
9	L	9.61
810	L, 340 6.59	6.61
1	L, 472 6.55, L 1959	10.62
2	L, 234 6.50	7.61
3	L	9.61
4	L	8.61
5	L	9.61
6	L, 897 6.58, 440 11.59	7.61
7	L, 444 6.52	9.61
8	L, 263 6.50, L 1959	8.61
9	L, 263 6.50, L 1959	2.60
820	L, 204 6.51	10.61
1	L	11.59
2	L, 444 6.52	10.61
3	L, 426 1.47, L 1948, 341 6.58	10.61
4	L, 341 6.58	10.61
5	L	12.59
6	L, 234 6.50	7.61
7	L, 340 6.58	6.61
8	L, 440 11.59	7.61
9	L, 341 6.59	10.61
830	L, 205 6.51	12.61
1	L, 309 10.47, L 1948	7.59
832	L	4.57
	Restriction "1"	
833	465, L c.33, 465 1941	12.61
4	465	7.61
5	466	7.61
836	466, L c.33, 466 1941	7.61
	Restriction "4"	
837	L, 209 6.51	10.61
8	L,	6.59
9	L	11.59
840	L, 207 6.51	10.61
1	L	8.61
2	L, 439 c.38, 434 11.59	12.61
3	L, 423 6.52	8.59
844	L, 244 1945, L 1.47, 897 6.58, 271 11.59	11.61
	Restriction "0"	
1019	L, 938 6.58	7.59
1020	L, 937 6.58	7.59
1	L, 937 6.58	9.59
1022	L, 937 6.58	7.59

No		Wdn
1023	L, 937 6.58	7.59
4	L	8.59
5	L	8.59
6	L, 476 1941	8.59
7	951	8.59
8	942	10.59
9	951	8.59
1030	951	8.59
1	951	8.59
2	948	9.59
3	943	8.59
4	950	8.59
5	949	10.59
6	945	10.59
7	944	9.59
8	941	9.59
9	946	9.59
1040	947	9.59
	Restriction "4"	
1113	L	10.61
1114	L, 760 5.43, L 6.55	8.61
	Restriction "0"	
1115	L	9.59
6	L	1.58
7	L	10.59
8	L, 939 6.55	10.59
9	939	9.59
1120	939	9.59
	Restriction "4"	
1121	L, 327 1945, L 1.47	10.61
2	204	10.61
3	205	12.61
4	206	2.62
5	L	8.61
6	L, 235 6.50	4.61
7	209	10.61
8	207	2.62
9	208	2.62
1130	L	10.61
1	L, 211 6.53, L 7.59	1.60
2	L, 439 1948, 434 11.59	10.61
3	L	10.61
4	204 1.47	10.61
5	L, 431 1948	11.61
6	L	8.61
7	L, 237 6.53, 429 11.59	6.61
8	L, 235 6.50	4.61
9	L	10.61
1140	L, 209 1.47	10.61
1	L	8.59
2	L, 468 6.60	7.61
3	L	11.61
4	L	9.61
5	L. Enemy action, Beighton	3.42
6	L. Enemy action, Beighton	3.42
7	L	10.61
1148	L, 803 6.57, 436 6.59	12.61

No		Wdn
1149	L	8.59
1150	L, 233 6.50	10.61
1	308, 201 11.59	11.61
2	L	11.61
3	L, 423 6.52, L 11.59	7.61
4	L, 236 9.48, L 1958	7.61
5	L, 233 6.50	10.61
6	L	9.61
7	L, 233 1942	10.61
8	L, 233 1942	10.61
9	L, 235 1941, L 1948	7.61
1160	L, 897 6.58	1.60
1	L, 237 1942, 429 11.59	6.61
2	L, 237 1942, 429 11.59	6.61
3	L, 237 1942, 429 11.59	6.61
4	308, 201 11.59	2.60
5	L, 201 6.60	11.61
6	L	12.61
7	L	10.61
8	L	9.61
9	L	10.61
1170	L, 236 1941	9.61
1	L, 236 1941	9.61
2	L, 236 1941	9.61
3	L, 234 6.57, L 2.61	9.61
4	L	2.60
5	L, 233 1941	11.61
6	L, 263 6.50, 456 11.59	12.61
7	L, 263 6.50, 456 11.59	12.61
8	L	6.61
9	L, 436 6.57	12.61
1180	L, 234 1945	7.61
1	L, 234 1945, L 6.61	5.62
2	L. Transfd to WR 1.63	7.64
3	L, 234 1941, L 1957. Accident damage, Ascot	11.63
4	L, 435 c.38, L 1.47. Transfd to WR 1.63	4.64
5	L, 432 c.38, L 1.47, 233 6.50	6.61
6	L, 208 1.47	2.62
7	247, 208 6.51	2.62
8	L, 442 1954	3.62
9	L, 432 6.63	4.64
1190	L	12.61
1	L	12.61
2	L, 955 6.62, 981 6.64	11.64
3	246, L 6.51	11.62
4	L, 431 c.38, L 1.47, 984 6.63	11.64
5	L	12.61
6	L, 442 1954	3.62
7	245, 208 6.51, L 2.62, 432 6.63	4.64
8	L, 468 1950	4.61
9	248, L 6.51	12.61
1200	L	12.61
1	L, 265 1945, L 1948, 442 6.54	3.62
1202	L, 276 6.58, 268 11.59	1.62

THIRDS -- continued

No		Wdn
1203	L	1.62
4	L, 436 c.38, L 1.47	12.61
5	L. Accident damage, Ascot	11.63
6	L, 267 1945, L 1948, 980 6.64	11.64
7	L, 267 1945, L 1.47, 955 6.62	4.64
8	327, L 1.47, 428 1963, 980 6.64	11.64
9	327, L 6.51	4.61
1210	L, 266 1945, L 1948, 212 6.60, L 6.62. Accident damage, Ascot	11.63
1	L, 265 1945, L 1.47, 854 6.64	10.64
2	L	7.65
3	L	5.64
4	L	12.61
5	328, L 6.51, 276 6.58, 268 11.59, L 1.62. Accident damage, Ascot	11.63
6	328, L 1.47, 207 6.60	4.61
7	L, 468 6.60, L 1961, 271 6.62	5.64
8	244, L 6.51, 271 6.60	12.61
9	L, 428 11.59	3.62
1220	L	11.62
1	330, L 6.51. Acc.dam.Ascot	11.63
2	330, L 1.47	12.61
3	330, L 1.47, 760 6.55, L 6.57	1.62
4	243, 209 6.51	1.62
5	329, L 1.47, 468 1950, L 6.61	4.64
6	329, L 6.51, 276 6.58 270 11.59	12.61
7	329, L 1.47	4.62
8	L	3.62
9	L, 442 1954, L 6.56	6.61
1230	L, 443 c.38, L 6.56	4.64
1	L, 194 6.47, 233 6.55	12.61
2	L, 194 6.47, 235 6.55, L 6.57	12.61
3	L, 194 6.47, 237 6.55, 429 11.59, L 6.61	2.62
4	L	12.61
5	L, 964 6.64	11.64
6	L, 206 1.47, L 2.62, 428 6.63, 980 6.64	11.64
7	L, 194 6.52, 471 6.55, 469 11.59, 212 6.61	12.61
8	L	12.61
9	L	12.63
1240	L, 266 1945, L 1.47	12.61

No		Wdn
1241	L	1.62
2	L, 459 1945, 428 1949	9.62
3	L, 221 1945, L 1948	12.61
4	L	2.62
5	L	1.62
6	L, 428 6.62	12.62
7	L, 209 1949, L 6.56, 234 6.60, 432 6.61	11.61
8	L, 269 9.54	3.62
9	L	6.61
1250	L, 308 6.51, 201 11.59	11.61
1	L	12.61
2	241, L 1945, 237 6.50, 471 6.57, 456 11.59, 953 6.62	5.64
3	L	2.62
4	L	12.61
5	L. Enemy action	5.41
6	L, 428 1949	12.62
7	L, 426 6.59, 433 6.62	5.64
8	L	12.62
9	L	12.61
1260	L, 434 6.58	2.62
1	L, 433 6.62	12.62
2	L	2.62
3	L. Enemy action, Newington	8.44
4	L	12.61
5	L, 855 6.64	10.64
6	L	2.62
7	L, 328 1944, L 1.47	1.62
8	L	5.64
9	L	3.62
1270	L, 983 6.62	12.62
1	L	6.62
2	L	6.61
3	L, 984 6.62	12.63
4	L, 984 6.62	12.62
5	L	3.62
6	L, 235 6.50, L 6.61, 983 6.62	4.64
7	L, 953 6.62, 958 6.63, 855 6.64	10.64
8	L, 340 6.58, L 6.61, 953 6.62	12.62
9	L, 433 6.62	5.64
1280	L, 436 6.62, 428 6.63	5.64

No		Wdn
1282	L	12.62
3	L, 308 1944, L 1948	12.62
4	L	12.62
5	L	12.63
6	L	12.62
7	L, 207 1.47, L 1948, 433 6.60, L 6.62	12.62
8	L	12.62
9	L	6.61
1290	L	12.63
1	L, 212 6.62	12.62
2	L	12.62
3	L, 212 6.62	12.62
4	L	12.62
5	L	12.62
6	L, 212 6.62	12.62
7	L	12.62
8	L, 430 11.59, L 6.62	12.62
9	L, 430 11.59, L 6.62	12.62
1300	L, 101 11.59	12.62
1	L, 212 6.62	12.62
2	L	12.62
3	L, 100 11.59	12.62
4	L, 103 11.59. To WR 1.63	7.64
5	L, 471 6.53, 430 6.55	12.62
6	L, 102 11.59. To WR 1.63	12.64
7	L, 434 6.60, L 10.61. To WR 1.63	9.64
8	L, 208 11.59, L 2.62	10.63
9	L	12.62
1310	L, 108 11.59	12.62
1	L, 212 6.62	12.62
2	L	8.62
3	L, 206 1.47, L 1948	6.61
4	L, 104 11.59, L 6.62	11.62
5	L, 432 6.61	11.61
6	L	12.61
7	L, 610 1960	10.64
8	L, 602 11.59	12.63
9	L	11.61
1320	L, 603 11.59	10.64
1	L	2.59
2	L	12.63
3	L, 611 1960	5.64
4	L	12.61
5	L, 110 11.59	12.61
6	L. Transferred to WR 1.63	7.64
7	L, 105 11.59	1.62
8	L, 606 11.59	11.64
9	L	12.61
1330	L, 608 11.59	10.64
1	L, 619 1960, L 1963	11.64
2	L	12.61
3	L	1.62
4	L	6.61
5	L	6.61
6	L	12.61
7	L	6.61
1338	L, 245 1945, 209 1.47, L 1948, 600 11.59	12.63

No		Wdn
1339	L, 109 11.59	4.62
1340	L	3.62
1	L, 615 1960	11.64
2	L, 618 1960, L 1963	11.64
3	430, L 1942, 607 11.59, L 1962	11.64
4	L, 430 6.55	12.63
5	L, 244 1945, L 1.47, 471 6.53, 430 6.55	12.63
6	L, 269 6.54, L 11.59	11.61
7	L, 613 1960	11.64
8	L	8.62
9	L, 605 11.59	12.63
1350	L	11.61
1	430, L 1942, 601 11.59	12.63
2	L	12.62
3	L, 609 11.59	11.64
4	L, 614 1960	10.64
5	L	6.62
6	L, 612 1960	5.64
7	L	11.61
8	L, 205 1.47, L 1948	11.61
9	L, 616 1960	10.64
1360	L, 208 1.47, L 1948, 604 11.59	11.64
1361	L, 617 1960	11.64
1369	L	6.61
1370	L, 106 11.59, L 6.62	12.62
1	L, 209 6.60	10.61
2	L	7.61
3	L	8.61
4	L	8.61
5	L	8.61
6	L	7.61
7	L	7.61
8	L	10.61
9	L	10.61
1380	L	9.61
1	L	10.61
2	L	2.62
3	L	10.61
4	L	6.60
5	L	9.61
6	L	10.61
7	L	7.61
8	L	7.61
9	L, 204 1.47, L 1948	10.61
1390	L	7.61
1	L. Burned out, Stewarts La.	11.61
2	L	2.61
3	L	12.62
4	L	9.61
5	L	6.61
6	L	12.59
7	L	8.61
8	L	9.61
9	L, 107 11.59	2.62
1400	L	9.61

OPEN THIRDS -- continued

No		Wdn
1410	241, L 1948, 107 6.62	12.62
1	L. Transfd to WR 1.63	7.64
2	242, L 1.47, 109 6.62	12.62
3	242, L 1948	12.62
4	L	12.62
5	L, 212 6.62	12.62
6	L, 212 6.62	12.63
7	L	12.62
8	L	12.62
9	241, L 1.47	12.62
1420	L	12.62
1	L	12.62
2	L	12.62
3	L	12.62
4	L, 430 1942	12.63
5	L, 430 1942	12.63
6	L	7.64
7	L. Transfd to WR 1.63	7.64
8	L	12.63
9	L	12.63
1430	L, 243 1945, L 1.47. To WR 1.63	7.64
1431	L Transfd to WR 1.63	7.64
2	L	12.63
3	L, 430 6.63	12.63
4	L	12.63
5	L, 110 6.62	12.63
6	L	12.63
7	L	12.63
8	L	12.63
9	L	12.63
1440	L, 430 6.63	12.63
1	L, 430 6.63	12.63
2	L	12.63
3	L	12.62
4	L	12.62
5	L	12.63
6	L	12.63
7	L	12.62
8	L	12.62
9	L	12.63
1450	L	12.63

THIRDS -- continued

No		Wdn
1801	L	6.61
2	L, 241 1945, L 6.51	2.62
3	L, 242 1945,308 6.51, L 1956, 980 6.62	12.63
4	L, 471 6.55, 469 11.59, 212 6.61, 980 6.62	12.62
5	L, 980 6.62	5.64
6	L, 269 1945	3.62
7	L, 269 1945, L 6.54, 804 6.57, L 1959	2.62
8	L, 426 6.59, 980 6.62, L 1964	11.64
9	L	11.62
1810	L, 984 6.62	12.63
1	L, 959 6.62	12.62
2	L, 271 6.62	12.63
3	L, 240 1945, L 1948, 956 6.62	7.64
4	L, 442 c.38, 952 6.62	5.64
5	L, 959 6.62	12.62
6	L, 459 1945, 432 9.61	12.62
7	L, 232 1945, L 1948	2.62
8	L, 459 1945, 432 9.61	12.63
9	L, 433 6.62	12.62
1820	L, 959 6.62	12.63
1	L, 245 1945, L 1.47, 959 6.62	12.63
2	L, 981 6.62, L 6.64	11.64
3	L, 960 6.62	12.62
4	L, 239 1945, L 1948, 456 11.59, L 2.61, 960 6.62,983 6.63,854 6.64	10.64
5	L	4.62
1826	L, 441 c.38, L 1948, 959 6.62	12.62
1827	202, 205 6.51, 250 6.62	12.62
8	L, 959 6.62	12.62
9	L, 205 1945, L 1.47, 269 6.54, 982 6.62,964 6.64	11.64
1830	L, 956 6.62	12.62
1	L, 440 c.38, L 6.58, 956 6.62	12.62
2	L, 955 6.62	5.64
3	L, 462 6.58, 469 11.59, 212 6.61, 428 6.62	12.62
4	L, 982 6.62	5.64
5	L, 204 6.51, 984 6.62	6.64
6	L. Enemy action,Newington	8.44
7	L, 270 6.54, 956 6.62, 433 6.63, 964 6.64	11.64
8	L, 270 1945, 249 6.62	12.62
9	L, 212 6.53, L 6.62	11.62
1840	L, 203 1945, L 1948. Damaged,W'loo 11.3.61	12.61
1	L, 268 1945, 77 2.62	12.62
2	L	2.62
3	L, 434 c.38, L 1.47, 340 6.58, L 6.61, 984 6.62, 983 6.63	12.63
4	L	12.62
5	L, 270 11.59	12.62
6	L, 803 6.57, 78 2.62	12.62
7	L, 328 1944, 270 1945, L 6.54, 264 9.58, L 2.61, 436 6.62, 428 6.63	6.64
8	249, L 6.51	12.62
9	L, 400 1947, L 1948, 269 9.54	3.62
1850	L	2.62

THIRDS -- continued

No		Wdn
1851	L	2.62
2	L, 961 6.62, 981 6.64	11.64
3	L, 982 6.63	5.64
4	L, 433 c.38, L 1.47, 961 6.62	12.62
5	L, 982 6.62	12.62
6	L	2.62
7	L, 803 6.57, L 11.61	12.62
8	L, 981 6.62	12.62
9	L, 961 6.62	12.62
1860	L, 204 1949, L 6.56	6.61
1	L, 212 6.53	4.62
2	L, 222 1945, L 1948, 442 9.61, 952 6.62	5.64
3	L, 984 6.64	11.64
4	L, 264 9.58, L 6.59, 982 6.63	12.63
5	L	6.64
6	L, 206 1949	2.62
7	L, 205 1945	2.62
8	L, 208 1949, 440 6.56, L 6.58	12.63
9	L	11.62
1870	L, 268 1945, 249 6.62, 433 6.63	12.63
1	L	5.64
2	L, 234 6.60, 432 6.61, L 12.61, 952 6.64	10.64
3	L, 271 1945	12.62
4	L, 804 6.57, L 6.59, 981 6.62	12.62
5	L, 456 2.61, L 9.61, 953 6.62	12.62
6	L, 207 1949, 432 6.62	12.62
7	L	11.62
8	L, 955 6.62, L 1964	12.64
9	L, 855 6.64	10.64
1880	L, 439 1948, 272 11.59, 250 6.62	12.62
1	L. Accident, Farnborough	11.47
2	L	3.62
3	L, 981 6.63	6.64
4	250, L 6.51, 804 6.57, 436 6.59	12.62
5	L	2.62
6	L, 439 1948, L 6.56	12.63
7	L, 206 6.51, 249 6.62, L 6.63, 854 6.64	10.64
8	L, 984 6.62	12.62
9	L	2.62
1890	L,981 6.62	11.64
1	L, 271 1945	12.62
2	L	4.64
3	L, 272 6.58, 250 6.62, 271 6.63	4.64
4	L, 272 1945, 250 6.62, 271 6.63	4.64
1895	L, 428 6.62	12.62
1896	L, 952 6.64	10.64
7	L, 272 1945, L 6.59, 960 6.62, 952 6.64	10.64
8	L	6.64
9	L, 443 6.54, 769 6.64	11.64
1900	L	5.64
1	L, 444 c.38, L 6.56, 960 6.62, L 1964	12.64
2	L, 437 c.38, 205 1949, L 6.56,960 6.62,803 6.63	4.64
3	L, 438 c.38, L 10.47, 443 6.54, 769 6.64	11.64
4	L, 961 6.62, L 1964	12.64
5	L, 443 6.54, 769 6.64	11.64
6	L, 211 6.55, 237 6.59, 429 11.59, L 9.61, 960 6.62, 952 6.64	10.64
7	L, 443 6.54, 769 6.64	11.64
8	L, 961 6.62, 803 6.63	4.64
9	L, 952 6.62	5.64
1910	L, 432 6.63, 952 6.64	10.64
1	L, 952 6.62	5.64
2	L, 436 6.62, 952 6.64	10.64
3	L	5.64
4	L, 430 1942, 472 6.55, L 7.59, 981 6.63, L 6.64	12.64
5	L	6.64
6	L, 952 6.64	12.64
7	L, 984 6.63	11.64
8	L, 207 6.51, L 6.56, 803 6.62	12.62
9	L, 803 6.63	4.64
1920	L, 433 6.63	5.64
2349	469	7.59
2350	469	7.59
1	469, L c.33, 469 1941	7.59
2	L	5.59
3	L, 469 6.54, L 7.59	6.61
4	470, L c.33	11.61
2355	470, L c.33	7.61

Restriction "1"

No		Wdn
2356	217, L 11.59	6.61
7	217, L 11.59, 456 2.61	12.61
8	218, L 11.59	11.61
9	218, L 11.59	8.61
2360	219, L, 466 1945	7.61
1	219, L, 466 1945	7.61
2	220, L, 465 1945, L 2.61	6.61
2363	220, L, 465 1945, L 2.61	6.61

THIRD BRAKES

No		Wdn
	Restriction "4"	
2754	225	7.59
5	226	6.61
6	226	6.61
7	227	10.61
8	227	10.61
9	228	9.61
2760	228	9.61
1	229	2.62
2	229	2.62
3	230	1.62
4	230	1.62
5	231, 444 6.60	10.61
6	231, 444 6.60	9.61
7	232	1.62
8	232	1.62
9	233	10.61
2770	233	10.61
2771	234	7.61
2776	168. Transfd to WR 1.63	12.63
7	172. Transfd to WR 1.63	11.64
8	196. Transfd to WR 1.63	12.64
9	197, 248 c.41, 436 6.62	12.62
2780	198	12.62
1	248, 436 6.62	12.62
2	248. Enemy action, Claph.Jn	9.40
3	249	12.62
4	249	12.62
5	250	12.62
6	250	12.62
7	400, 28 1948	12.62
8	400, 29 1948. To WR 1.63	11.64
9	L, 469 1945, L 6.54, 270 6.61, 271 6.62	12.63
2790	L, 265 1945, 22 1948. Transfd to WR 1.63	12.64
1	L, 465 1945, 270 6.61, L 9.61, 433 6.62	12.63
2	L, 265 1945, 23 1948. Transfd to WR 1.63	11.64
3	234, 760 6.57	8.61
4	235	4.61
5	235	4.61
6	236	9.61
7	236	9.61
8	237, 803 6.57	11.61
9	237, 804 6.57, 803 6.59	11.61
2800	238	4.61
1	238	4.61
2	239	8.62
3	239. Damaged, Hastings	8.59
4	240	7.59
2805	240	7.59
2831	L, 267 1945, 26 1948. Transfd to WR 1.63	7.64
2	L, 266 1945, 24 1948. Transfd to WR 1.63	7.64
2833	L, 760 5.43, 199 9.61	12.62

No		Wdn
2834	L, 430 c.42	12.62
5	L, 430 c.42	12.62
6	178. Transfd to WR 1.63	?
7	202, 179 2.62. To WR 1.63	11.64
2838	202, 31 2.62. To WR 1.63	11.64
3214	390	11.61
5	390	11.61
6	391	4.58
7	391	4.58
8	392	10.59
9	392	10.59
3220	393	7.58
1	393	7.58
2	394	11.61
3	394	11.61
4	395	11.61
5	395	11.61
6	397	11.61
7	398	12.61
8	396	11.61
9	396	11.61
3230	398	12.61
1	397	11.61
2	399	11.61
3233	399	11.61
	Restriction "0"	
3234	940	9.59
5	940	9.59
6	939	10.59
3237	939	10.59
	Restriction "4"	
3664	458, 440 6.58	8.61
5	458, 440 6.58	7.61
6	459	10.61
7	459	10.61
8	427, L 6.57, 341 6.58	10.61
9	427, L 6.57, 341 6.58	10.61
3670	428	9.61
3671	428	9.61
	Restriction "0"	
3672	475, L c.38, 951 1948	8.59
3	475, L c.38, 937 6.58	7.59
4	476, L c.38, 951 5.44	8.59
5	476, L c.38, 937 6.58	7.59
6	477, L c.33, 938 6.54	7.59
7	477, L c.33, 460 1947, L 6.51, 938 6.54	7.59
8	478	9.59
9	478	9.59
3680	479, L 1960, 214 9.61	11.61
1	479, L 1960	6.61
2	480	9.59
3	480	9.59
4	213	9.62
5	213	9.62
3686	214	9.61

No		Wdn
3687	214	11.61
8	215	9.59
9	215	9.59
3690	216, L 6.60	10.61
3691	216, L 6.60	10.61
	Restriction "1"	
3692	185, 184 6.63	1.65
3	185	2.65
4	186	3.65
5	186, 444 6.63	3.65
6	187	1.65
7	187, 445 6.63	3.65
8	188	3.65
9	188, 446 6.63	3.65
3700	217	5.64
1	217, 457 6.63	5.64
2	218	1.65
3	218, 458 6.63	10.64
4	189	3.65
5	189, 447 6.63	3.65
6	190	7.65
7	190, 448 6.63	1.65
8	191	1.65
9	191, 455 6.63	1.65
3710	192	7.65
1	192, 456 6.63	3.65
2	219	3.65
3	219, 459 6.63	11.64
4	220. Fire damage ?	3.38
3715	220, L 6.59, 182 9.61	10.64
	Restriction "4"	
3716	204	10.61
7	204	10.61
8	205	12.61
9	205	7.61
3720	208	2.62
1	208	2.62
2	209	10.61
3	209	10.61
4	207	2.62
5	207	2.62
6	202? 308 1933	12.59
7	202? 308 1933	12.59
8	206	2.62
9	206	2.62
3730	201	11.61
1	201	11.61
2	179	1.62
3	180	12.62
4	203 ? L 1933, 962 5.43	6.61
5	203 ? L 1933, 962 5.43	6.61
6	199	8.61
7	200	12.62
8	193	10.59
9	193	10.59
3740	194	11.61
1	194	11.61
3742	195	9.61

No		Wdn
3743	195	9.61
4	464	8.59
5	464	8.59
6	426	10.61
7	426	10.61
8	429	11.59
9	429	11.59
3750	221, 429 6.60	7.61
1	221, 429 6.60	7.61
2	222, 268 6.61	9.61
3	222, 268 6.61	9.61
4	223, 455 1957	10.59
5	223, 455 1957	7.59
6	224	12.61
7	224	? 12.61
3758	225	7.59
3771	246, 271 6.62	12.63
2	L, 821 1956, 239 11.59, 433 6.62	12.63
3	327, 443 6.62	12.63
4	327, 443 6.62	12.63
5	430, L c.42, 267 1945, 27 1948. To WR 1.63	3.65
6	430, L c.42, 436 1958	12.62
7	247. Transfd to WR 1.63	12.64
8	243, 443 1960, L 6.62	10.62
9	243, 443 1960, L 6.62	10.62
3780	L, 266 1945, 25 1948. Transfd to WR 1.63	7.64
1	203	2.62
2	330, 434 6.58, L 2.62	10.62
3	330. Damaged, B'mouth West	8.56
4	203	2.62
5	245	11.62
6	244	6.62
7	244	6.62
8	246, 30 2.62. To WR 1.63	12.64
9	L, 245 1948	11.62
3790	242, L 6.62	11.62
1	242	6.62
2	329, 428 6.62	12.63
3	329, 428 6.62	12.63
4	247	12.62
5	L, 434 6.58	2.62
6	245. Accident, Farnborough	11.47
7	328, 432 6.59	12.63
8	328, 432 6.59	12.63
9	241	12.62
3800	241	12.62
4048	469, L 6.54, 234 6.60	7.61
9	469. Enemy action	9.44
4050	470, L 7.59	9.61
4051	470, L 7.59	10.61
4055	445	11.58
6	445	11.58
7	446	4.61
4058	446	4.61

THIRD BRAKES -- continued

No		Wdn
4059	447	7.59
4060	448	10.58
1	447	7.59
4062	448, 436 6.59	12.61
	Restriction "1"	
4063	467, 466 6.63	3.65
4	467	3.65
5	468. Damaged, Haywards Hth?	9.45
6	468, 460 6.51, L 11.59	11.61
7	449	3.65
8	449, 460 6.63	3.65
9	450	1.62
4070	450	1.62
1	451	5.64
2	451, 463 6.63	5.64
3	452	11.59
4	452	11.59
5	453	10.59
6	453	10.59
7	454. Enemy action	12.40
8	454, 465 6.63	12.63
9	465, 454 c.40	12.63
4080	465, 466 1947, 453 11.59, 464 6.63	11.64
1	466. Accident, Woking ?	11.45
4082	466, 453 7.61	11.64
	Restriction "4"	
4083	456	12.61
4	456	12.61
5	387	1.62
4086	387	1.62
	Restriction "1"	
4087	181	1.62
8	181	1.62
9	182	6.61
4090	182, 183 6.63	10.64
1	183	7.58
2	183, 156 6.59, 453 11.59	6.61
3	184	9.58
4094	184	9.58
	Restriction "4"	
4095	L, 468 1946	10.59
6	L, 469 6.54	8.61
4097	L, 469 6.54	6.61
4231	952	12.63
2	952	12.63
3	953	12.62
4	953	12.62
5	954, L 6.59	12.63
6	954, L 6.59, 960 11.60	12.62
7	955	12.63
8	955	12.63
9	956	12.62
4240	956. Transfd to WR 1.63	11.64
1	957	12.62
2	957	12.62
3	958	12.63
4	958	12.63
5	959. Transfd to WR 1.63	11.64
6	959. Transfd to WR 1.63	11.64
7	960	12.62
8	960. Damaged, Templecombe	6.60
9	961	12.62
4250	961	12.62

NONDESCRIPT BRAKES *

No		Wdn
4431	L, 212 6.60, L 9.60	6.61
2	L, 452 6.62	3.65
3	L, 428 9.61, L 6.62	12.62
4	L	12.64
5	L	12.64
6	L	12.62
7	L, 428 9.61, L 6.62	12.62
8	L. To Ambulance 7920,5.59	c.67
9	L. To 2nd, 1939. 181 6.62, 180 6.63	12.63
4440	L	12.63
4441	L, 181 6.62	3.65
2	L. To 2nd,1939. 212 9.60, 180 3.64	10.64
3	L, 452 6.62, 462 6.63	3.65
4	L. To Ambulance 7921,5.59	6.68
5	L. To Ambulance 7922,5.59	6.68
6	L	12.62
7	L, 450 6.62	3.65
8	L, 450 6.62, 461 6.63	12.63
9	L. To Ambulance 7923,5.59	c.67
4450	L, 212 6.62, 461 3.64	1.65

*All classed as Open Brake Seconds from June, 1956

SECOND BRAKES

No		Wdn
4481	L. To 3rd Bke 2772, 10.54 L, 234 6.57	12.58
4482	L. To 3rd Bke 2773, 10.54 L	10.59

SECONDS

No			Wdn
4483	L. To 3rd 1921, 1.55.	L	12.61
4484	L. To 3rd 1922,10.54.	L	10.61
4485	L. To 3rd 1923,10.54.	L	12.61
4486	L. To 3rd 1924,10.54.	L	12.59

COMPOSITES

No		Wdn
	Restriction "4"	
5137	393	7.58
8	390	11.61
9	391	4.58
5140	396	11.61
1	392	10.59
2	397	11.61
3	394	11.61
4	398	12.61
5	399	11.61
6	395	11.61
7	445	9.58
8	446	4.61
9	447	6.59
5150	448	10.58
	Restriction "1"	
5151	467, 217 6.50	7.59
2	467, 218 6.50	8.59
3	467, 466 6.63	3.65
4	467	3.65
5	468, L 1946, 696 6.57, L 7.59, 468 6.60	7.61
6	468. Damaged, Haywards Hth?	9.45
7	468, L c.33, 468 1946	10.59
8	468, L c.33, 468 1946	9.59
9	449	3.65
5160	449, 460 6.63	3.65
1	450	1.62
2	450	1.62
3	451, 463 6.63	5.64
4	451	6.64
5	452	11.59
6	452	11.59
7	453	10.59
8	453	10.59
9	454	12.63
5170	454, 465 6.63	12.63
	Restriction "4"	
5171	387	1.62
5172	456	11.58
	Restriction "1"	
5173	181	1.62
4	181	1.62
5	182	12.61
6	182	12.61
5177	183	7.58
	Restriction "0"	
5578	939	7.59
5579	939	7.59
	Restriction "1"	
5582	183	7.58
3	184	9.58
5584	184	9.58

No		Wdn
	Restriction "4"	
5585	458? L, 275 6.54, 440 11.59	7.61
6	L, 212 6.53, L 1959	11.61
7	459	10.61
8	427, 276 6.54, 440 11.59	7.61
9	459	10.61
5590	428	9.61
5591	L, 263 6.55, L 7.59, 468 6.60	7.61
	Restriction "0"	
5592	475, L c.38, 938 6.54, 479 6.59, L 1960	10.61
3	476, L c.38, 938 6.54, 480 6.59	9.59
4	477, L c.33, 938 6.54, 940 6.59	9.59
5	478, L, 937 6.58	7.59
6	479, L, 937 6.58	8.59
7	480, L, 215 6.59	9.59
8	L, 213 6.59	9.62
9	L, 216 6.59, L 1960	9.61
5600	L, 478 6.59	9.59
5601	L, 214 6.59	11.61
	Restriction "1"	
5602	185, 184 6.63	1.65
3	185	1.65
4	186	3.65
5	186, 444 6.63	3.65
6	187	3.65
7	187, 445 6.63	10.64
8	188	3.65
9	188, 446 6.63	3.65
5610	217, L, 456 6.57, 452 6.62	11.64
1	217	5.64
2	217, 457 6.63	5.64
3	217, L 11.59, 429 6.60, L 9.61, 182 6.62	3.65
4	218, L 11.59, 182 6.62, 183 6.63	10.64
5	218	1.65
6	218, 458 6.63	10.64
7	218, L, 455 6.57, 453 11.59	11.64
8	189, L, 189 c.35	3.65
9	189, 447 6.63	10.64
5620	190, L, 190 c.35	7.65
1	190, 448 6.63	1.65
2	191, L, 191 c.35	3.65
3	191, 455 6.63	1.65
4	192, L, 429 6.57, L 6.61, 181 6.62, 180 6.63	3.65
5	192, L, 192 c.35	7.65
6	219, L, 464 6.57, 453 11.59, 464 6.63	11.64
7	219, L, 219 c.35	7.65
5628	219, 459 6.63	1.65
5629	219, 192, 456 6.63	3.65

COMPOSITES -- continued

No		Wdn
5630	220, L, 212 6.53, L 1959, 450 6.62	3.65
1	220, L, 181 6.62	3.65
2	220, L, 220 c.35, L 6.59, 450 6.62, 461 6.63	10.64
5633	220, L 6.59, 341 6.60, 428 9.61,452 6.62, 462 6.63	3.65
	Restriction "4"	
5634	L, 269 1945, 330 6.54,273 6.58	8.59
5	201, 470 6.57, 204 11.59	10.61
6	203? L, 273 1945	8.59
7	L,221 1945,L 1948,237 6.50, L 6.53,328 6.54,270 6.59	12.61
8	L, 239 1945, L 1948, 202 6.51	4.61
9	L, 232 1945, L 1948, 241 6.51	10.61
5640	193, L c.33, 268 1945	12.61
1	193, 226 11.59, 202 6.61	12.61
2	194	11.61
3	194, L 6.54, 469 1956	6.61
4	195	9.61
5	195, 962 5.43	6.61
6	L, 270 1945	12.61
7	464	8.59
8	L, 459 1945, 428 1949	10.59
9	426, 271 6.59	11.61
5650	L, 271 1945	11.61
1	429	7.59
2	L, 222 1945, L 1948, 327 6.51	1.62
3	L, 203 c.33	2.62
4	L, 400, L 1.47, 246 6.51	1.62
5	L, 250 6.51	6.61
6	L, 470 c.33, 204 11.59	10.61
7	L, 272 1945	12.61
8	L, 240 1945, L 1948, 245 6.51	1.62
9	L, 426 1.47, L 1948, 244 6.51, L 6.54, 247 1955	11.61
5660	L, 458, 244 6.58	6.62
1	L, 248 6.51	12.61
5662	L, 429 1.47, L 1948, 243 6.51	12.59

No		Wdn
5663	L, 242 6.51	7.61
4	221	11.59
5	222	6.61
6	223, 455 1957	2.59
7	224	12.61
8	225	7.59
9	226	10.59
5670	227	10.61
1	228	9.61
2	229	2.62
3	230	1.62
4	231	12.59
5	232	1.62
6	233, L 6.55, 430 6.57	10.59
7	233, L 6.55, 237 6.57, 429 1959	11.59
8	234, L 6.55, 760 6.57	9.61
9	234, L 6.55, 272 6.58	12.61
5680	235	12.59
1	235	12.59
2	236, L 6.55, 236 6.58	9.61
3	236, L 6.55, 236 6.58	9.61
4	237, L 6.55, 237 6.57, 429 1959	11.59
5	237, L 6.55, 469 1956	6.61
6	238, L, 237 5.44, L 6.53, 329 6.54	3.62
7	238	2.60
8	239, L, 236 1945, L 1948, 235 5.49,L 6.50,249 6.51	12.61
9	239	8.59
5690	240	7.59
1	240, L, 203 1945, L 1948, 247 6.51, 269 6.54	3.62
2	952	12.63
3	953	12.62
4	954, 456 6.59, 953 6.62	12.62
5	955	12.63
6	956	12.62
7	957	12.62
8	958	12.63
9	959, 958 6.63	12.63
5700	960	12.62
5701	961	12.62

COMPOSITE BRAKES

No		Wdn
	Restriction "4"	
6565	L, 263 6.53	7.59
6	L, 263 6.53	7.59
7	L, 29 1948	12.59
8	L, 271 11.59	11.61
9	L, 28 1948	12.61
6570	L, 353 6.51, L 6.57, 340 6.58	1.59
1	L, 273 1945	8.59
2	L, 101 1958	10.59
3	L, 106 1958	12.62
6574	L, 273 1945	8.59

No		Wdn
6575	L, 23 1948	12.59
6	L, 105 1958	4.59
7	L, 102 1958	3.62
8	L, 696 6.57, L 11.59	6.61
9	L, 261 6.54.Damage,Maze H.	7.58
6580	L, 261 6.54.Damage,Maze H.	7.58
1	L, 262 6.54	5.59
2	L, 471 1946, L 11.59	12.61
3	L, 107 1958	9.59
4	L, 468 6.51	10.59
5	L, 103 1958	8.59
6586	L, 26 1948	12.61

COMPOSITE BRAKES -- continued

No		Wdn
6587	L, 351 6.51, 433 6.57	12.59
8	L, 200 c.31, L 6.62	11.62
9	L, 104 1958	12.62
6590	L, 108 1958	12.62
1	L,276 6.54,270 11.59, 28 6.62	12.62
2	L, 262 6.54, 107 11.59. Transfd to WR 1.63	7.64
3	L, 276 6.54, 270 11.59, 26 6.62	12.62
4	L, 109 1958	12.62
5	L, 110 1958, L 4.61. Transfd to WR 1.63	11.64
6	L, 274 6.54, 268 11.59, 77 2.62	12.62
7	L, 275 6.54, 268 11.59, 78 2.62	12.62
8	L, 274 6.54, 271 11.59, L 1962	12.62
9	L, 100 1958	12.62
6600	L, 275 6.54, 269 11.59, 102 1962	11.62
1	L, 350 6.51, 431 6.57,442 9.61,L 6.62. To WR 1.63	?
2	L, 24 1948. To WR 1.63	7.64
3	L, 27 1948	12.62
6604	L, 212 6.53, L 6.62. Transfd to WR 1.63	11.64
6643	L, 29 9.60, L 4.61. Transfd to WR 1.63	11.64
4	L, 354 6.51, L 6.57, 340 6.59, L 6.61	12.62
5	L, 350 6.53, 431 6.57, 442 9.61, L 6.62	12.62
6	L,23 9.60,L 11.60. WR 1.63	10.65
7	L, 269 11.59, L 6.62	12.62
8	L, 22 9.60, L 11.60, 25 6.62, To WR 1.63 ?	?
9	L, 350 6.51, L 6.53, 105 6.59. Transfd to WR 1.63	7.64
6650	L, 352 6.51, L 6.57, 180 9.61. To WR 1.63 ?	5.64
1	L, 353 6.51, L 6.57, 340 6.58, L 6.61	11.62
2	L, 23 11.60	12.62
3	L, 29 4.61	12.62
4	L, 110 4.61. To WR 1.63?	7.64
5	L,168 9.60,L 11.60.WR 1.63	11.64
6	L. ReNo 6905 1947. L, 103 11.59. To WR 1.63	7.64
7	L, 199 c.31	12.62
8	L, 179 2.61	12.62
9	L, 168 11.60. To WR 1.63?	?
6660	L. ReNo 6906 1947. L, 101 11.59. To WR 1.63	7.64
1	L, 212 6.53, L 6.60. Transfd to WR 1.63	7.64
2	L, 351 6.51, 433 6.57, L 11.60, 31 2.62. WR 1.63	11.64
6663	L, 272 1945, L 6.62	12.62

No		Wdn
6664	L, 172 6.60. To WR 1.63	11.64
5	L, 25 1948, L 6.62. To WR 1.63	7.64
6	L, 178 6.60	11.62
7	L, 196 6.60. To WR 1.63	5.65
8	L, 272 1945, 30 2.62	12.62
9	L, 352 6.51, L 6.57, 22 11.60. To WR 1.63	5.65
6670	L, 198 6.60	12.62
1	L, 433 11.60, L 6.62	11.62
2	L, Transfd to WR 1.63	11.64
3	179, L 2.61. To WR 1.63	11.64
4	180. Damaged, Tavistock	7.61
5	L, 269 1945, L 6.54, 603 11.59	10.64
6	L, 268 1945, 604 11.59	11.64
7	L, 269 6.54, 605 11.59	12.63
8	L, 268 1945, 606 11.59	11.64
9	L, 610 6.60	10.64
6680	L, 269 1945, 611 6.60	5.64
1	L, 602 11.59	12.63
2	L, 271 1945, 607 11.59. Damaged,Eastbne 15.9.61	11.61
3	L, 612 6.60	5.64
4	L	10.53
5	L	1.67
6	L	9.66
7	L, 270 1945, 601 11.59	12.63
8	L, 613 6.60	11.64
	Re-instated. L	9.66
9	L, 271 1945, 608 11.59	10.64
6690	178, 614 6.60	10.64
1	L, 22 1948, 615 6.60	11.64
2	L	11.62
3	L, 270 1945, 600 11.59	12.63
4	L, 609 11.59. To WR 1.63	11.64
5	168, 616 6.60	10.64
6	172, 617 6.60	11.64
7	196, 618 6.60, L 1963	12.63
8	197. Enemy action	1.41
6699	198, 619 6.60, L 1963	12.63
	Restriction "0"	
6881	941	9.59
2	941	9.59
3	942	8.59
4	942. Enemy action	c.44
5	951, L 1948	8.59
6	951, 942 1944	8.59
7	476	8.59
8	476	8.59
9	944	9.59
6890	944	9.59
1	945	8.59
2	945	8.59
3	946	9.59
4	946	9.59
5	947	9.59
6	947	9.59
7	948	c.59
6898	948	9.59

COMPOSITE BRAKES -- continued

No		Wdn
6899	949	9.59
6900	949	9.59
6901	950	8.59
6902	950	8.59
3	943	8.59
6904	943	8.59

FIRSTS

No		Wdn
	Restriction "4"	
7208	L	10.58
9	L, 265 1945, L 1948, 426 6.60	10.61
7210	L	7.59
1	L, 245 1933, L 6.51, 431 6.58	8.61
2	L, 247 1933, L 6.51	11.59
3	L, 246 1933, L 6.51, 436 6.59, L 6.60	9.61
4	L,	8.59
5	L, 244 1933, L 6.51	10.59
6	L, 248 c.36, L 6.51	9.59
7	L, 400 1947, L 1948	8.59
8	L, 207 c.31	12.59
9	L, 206 c.31	10.59
7220	L, 266 1945, L 1948	9.59
1	L, 430 c.42, L 6.55	11.61
2	L, 249 c.36, L 6.51	11.59
3	L, 327 1933, L 6.51	8.59
4	L, 442 6.59, L 1960	9.61
5	L, 430 c.33, L 6.55	6.59
6	L, 194, L 9.52	12.59
7	L. Burnt out, Micheldever	8.36
8	204, L 11.59	1.62
9	205	12.61
7230	L, 329 1933, L 6.51, 432 6.60, L 6.62	10.62
1	L, 330 1933, L 6.51, 442 9.61	3.62
7232	L, 433 6.60	12.61
	Restriction "1"	
7390	465, L 6.59	7.61
1	465, L 6.59	7.61
2	465, L c.33, 466 1.47	7.61
3	465, L c.41. To 3rd 656 6.54. 262, 455 6.59, 456 11.59, L 2.61	12.61
4	466, L 1.47. To 3rd 657 6.54. L	6.61
5	466, L c.33. Enemy action	12.40
6	466, L c.33. To 3rd 658 5.54. 211 6.55, L 7.59	12.61
7397	466	7.61
	Restriction "4"	
7398	L, 308, L 9.52, 444 6.59	12.59
7399	L, 433 6.58	12.59
	Restriction "0"	
7400	L, 480, L 6.59	8.61
7401	L	7.61
7402	L, 479, L 6.59	7.61
3	L, 478, L 6.59	7.61
4	213, L 6.59	6.61
7405	214, L 6.59	8.59
	Restriction "4"	
7406	L, 328 1933, L 6.51	3.62
7	208	2.62
8	L	12.61
9	L, 430 c.33, L c.42. Damaged, Clapham J.21.9.61	10.61
7410	L	1.62
1	209	12.61
7412	L, 243 1933, L 6.51, 194 9.52, 233 6.55, L 1960	11.62
	Restriction "0"	
7414	940, L 6.59	7.61
5	216, L 6.59	7.61
7416	215, L 6.59	9.59
7418	939, L 6.59	7.61
9	951	8.59
7420	L, 951 6.54	8.59
1	L, 951 6.58	8.59
7422	L, 951 6.58	8.59
	Restriction "4"	
7665	469, L 6.54, 897 6.58	12.59
6	469, L c.33, 430 c.42, L 6.57	7.59
7	469, 430 c.33, L c.42	10.59
8	L	10.59
9	L, 267 1945, L 1948	10.59
7670	L	9.59
1	470, L c.33, 443 6.50, L 6.54	10.59
2	470, L c.33, 202 c.36, L 6.51	11.59
3	470, L c.33, 760 5.43, L 6.57, 432 6.59	12.59
4	470, L c.33, 250 c.36, L 6.51	8.59
5	L, 242 1933, L 6.51, 439 6.59, 434 6.50	2.62
7676	L, 241 1933, L 6.51, 308 9.52, 201 6.60	12.61

FIRST BRAKES

No		Wdn
7715	L	12.61
7716	L, 356 6.51, L 6.52	10.61

NONDESCRIPT SALOONS (LATER CLASSED AS OPEN SECONDS)

No		Wdn
7781	L	8.59
2	L	7.59
3	L	7.59
4	L, 444 6.56	12.59
5	L, 207 6.56	12.59
6	L, 441 6.56	8.59
7	L, 433 6.56	12.59
8	L, 436 6.56	2.60
9	L, 431 6.56	9.61
7790	L, 204 6.56	7.59
1	L, 205 6.56	2.60
2	L, 429 6.57	7.59
3	L. ReNo 4391 1939. 696 6.57	7.59
4	L, 429 6.57	7.59
5	L, 201 6.57	10.61
6	L, 443 6.56	8.62
7	L, 429 6.57	7.59
8	L, 434 6.56	10.59
9	L, 442 6.56	12.59
7800	L. ReNo 4392 1939.470 6.57	7.59
7901	L, 308 6.56	12.59
2	L. ReNo 4393 1939. Enemy action	11.40
3	L	8.59
4	L. ReNo 4394 1939. 456 6.57, L 11.59	10.61
5	L. ReNo 4395 1939.696 6.57	7.59
6	L. ReNo 4396 1939.696 6.57	7.59
7907	L	8.59
7908	L, 429 6.57	7.59
9	L, 455 6.57	7.59
7910	L, 460 6.57	7.59
7911	L.ReNo 4397 1939. 696 6.57	7.59
7959	L, 209 6.56	2.60
7960	L, 460 6.57	7.59
1	L, 206 6.56	10.59
2	L, 437 6.56, 426 6.60	10.61
3	L, 917 6.57	7.59
4	L, 440 6.56	12.59
5	L, 456 6.57, 205 6.60	12.61
6	L, 917 6.57	7.59
7	L, 696 6.57	7.59
7968	L, 456 6.57	7.59
7974	L, 917 6.57	7.59
5	L, 456 6.57	7.59
6	L, 917 6.57	7.59
7	L, 470 6.57	7.59
8	L, 208 6.56	10.59
9	L, 917 6.57	7.59
7980	L, 917 6.57	7.59
1	L, 455 6.57	7.59
2	L, 455 6.57	7.59
3	L, 432 6.56	12.59
4	L, 455 6.57	7.59
5	L, 470 6.57	7.59
6	L, 464 6.57	7.59
7	L, 455 6.57	7.59
8	L, 470 6.57	7.59
9	L, 435 6.56	8.59
7990	L, 438 6.56, 426 6.59	2.60
1	L, 464 6.57	7.59
2	L, 464 6.57	7.59
3	L, 464 6.57	7.59
7994	L, 439 6.56	9.59

KITCHEN/DINING FIRSTS

No		Wdn
7858		12.60
9	Altered to Buffet 1953	12.62
7860	Altered to Buffet 1953	3.62
1		5.61
2	Altered to Buffet 1954	12.62
3	Altered to Buffet 1953	12.62
4	To Kitchen/Buffet 1947	1.62
5	To Kitchen/Buffet 1947	9.61
6	Altered to Buffet 1954	12.63
7	To Kitchen/Buffet 1947	12.62
8		6.61
9	Altered to Buffet 1954	12.63
7870	Altered to Buffet 1954	12.62
7871	Altered to Buffet 1954	12.62
7878	To Kitchen/Buffet 1947	12.63
7880		12.62
7931		5.62
2		2.61
3		12.62
7934	Altered to Buffet 1953	12.63
7939	Altered to Cafeteria 8.52	12.62
7940	To Kitchen/Buffet 1954	12.60
1	Altered to Buffet 1953	12.60
2	Altered to Buffet 1953	2.62
3		12.60
4	Altered to Buffet 1953	12.60
5	Altered to Buffet 1953	1.61
6		1.62
7	Altered to Buffet 1953	2.62
8	Altered to Buffet 1954	12.63
9		1.61
7950	Altered to Buffet 1954	1.62
1	Altered to Buffet 1954. Damaged, Clapham Jn.	11.62
2		11.61
3	Altered to Buffet 1954	1.61
4	Altered to Cafeteria 8.52	12.62
5	To Kitchen/Buffet 1953	10.61
6	Altered to Buffet 1954	2.62
7957	Altered to Buffet 1954	12.63

KITCHEN/DINING FIRSTS -- continued

No		Wdn	No		Wdn
7958	Altered to Buffet 1954	12.62	7998		12.62
7969	To Kitchen/Buffet 1947	12.67	7999	To Kitchen/Buffet 1947	12.63
7995	Altered to Buffet 1954	12.63	8000		12.62
7997		12.62			

RESTAURANT SALOONS

No	To Open Third	To Composite Saloon	Wdn	
7864	1363, 2.34	7846, 1947 *	12.62	
5	1364, 12.33	7847, 1947 *	12.62	
6	1365, 12.33	7841, 1947	9.61	
7	1366, 2.34	7842, 1947	2.62	* Unclassed
8	1367, 12.33	7843, 1947	12.61	
7869	1368, 1.34	7844, 1947	4.54	

QUANTITIES OF MAUNSELL COACHES BUILT FROM 1926 TO 1936

401 Thirds
153 Open Thirds
272 Third Brakes
20 Nondescript Brakes
4 Seconds
2 Second Brakes
163 Composites
121 Composite Brakes
68 Firsts
2 Pantry First Brakes
62 Unclassed Saloons
46 Kitchen/Dining Saloons
6 Restaurant Saloons

Total : 1,320 coaches.

MAUNSELL 59 ft STOCK CONVERTED TO SERVICE VEHICLES

SECONDS

790 to 081321 Internal Use , after 1959.
1019 to DS 70129, 1962. Motive Power Department Breakdown Van.
1020 to DS 70134, c.62. Sold to KESR 11.71
1022 to DS 70119, 5.61. Staff & Tool, Three Bridges. Condemned 10.74
1023 to DS 70130, 1963. Motive Power Dept Brighton Breakdown Van.
1025 to DS 70118, 3.61. Staff & Tool, Ashford. Condemned 8.72
1026 to DS 70135, 6.61. Staff & Tool, Ashford. Condemned 12.70
1145 u'frame to 61328, 1947. Dover Ferry Berth Shunting Truck.
To DS 89, 12.57. Condemned c.81
1232 u'frame to DS 70170, 5.62. Match Wagon. Condemned c.83
2356 to 081315 Internal Use , after 1961. Streatham Com. To Bluebell Railway, 10.73

OPEN SECONDS

1306 to 082274, c.65. To DS 70267, 1967. Staff/Tool, ME. Condemned 9.78
1309 to 081642, c.63. Sold to Bluebell Ry 3.73
1310 to 081810, c.63.
1313 to DS 70146, 11.61. Staff Van. Condemned 12.66
1319 to DS 70206, 3.65. "Work Study Coach". Condemned 11.80
1323 to 082232, c.64. To DS 70266, 1967. Instruction Car. ?
1327 to DS 70176, 11.62. Staff/Tool, Purley. Condemned 10.71
1329 to DS 70195, 4.63. Staff/Tool. Basingstoke. Condemned c.83
1333 to DS 70196, 4.63. Staff/Tool, Hither Green. Condemned 8.81
1336 to 081901, c.62. To DS 70313, 1970. Office.
1346 to DS 70201, 12.61. To 083181, 1975. Instruction Coach. Sold to KESR 9.82
1358 to 081809, c.62.
1369 to DS 70149, 10.61. Dormitory Coach, Exeter District. Condemned ?
1371 to DS 70213, 8.64. Dormitory Coach. Condemned 12.81
1373 to DS 70151, 11.61. Dormitory Coach, Exeter District. Condemned 7.73

OPEN SECONDS -- continued

1378 to DS 70157, 3.62. Staff/Tool. Condemned 7.66
1379 to DS 70177, 9.62. Staff/Tool, Purley. Condemned 12.69
1380 to DS 70179, 12.62. Staff/Tool, Exeter Central. Condemned ?
1381 to DS 70175, 7.62. Staff/Tool, ME. Horsham. Sold to Swanage Ry 10.79
1385 to DS 70150, 11.61. Dormitory Coach, Exeter District. Condemned 1.68
1386 to DS 70212, 7.64. Dormitory Coach. Condemned 12.74
1387 to DS 70152, 12.61. Dormitory Coach, Exeter District. Condemned 2.69
1388 to DS 70153, 12.61. Dormitory Coach, Exeter District. Condemned 11.67
1394 to DS 70158, 4.62. Staff/Tool, Wimbledon. Condemned 69
1397 to 081818, c.62.
1399 underframe to DS 70193, 11.63. Match Wagon to Crane.
1400 to DS 70169, 6.62. Staff/Tool, Brighton. Condemned 5.70

SECOND BRAKES

2768 to DS 70172, 1963. S & T Central Division. Sold to Swanage Ry 11.81
2772 (ex 4481) to 081037, c.59.
3675 to DS 70136, 9.61. Dormitory Coach, Exeter District. Condemned 10.68
3676 to DS 70126, 1963. Breakdown Van (Tool).
3677 to DS 70125, 1962. Breakdown Van (Tool).
3679 to DS 70082, 7.60. Staff/Tool, Faversham. Condemned 10.68
3680 to DS 70159, 11.62. Office, Emergency Control Train.
3687 to DS 70160, 11.62. " " " " To 083409, 2.81
3690 to DS 70163, 12.62. Mobile Office
3691 to DS 70164, 12.62. Mobile Office.
3718 to DS 70167, 4.62. Staff/Tool, Exeter Central. Condemned 9.72
3719 to DS 70168, 4.62. Staff/Tool, Yeovil Junction.
Sold to Mid Hants Railway, 3.76
3721 to DS 70178, 11.62. Staff/Tool, Woking. Condemned 11.70
3724 to CWT 7, Chipman Chemical Co. Horsham. Sold to Bluebell Ry 87
3725 underframe to DS 70192, 3.64. Match Wagon to Crane.
3729 to DS 70184, 2.63. Mobile Office. Condemned 4.77
3732 underframe to DS 70194, 5.63. Match Wagon to Crane.
3741 to 081340, c.62.
3756 to DS 70180, 12.62. Tool Coach, Three Bridges. Condemned 8.72
4077 u'frame to 61329, 1947. Dover Ferry Berth Shunting
Truck. To DS 88, 12.57 Condemned c.81
4441 to 082444, c.1965. Streatham Common. Sold to Bluebell Railway 10.73

COMPOSITES

5579 to DS 70122, 1963. M.P. Breakdown Van (Riding).
5595 to DS 70121, 1963. M.P. Breakdown Van (Riding).
5599 to DS 70161, 11.62. Office, Emergency Control Train.
DS 70159-61 ran as a set.
5600 to DS 70155, 1962. Inspection Saloon, then Instruction Coach.
5601 to DS 70162, 12.62. Mobile Office. DS 70162-4 ran as a set.
5644 to CWT 8, Chipman Chemical Co, Horsham.

COMPOSITE BRAKES

6574 to DS 70088, 11.60. Staff Coach, Exmouth Junction. Condemned 4.69
6581 to DS 70034, 10.59. Staff Coach, Broad Clyst. Condemned 5.79
6601 to DW 150386, Western Region. Sold to Mid Hants Ry, 11.78
6697 to CWT 9, Chipman Chemical Co, Horsham.
6699 to CWT 11, Chipman Chemical Co, Horsham. Sold to Mid Hants Ry, c.83
6886 to DS 70042, 11.59. Staff Coach, Ashford District. Condemned 9.81
6887 to DS 70171, 12.62. Staff/Tool. Condemned 7.76
6888 to DS 70070, 2.60. Weedkilling Coach, Horsham.
To Eastern Region 3.74. Condemned 11.80
6895 to DS 70137, 1961. U'frame. Wheel wagon, Ashford-E'leigh Wks. ?
6903 to DS 70060, 5.60. Staff Coach, Woking. Condemned 8.68
6904 to DS 70073, 5.60. Staff Coach, Woking. Condemned 2.72

FIRSTS

Coach	Conversion	Disposal	Date
7216	to 081256 Internal Use , after 1959.		
7400	to 081621 Internal Use , after 1961.	Sold to K&ESR	11.71
7404	to DS 70143, 7.61. Staff/Tool , Ashford.	Condemned	5.67
7405	to DS 70035, 10.59. S&T Instruction Coach. "Work Study Vehicle", Basingstoke. To 083229, 9.76.	Broken up	5.80

OPEN SECONDS (ex NONDESCRIPTS)

Coach	Conversion	Disposal	Date
7781	to DS 70147, 1.62. Mobile Office.	Condemned	4.71
7784	to 081152 Internal Use, after 1959.		
7798	to DS 70109, 1960. "Mess & Tool Van Purley District (Painters)."	Sold to K&ESR	11.71
7901	to DS 70108, 12.60. Staff/Tool, Eastleigh.	Condemned	8.72
7959	to 081297, c.60.		
7982	to 081158, c.59.		
7984	to 081159, c.59.		
7990	to 081324, 5.62.		

INVALID SALOONS

Coach	Conversion	Disposal	Date
7920	to DB 975279, c.73. Dover Marine.	Sold to K&ESR	6.80
7923	to DB 975406, 10.74.	Sold to Mid Hants Ry	11.78

Few Maunsell coaches ended as grounded bodies. Those at New Cross Gate were painted grey, as in all probability were the others. These are the only examples known :

1143 (?)	New Cross Gate, C & W Examiners accommodation. Broken up 1980.
1152 (?)	New Cross Gate, C & W Examiners accommodation. Broken up 1980.
1332	Lancing. Office.
1348	Lancing. Office.
1376	Eastleigh Carriage Works.
7964	? Office.
7983	Eastleigh. Office.

Open Third No. 1371 of 1930 as converted in May 1964 to a dormitory coach, DS 70213; seen here at Stewarts Lane. *Lens of Sutton*

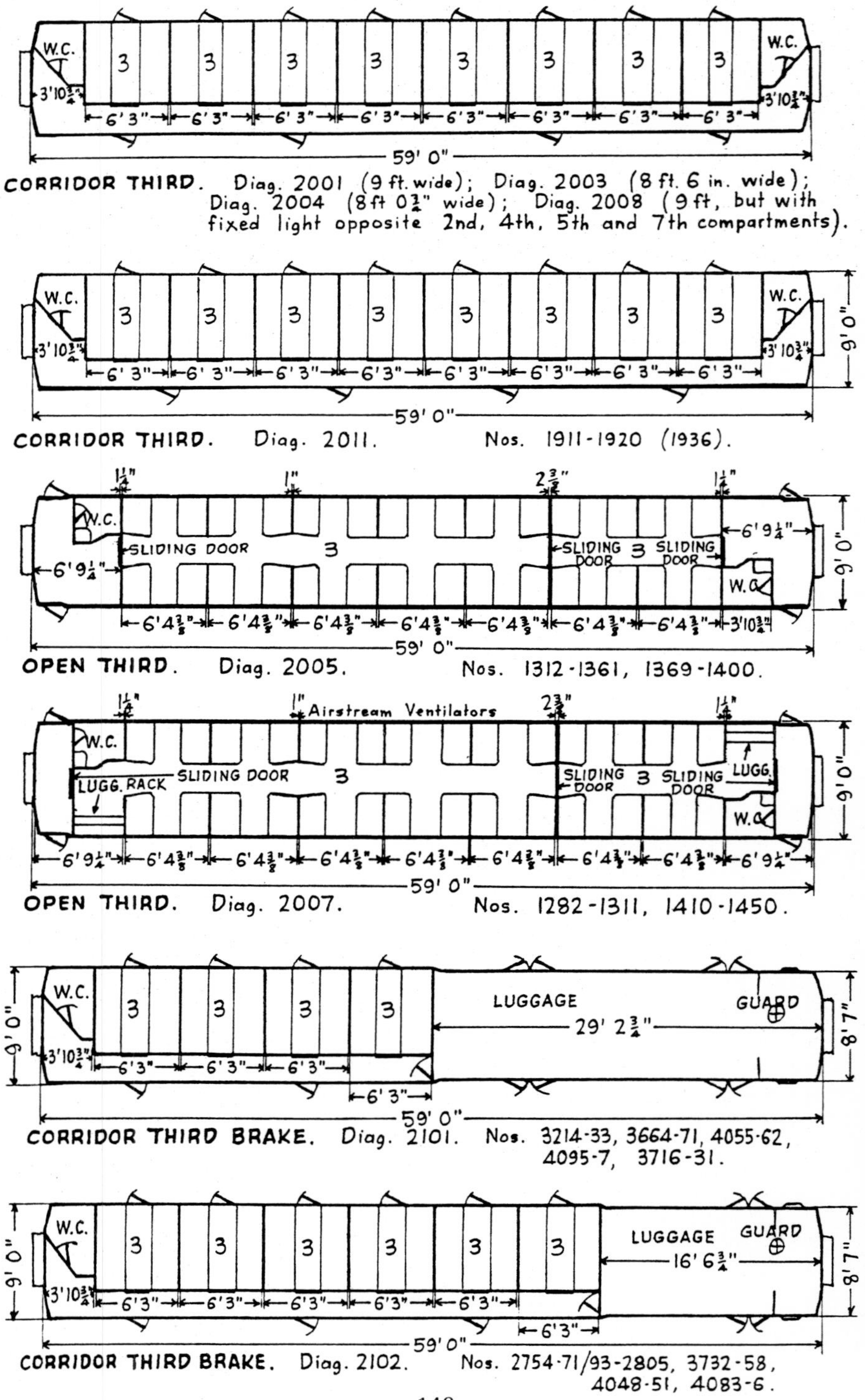

CORRIDOR THIRD. Diag. 2001 (9 ft. wide); Diag. 2003 (8 ft. 6 in. wide); Diag. 2004 (8 ft 0¾" wide); Diag. 2008 (9 ft, but with fixed light opposite 2nd, 4th, 5th and 7th compartments).

CORRIDOR THIRD. Diag. 2011. Nos. 1911-1920 (1936).

OPEN THIRD. Diag. 2005. Nos. 1312-1361, 1369-1400.

OPEN THIRD. Diag. 2007. Nos. 1282-1311, 1410-1450.

CORRIDOR THIRD BRAKE. Diag. 2101. Nos. 3214-33, 3664-71, 4055-62, 4095-7, 3716-31.

CORRIDOR THIRD BRAKE. Diag. 2102. Nos. 2754-71/93-2805, 3732-58, 4048-51, 4083-6.

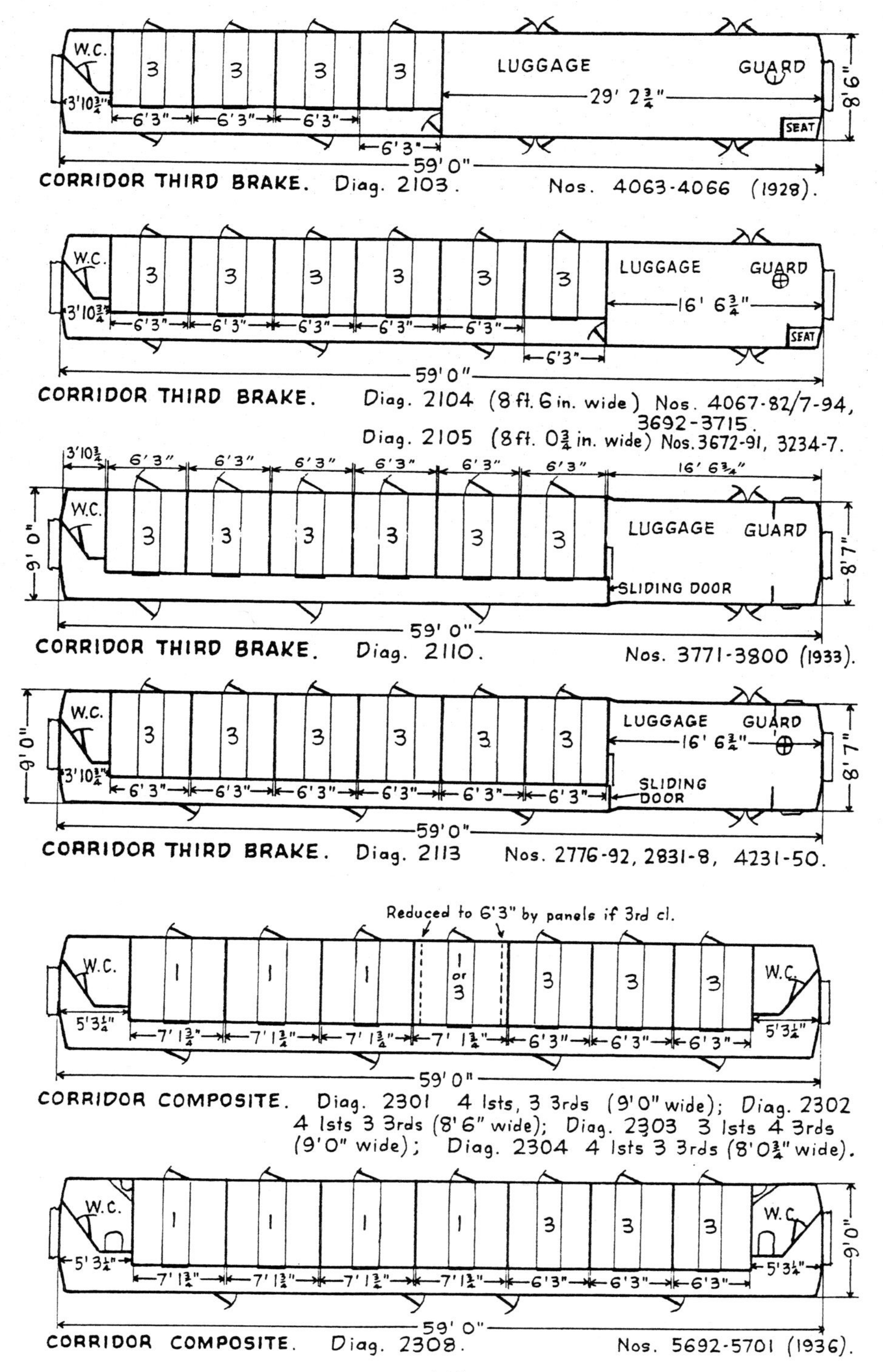
W.C.
3
LUGGAGE
GUARD
29' 2¾"
SEAT
3'10¾"
6'3"
59' 0"
8'6"
CORRIDOR THIRD BRAKE. Diag. 2103. Nos. 4063-4066 (1928).
16' 6¾"
CORRIDOR THIRD BRAKE. Diag. 2104 (8 ft. 6 in. wide) Nos. 4067-82/7-94, 3692-3715.
Diag. 2105 (8 ft. 0¾ in. wide) Nos. 3672-91, 3234-7.
9' 0"
8' 7"
SLIDING DOOR
CORRIDOR THIRD BRAKE. Diag. 2110. Nos. 3771-3800 (1933).
CORRIDOR THIRD BRAKE. Diag. 2113 Nos. 2776-92, 2831-8, 4231-50.
Reduced to 6'3" by panels if 3rd cl.
1
1 or 3
5'3¼"
7' 1¾"
CORRIDOR COMPOSITE. Diag. 2301 4 1sts, 3 3rds (9'0" wide); Diag. 2302 4 1sts 3 3rds (8'6" wide); Diag. 2303 3 1sts 4 3rds (9'0" wide); Diag. 2304 4 1sts 3 3rds (8'0¾" wide).
CORRIDOR COMPOSITE. Diag. 2308. Nos. 5692-5701 (1936).

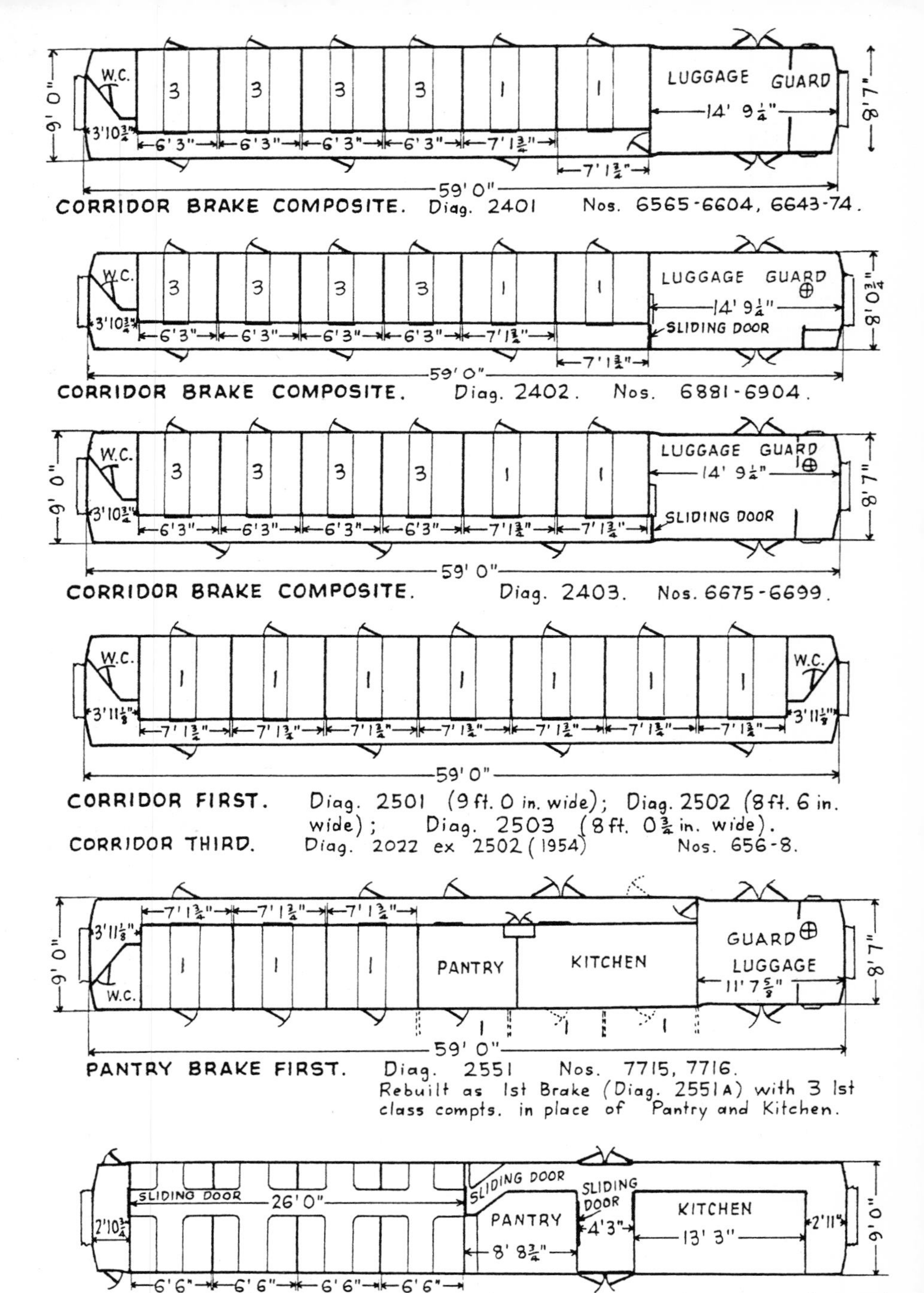

CORRIDOR BRAKE COMPOSITE. Diag. 2401 Nos. 6565-6604, 6643-74.

CORRIDOR BRAKE COMPOSITE. Diag. 2402. Nos. 6881-6904.

CORRIDOR BRAKE COMPOSITE. Diag. 2403. Nos. 6675-6699.

CORRIDOR FIRST. Diag. 2501 (9 ft. 0 in. wide); Diag. 2502 (8 ft. 6 in. wide); Diag. 2503 (8 ft. 0¾ in. wide).
CORRIDOR THIRD. Diag. 2022 ex 2502 (1954) Nos. 656-8.

PANTRY BRAKE FIRST. Diag. 2551 Nos. 7715, 7716.
Rebuilt as 1st Brake (Diag. 2551A) with 3 1st class compts. in place of Pantry and Kitchen.

1ST RESTAURANT/KITCHEN. Diag. 2650 (Fletcher Russell Range) Nos. 7870/1, 7931/2. Diag. 2651 Nos. 7858-63, 7939-58. Stills Boiler and coffee-making equipment in Nos. 7940/3/55, 7.38. Diag. 2655 (Slater's new type Stove) Nos. 7878/80, 7933/4/69, 7995/7/8. Diag. 2656 (Slater's old type Stove) Nos. 7864-9, 7999, 8000.

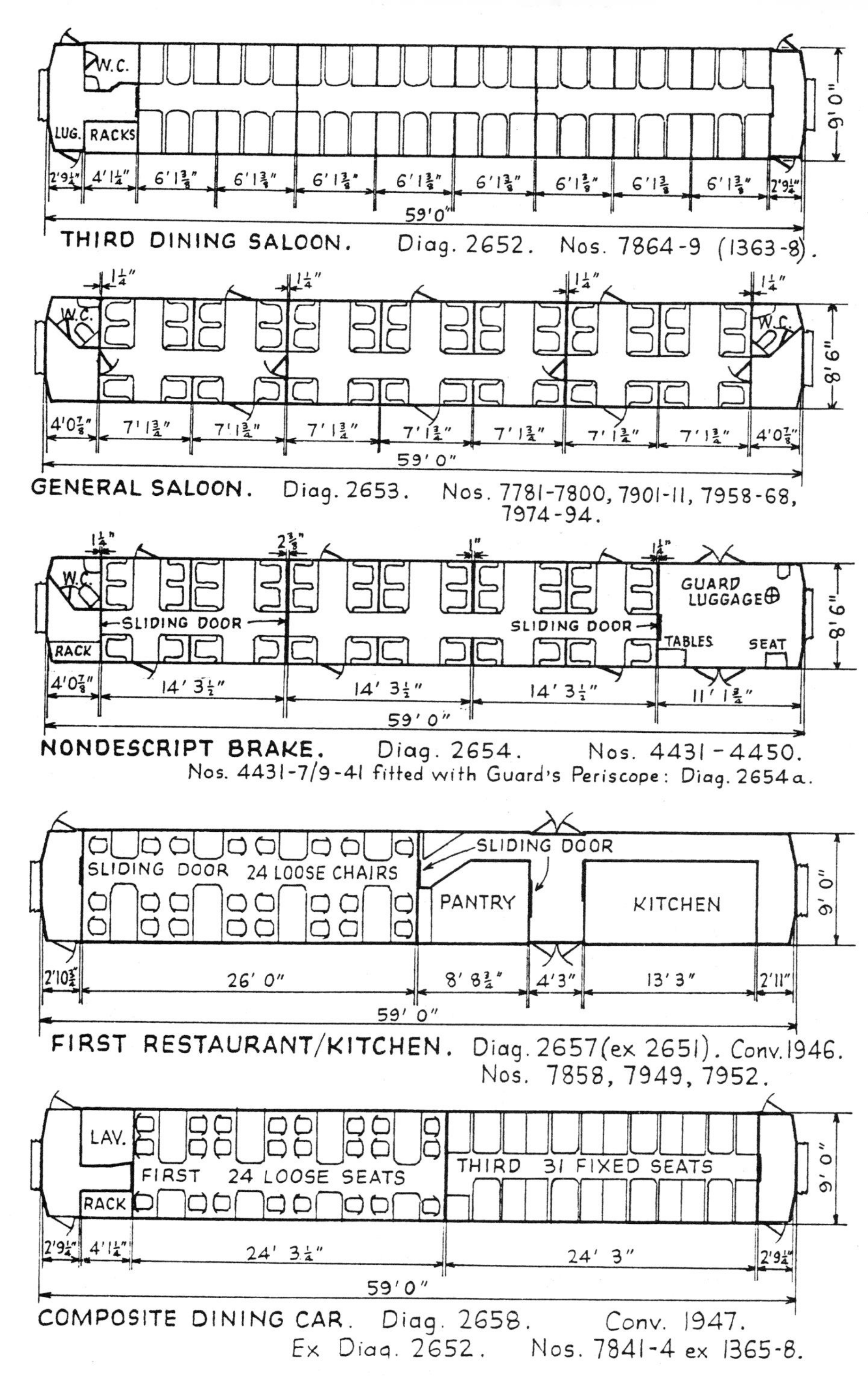
W.C.
LUG.
RACKS
2'9¼"
4'1¼"
6'1⅜"
2'9¼"
59'0"
9'0"
THIRD DINING SALOON. Diag. 2652. Nos. 7864-9 (1363-8).
1¼"
W.C.
W.C.
4'0⅞"
7'1¾"
4'0⅞"
59' 0"
8'6"
GENERAL SALOON. Diag. 2653. Nos. 7781-7800, 7901-11, 7958-68, 7974-94.
1¼"
2⅜"
1"
W.C.
SLIDING DOOR
SLIDING DOOR
GUARD
LUGGAGE
TABLES
SEAT
RACK
4'0⅞"
14' 3½"
11' 1¾"
59' 0"
8'6"
NONDESCRIPT BRAKE. Diag. 2654. Nos. 4431-4450.
Nos. 4431-7/9-41 fitted with Guard's Periscope: Diag. 2654a.
SLIDING DOOR
SLIDING DOOR 24 LOOSE CHAIRS
PANTRY
KITCHEN
2'10¾"
26' 0"
8' 8¾"
4'3"
13' 3"
2'11"
59' 0"
9'0"
FIRST RESTAURANT/KITCHEN. Diag. 2657 (ex 2651). Conv. 1946.
Nos. 7858, 7949, 7952.
LAV.
FIRST 24 LOOSE SEATS
THIRD 31 FIXED SEATS
RACK
2'9¼"
4'1¼"
24' 3¼"
24' 3"
2'9¼"
59'0"
9'0"
COMPOSITE DINING CAR. Diag. 2658. Conv. 1947.
Ex Diag. 2652. Nos. 7841-4 ex 1365-8.

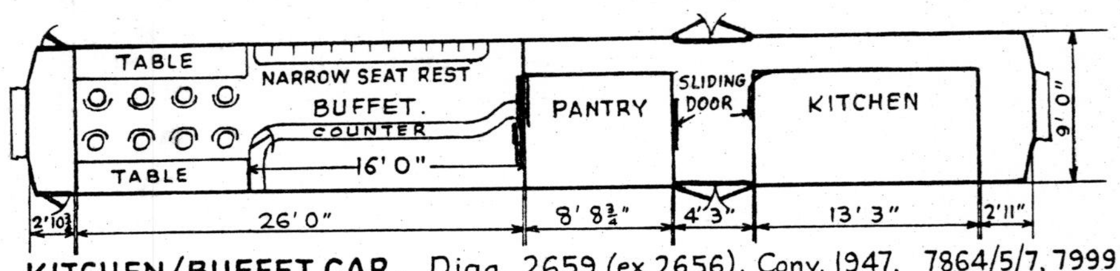

KITCHEN/BUFFET CAR. Diag. 2659 (ex 2656). Conv. 1947. 7864/5/7, 7999.
Diag. 2661 (ex 2655). Conv. 1947. 7878, 7969.

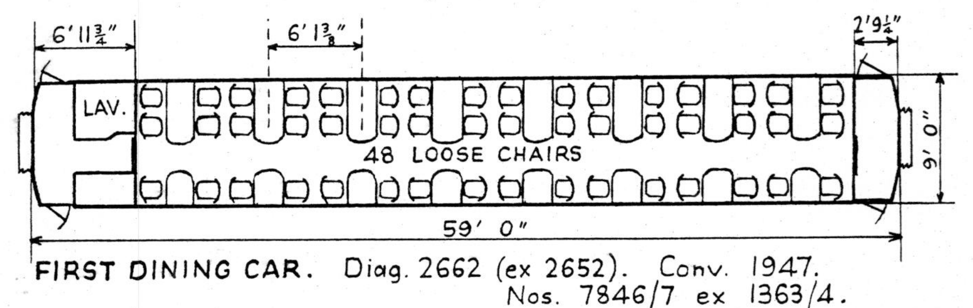

FIRST DINING CAR. Diag. 2662 (ex 2652). Conv. 1947.
Nos. 7846/7 ex 1363/4.

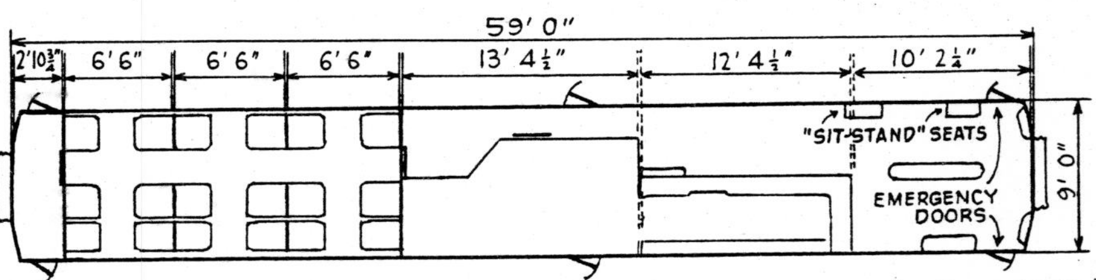

BUFFET CAR. Diag. 2666 (ex 2650, 2651, 2655, 2656). Conv. 1953/4.
Nos. 7859/60/2/3/6/9/70/1, 7934/41/2/4/5/7/8/50/1/3/6/7/8/95.

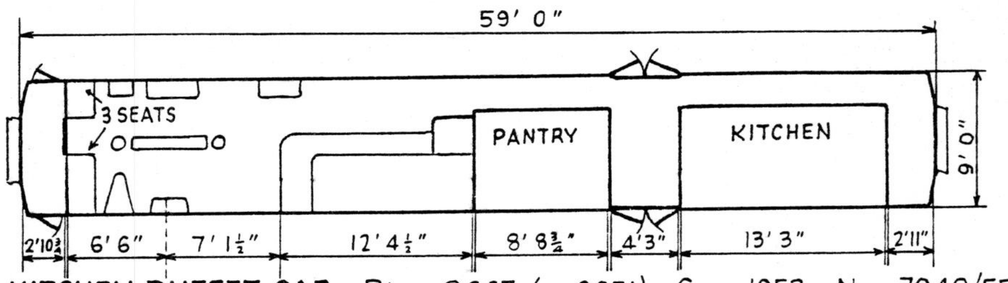

KITCHEN BUFFET CAR. Diag. 2667 (ex 2651). Conv. 1953. Nos. 7940/55.

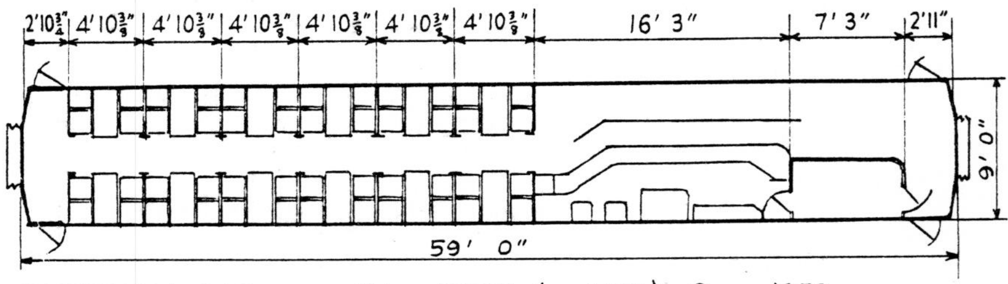

CAFETERIA CAR. Diag. 2675 (ex 2651). Conv. 1952.
Nos. 7939, 7954.